DOUBLE LIVES

DOUBLE LIVES

An Autobiography

by

WILLIAM PLOMER

JONATHAN CAPE
THIRTY BEDFORD SQUARE
LONDON

FIRST PUBLISHED 1943
SECOND IMPRESSION 1944

JONATHAN CAPE LTD. 30 BEDFORD SQUARE, LONDON W.C.I
AND 91 WELLINGTON STREET WEST, TORONTO

THIS BOOK IS PRODUCED IN
COMPLETE CONFORMITY WITH THE
AUTHORIZED ECONOMY STANDARDS

PRINTED IN GREAT BRITAIN
BY BUTLER AND TANNER, LTD., FROME AND LONDON
BOUND BY A. W. BAIN AND CO., LONDON

Hihito no nukagama yueru
Shimeyū no shiminishi kokoro
Ware wasuremeya.

As the *yū* cloth is dyed fast and deep
Which ties the forelocks of the men
In the land of Hi,
So is my heart coloured with love:
How can I forget?

KAKINOMOTO HITOMARO, c. 700 A.D.

NOTE

1 HAD not intended to write anything resembling an autobiography until advanced middle age might enable me to look back a longish way, but during the third year of the present war I suddenly found that I could see the earlier part of my life as a unity and in perspective. I knew that it was not much like the lives of any of my acquaintances and I felt that they and others might like to read about some aspects of it. I also felt that I should enjoy writing about it, as a distraction from duties imposed by the war. I have therefore given some account of the first twenty-five years of my existence, and since it seems to me highly unreasonable (though it is often almost inevitable) that a man's birth should be treated as the real starting-point of his life, I have had something to say about the lives of my parents and their respective origins and backgrounds.

CONTENTS

Part I : PRENATAL

Part II : CHILDHOOD AND ADOLESCENCE

Part III : NOT BY EASTERN WINDOWS ONLY

Part I

PRENATAL

1. A BOURGEOIS FAMILY

It was in 1903 (when men were at last beginning to fly, though in contraptions more like birdcages than birds) that I first, to use an old phrase, saw the light. It was dazzling, for the scene of this event was, of all places, the Northern Transvaal; but since nobody, if a cat happens to have kittens in an oven, regards them as biscuits, I should be no more justified in pretending to be a South African than in declaring myself a Bantu. Yet the African sun warmed my young bones, and to Africa I must always partly belong, though my parents, of whom I was the first child, were in fact very English. They came from that stratum of society which may be called the stranded gentry, and were of a nomadic habit. To explain what they were doing in the Northern Transvaal in 1903, it will be best to go back a bit.

A Victorian poet observes, albeit rather prosily, that

'If one is born a certain day on earth,
All times and forces tended to that birth.'

A truism, but an important one; and it will not be out of place to give some indication of the more recent times and particular forces tending to my entry into this world. It has been suggested that pedigrees pretending to accuracy should only be traced through the female line. This cynical proposal shall not deter me from giving some account of my father's family, although it is not in the least illustrious, but a bourgeois line of which the fortunes have gone up and down and which has seldom stayed long in one place.

The name Plomer was originally le Plomer or le Plumer, and is said to have signified either a plumber, or worker in lead, or a *plumier*, a person concerned with feathers — whether for stuffing

9

mattresses, tipping arrows, personal adornment or writing purposes
I don't know, but to descend from a *plumier* rather than a plumber
might be conducive to a lighter touch. A certain Bruce, who published a Plomer genealogy in 1847, was candid enough to observe
that 'the remote antiquity of the family of Plomer, or Plumer,
precludes all accuracy of the development of its origin.' If by
developing an origin he meant proving a descent, the remark is true
of every family on earth. He gives Burke as his authority for saying
of the Plomers that 'traditionally they derive from a noble Saxon
knight, who lived in the time of King Alfred.' This is fiddlesticks,
or, to be more exact, early Victorian romantic snobbery. The truth
is that Bruce's son, a judge in Jamaica, had married my great-aunt
Louisa, and he probably wished to make out that this alliance was as
distinguished as it was lucrative — for Louisa was something of an
heiress. The Plomers, he declared,

'have long been seated in Hertfordshire, where they ranked with the
most distinguished of the gentry of that county; so far back as the
year 1361 Peter le Plomer, a person of considerable note and great
opulence, was M.P. for St. Albans, and Robert Plomer was sheriff
of the county in 1495.'

This is a far cry from King Alfred, and why opulence should in
itself be thought interesting so long afterwards, it would be hard to
guess. It would be better to know what Peter and Robert did in
their spare time, or what they looked like, or what their friends said
about them; but there they are, without glory or disgrace or the
faintest savour of reality, mere names and dates. Give me rather
Christopher Plomer, a canon of Windsor who was unfrocked and
clapped into the Tower in 1535 for criticizing, as well he might, the
behaviour of his royal master, Henry VIII. There at least is a
voice.

It is supposed that the two main branches of the Hertfordshire
Plomers or Plumers came from a common stem. One lot lived at
Blakesware Hall in the parish of Ware — the 'Blakesmoor'
described by Charles Lamb — and after producing at intervals a
sheriff of the county and a couple more members of Parliament,

ended with yet another, William by name, who, leaving no children, was survived by the cousin he had married. She was Jane Hamilton, daughter of a canon of Windsor and granddaughter of an Earl of Abercorn, from whom possibly she derived her arrogant feudal habits: she lived in great state and drove abroad in a four-horse chariot so large that gaps had to be cut in the hedges of the Hertfordshire roads to enable other vehicles to get out of its way. She married, as her third husband, Robert Ward, who took her name and arms in addition to his own, and who, as Robert Plumer Ward, had some success as a novelist. He was the author of the long-winded *Tremaine, or the Man of Refinement*, and of *De Vere, or the Man of Independence*, a *roman à clef* which contains a portrait of Canning, under whom he had served at the Admiralty. He led the opposition to Cobden during the legislation over the repeal of the Corn Laws, had been a judge, and wrote several books on international law. Canning said that Plumer Ward's law books were as pleasant as novels, and his novels as dull as law books.

My father's branch was settled in Elizabethan times at Radwell House, on the Ivel near Baldock. William, who died in 1625, had been knighted by James I in 1616, no doubt in exchange for some timely contribution to the expenses of that queer monarch. For the sake of clarity, we will call him William II, his father having also been William. He can be seen in effigy, kneeling and wearing armour, in Radwell Church. In the chancel is an alabaster monument to his wife Mary and their children. It represents a seated woman in the dress of the period, with a ruff round her neck and a short coif-like mantle over her head. Her right hand appears to have once held a flower or some small object now lost; her left rests on an hour-glass which stands upon an altar-shaped pedestal, upon which also lies an infant in swaddling clothes. (Poor Mary, she died in 1605 at the age of 30 of this, her eleventh child.) Below are carved in high relief the kneeling figures of six sons (the three elder ones wearing long cloaks) looking west and facing four eastward-looking daughters, a double prayer-desk between them; and on a tablet of black marble is Mary's fancy epitaph, which has sometimes found its way into printed collections of such things :

'See Virtue's Jewel, Beauty's Flower,
Cropt off in an untimely hour,
Religion, Meekness, Faithful Love
To Parents, Husband, God above:
So that the stone itself doth weep
To think of her which it doth keep;
Weep thou, whoe'er this stone may see,
Unless more hard than stone thou be.'

Not a word, of course, about excessive child-bearing.

William II married again, adding four more children to his quiverful. His eldest son, William III, was sheriff of the county, but failed to establish a county family: he sold Radwell and left no children. Perhaps it was just as well. If we had become a settled, landed line we might in course of time have dishonoured ourselves, like so many, by enclosing woods and commons, interfering with ale-houses, fairs, morris-dances and other rustic sports, setting man-traps and spring-guns to catch those poachers not already shot, caught or convicted, and generally busying ourselves with the preservation of game and public morals at the expense of the welfare and contentment of the poor.

William III's brother, Thomas, was vicar of Stone in Bucking-hamshire. From him descended John, another parson, and William IV. John was headmaster of Rugby from 1731, when the number of boys was low, until 1759, when it was lower still. William IV had two sons, William V and John, whose son was sheriff of Northamptonshire, took the name and arms of Clarke in addition to his own, and sired the family of Clarke of Welton Place in that county.

William V, born in 1725, was a man of shrewd and genial appearance who, having made his fortune in trade, became Lord Mayor of London, and received a knighthood. This was quite in the tradition, for John Plomer, a Knight of the Bath, had been sheriff of London in 1454. William V introduced — for the first time, perhaps, since that nebulous 'Saxon Knight' — a military tendency into the family, for in 1793 he was president of the

Honourable Artillery Company. His wife Susannah, seeking a change from the opulence of the City, went in her old age to live in a log cabin in Epping Forest, and there exists a print of her sitting before this leafy hermitage, which was ironically known as Lady Plomer's Palace: she looks as placid and meditative as a Chinese sage in a mountainous landscape, seated on a bench before her door, while comfortable smoke rises from her chimney in the background, where perhaps a kettle was getting ready to provide her with a nice cup of tea. Her son, William VI, also knighted, was a sheriff of London, a Whig, and, for seven years in Napoleonic times, a colonel of militia. His son, William VII, was a deputy lieutenant for Edinburgh, and married in 1819 a lady with the gratifying surname of Pagan. The Pagans were Scotch, had made a fortune in the West Indies out of sugar and slaves, and had settled at Linnburn in Midlothian.

William VII and his wife Catherine Pagan (who survived him and lived to a ripe old age in Norfolk Square, peering through horn-rimmed spectacles at a pet parrot) had three sons and two daughters. The eldest son, William VIII, died at the age of 30, under a cloud of some sort, whose shade I hope he found comforting. The second son, remarkably christened John Thomas, also provided himself with a cloud, for he married very happily into the working class (his wife being known later as Aunt Polly), was banished to Australia, where he made a fortune out of wool, and returned to live comfortably in England, thus vindicating the truth of the rhyme:

> 'Baa, baa, black sheep, have you any wool?
> Yes, sir, yes, sir, three bags full.'

The third son, Alfred, born in 1829, was my grandfather.

I don't know whether my grandfather was called Alfred because of that mythical 'noble Saxon knight' who was supposed to be a contemporary of the monarch so named, or simply because Saxon names were coming into fashion. He entered the Indian Army, helped to pursue (goodness knows why) the Persian army with Outram in 1856–7 and to suppress the Indian Mutiny (during which his life was saved by his Indian butler), and was on active service until the capture of Gwalior in 1858. In the following year he returned to England and in 1860 he married. His wife returned with him to India, where his three eldest children were born. He continued his career in the Bombay Staff Corps until 1880, when he retired, after thirty-five years of useful service, on full pay, with the rank of Colonel and a frizzy black beard like a Sikh's. It will do his memory no injustice to say that he was steady rather than brilliant. His nose was large, his eyes small, his heart kind, his politics Conservative, his manners and opinions rigidly conventional, and his temper placid; he had great strength of body, and measured 48 inches round the chest; and it pleased him at times to play *The Two Obadiahs*, a popular song of the period, on the flute.

He married a woman of very different character. His wife was Helen Lucretia, the only daughter of Francis Bush, a doctor at Bath, who, failing to stick to pills and plasters, dropped down dead while making a vehement speech against those very Corn Laws which Robert Plumer Ward was concerned to defend. Helen's mother died at an early age, and the orphan was brought up in the household of a relation, an Admiral Edgell of Frome in Somerset. Through the Edgells my grandmother was descended from an interesting man, Martin Folkes, or Ffoulkes (1690–1754), a friend of Newton, a President of the Royal Society, and a member of the Académie Française. He gave help to Theobald for his notes on Shakespeare, missed a baronetcy because of his Jacobite leanings, and sat to Hogarth and Roubiliac. He is said to have been 'upright, modest and affable,' and is commemorated by a monument in Westminster Abbey, of which the following account is taken from an old guide-book:

'A monument to Martin Folkes, esq., a sublime philosopher. He is sitting in a contemplative mood, resting his hands on a shut book. Above is an urn, hung with drapery, which is held up by a boy. Another boy is measuring the globe with a pair of compasses; and a third is struck with astonishment from looking through a microscope.'

A man of learning and culture rather than a 'sublime philosopher,'

Folkes married Lucretia Bradshaw, a handsome actress, described as 'one of the greatest and most promising genii of her time,' whom he took off the stage for her 'exemplary and prudent conduct' — though let us hope he had other and more interesting reasons. It was from Lucretia Folkes, who died mad, that my grandmother derived her second name.

Helen Lucretia Bush is thought to have been unduly indulged by the Edgells. She was a dark beauty, intelligent and lively, but imperious, with a streak of perversity and a tendency to violent outbursts of temper. In the earliest of these that is remembered, she took the corner of a tablecloth firmly in her hand and walked out of the room, bringing down nobody now knows what an elaborate setout of plate, glass and crockery in noisy ruin. But to the unsuspecting, whom she might wish to please, her erratic temper was not evident, and she became engaged in due course to an eligible and well-to-do young man whom we will call Maitland. He was a soldier, tall, fair and virile, with curly golden hair and a beard to match. For a time all went well. Maitland used to take her out riding, but one morning he arrived at the door leading a horse which she did not choose to ride: she made a terrible scene, and after an outburst of scarcely comprehensible anger, snatched off her engagement ring, threw it down, and ground it under her heel. The young man, instead of putting her in her proper place (which was obviously over his knee) withdrew dumbfounded, and the engagement came to an end. Maitland was much handsomer than Alfred Plomer, and Helen is thought to have been as much in love with him as he was certainly infatuated with her, but, as a neurotic, she was probably wise to marry my grandfather, a stolid, patient, reliable being, who was also comfortably off.

My uncles William IX and Durham, and my aunt Laura, were all born in India, two of them at Poona (that byword for the limitations of the Anglo-Indian), where my grandfather was then brigade-major. For the sake of their health, he brought his wife and children home to England, took a house for them at 2 Stanhope Street, near Lancaster Gate, and returned to India.

In the sixties there might have been seen, at fashionable seaside resorts in the summer, a man in his thirties, dressed in black, with black cotton gloves, and moving with rather a peculiar gait, like that of a clockwork toy, along the sands. He was seen to pay particular attention to little girls. He was a clergyman and a don, and among his pleasures was that of dressing little girls up as gypsies or shepherdesses and then photographing them. One fine morning he was prowling about a beach in the Isle of Wight, when his attention was arrested by the sight of a pretty little girl with a pink complexion, bright eyes, fair ringlets, and a red skirt which stuck out stiffly round her, as she afterwards said, 'like a penwiper.' She was digging in the sand, and her nurse, some way off, was sitting gossiping with a crony and eating cherries out of a bag.

'Good morning, my pretty dear,' said the stranger in black.

The little girl drew herself up.

'Mamma says that I am not to speak to *anybody* on the beach.'

The stranger was not to be rebuffed.

'Ah,' he said, 'then it's quite all right. You see I'm not *anybody*, I'm *somebody*.'

True enough: he was Lewis Carroll.

The next step was to call on the little girl's mother, but he was not cordially received, for two reasons. The first was that my grandmother rightly thought that there was something fishy about a grown-up man who picked up strange little girls on beaches; the second was that she resented attention being paid to her daughter rather than herself. The little Laura received a copy of *Alice in Wonderland* from its author, with some verses inscribed to herself, and that was the end of her relationship with Lewis Carroll: but her relationship with her mother was to continue off and on for the best part of half a century, and it was not a happy one.

It is not rare for a mother to make a favourite among her children; it is less common for her to show unkindness to the others. According to my father, who was her youngest son, his mother frankly disliked all her children except Durham, whom she adored. But she did not neglect them and took care that they were all properly clothed and fed and made to behave properly. She was a capable housewife. In those days there was still a good tradition in

16

this matter, and it was not thought that because a woman could afford to do nothing, it therefore became her to be idle. My grandmother not only practised with skill the arts of cooking and sewing, but she used to make from ancient recipes both soap and pomatum for the whole family — possibly an uncommon accomplishment at so late a period. On the other hand she dressed with style, was fond of social gaieties, and was considered 'fast.' She was in the habit of smoking cigarettes, and considerable excitement was caused when she was seen, in what was known as respectable society and some time before 1870, not only smoking, but sitting on a table and *swinging her legs.*

2. THE YOUNGEST SON

THE characters of the children began to take shape. William IX, the eldest, had that air of reserve so often found in eldest sons, as if even when young he felt life to be a strain and responsibility. Laura was pretty and lively, but the more winsome and vivacious she grew, the more open became her mother's hostility towards her. Durham, the apple of his mother's eye, was a handsome, hearty extravert obviously destined for the polo ground and the ballroom, to wear a uniform, break hearts, get drunk, and not give a damn for anybody or anything unable to contribute to his pleasure.

At the time of the Franco-Prussian war my father was born at the house in Stanhope Street, and was christened Charles Campbell, the latter name after a Scotchman with a title who had married one of his great-aunts. He was the most highly strung of the children, pale, with silky black hair and startled dark brown eyes. He had his mother's tendency to violent outbursts of temper, and a fiery independence of his own: at the same time he had a great need for the give-and-take of affection of a demonstrative kind. This was certainly not forthcoming from his mother. He respected and loved his father, whom he always remembered as just and kind, although

17

the old colonel, a bit of a martinet perhaps, used to beat him for his childish misdemeanours. His sister was good to him, and did something to make up for the want of maternal love — which nothing can really ever make up for.

When Charles was still a small child his mother told him one day that his father had come home from India and would arrive late that very night, after he himself had gone to sleep. She came to say good night to him before going down to dinner, and he asked her, in solemn innocence, 'Is my papa black?' This was always considered a great joke in the family.

His innocent air appealed to an old apple-woman who knew him by sight. One day she offered him an orange and asked for a kiss in return. Just as he was about to oblige her, his mother came round the corner of the street, bore down and prevented him, possibly from fear of infection. In any case the caste system in Bayswater in the early seventies was no less rigid than in the India that she had left, and the apple-woman was clearly an untouchable. At the same time there may have been some obscure resentment, something like jealousy, at this display of affection. The child's mother forbade him ever to speak to the old woman again or even to go near her, and this struck him as bitterly unjust. The reproof went deep, and I doubt if he ever forgave it. This was one of those incidents of childhood which mark a man for life, and it is not surprising that at an early age my father developed a tendency to try and escape from his surroundings. One afternoon his mother, while entertaining a female friend to tea, looked out of the window and was astonished to see a growing and excited crowd staring up at the house. Thinking a chimney must be on fire, she rang the bell to find out, whereupon an agitated manservant informed her that Master Charles had somehow got through the bars of the nursery window and was at large on the very narrow parapet at the top of the house.

A little later, when he was attending a day school in Albion Street, Charles and another boy decided to run away. His friend had tenpence, Charles had half-a-crown and three pennies, and off they went into the great world. They got as far as Richmond Park, where they lay down in the bracken and fell asleep. Emerging at evening, they were questioned by a policeman and promptly returned to their homes in a hansom cab. Corporal punishment again.

One day, when Helen was taking her children for a walk in the Park, Charles ran on ahead, climbed a railing, could not get down, and burst into tears. A handsome, well-dressed man who happened to be passing, kindly lifted him down and was consoling him when Helen approached. The man took off his hat and bowed, and she was about to thank him when she was startled to recognize Maitland, her erstwhile fiancé. His old feeling for her instantly revived, and he became a constant visitor at Stanhope Street and elsewhere. The children detested him, seeing him no doubt as a usurper of their mother's affection, and one summer, when he was staying with the family at a house my grandfather had taken in the Lake district, they demonstrated their feelings about their mother's double life by emptying quantities of salt, pepper and mustard into Maitland's top hat.

At the age of nine, Charles was sent to the Imperial Services College at Westward Ho, the school about which Kipling wrote *Stalky & Co.* He was fairly contented there, and the boys used to brew quantities of sloe gin, which made them so jolly that they were often late for call-over. While he was at this school, his father retired from the Indian Army, and took a house in Chesterfield Street. During one of Charles's holidays there, Disraeli was dying a few yards away, in Curzon Street, and every morning after breakfast the boy was sent by his father to report on the latest bulletin outside the invalid's house. One morning he had the satisfaction of rushing back and crying, 'Dizzy's dead! Dizzy's dead!' — news which was received by my grandfather with the gravity becoming to a diehard Conservative, now convinced that the country's progress towards that mysterious destination 'the dogs,' would be greatly accelerated. Whether he was right or not depends entirely on his definition of these metaphorical creatures, but he undoubtedly regarded liberals and radicals as having designs on the pockets, property and privileges of those who had inherited wealth and position, and he had a belief that a kind of divine right to these things was innate in their possessors.

Charles had suffered for some time from a painful eczema on the legs, and it was suddenly decided that he should be taken away from Westward Ho and sent to a small school in France, ostensibly for the good of his health, though it is not improbable that his mother wished him well out of her way. It is significant that he was not allowed to return home for the holidays, though the school was no further off than Guînes, in the Pas-de-Calais. He was, however, happy and well cared for at this school, where he was fined one sou for each word of English inadvertently uttered. On Sundays there was always calf's head with sauce piquante for luncheon, and it was so carved that each boy had a small piece of the tongue: this was followed by an *omelette à la confiture*.

But the eczema remained uncured and in fact got worse, and the schoolmaster thought it best that the boy should return home. The ravages of the disease made such an impression on my grandmother that she wept: it was the only time my father ever saw her in tears. To her credit she nursed him carefully, and took him to an eminent dermatologist in Manchester Square, who sent him to Bath to take the waters externally and internally.

At Bath he was housed with one Willan, an assistant master at a local public school, which he attended. The headmaster was a ferocious sadist, and when he attacked Charles's hands with a cane (which he used with a skilful technique in order to break the skin) the gloating expression on his face was too much for the boy who flew at him and kicked him hard on the shins. When Willan decided to set up on his own as a crammer, Charles remained with him and spent a happy time under his roof. Willan took him and another boy to France, Germany and the Tyrol, and in order that he might brush up his German, Charles was placed for a time in the family of a kind Lutheran pastor near Hanover.

When he was nearly fourteen his eczema had almost healed, but the dermatologist said that when it disappeared it would leave him either consumptive or asthmatic, and he was right, for my father suffered from asthma all his life. This is a good illustration of a saying of Hardy's, that 'a physician cannot cure a disease, but he can change its mode of expression.' Disease, in fact, like romantic art, is a kind of protest of the individual against his environment, and when this protest is against not only the way that his life, but the way that the world is ordered, then the disease is deep-seated indeed — like Hardy's art.

Charles was now sent to Sherborne, his fifth school, where he was again pretty content. It was the custom there to toss new boys in a blanket, and at the beginning of his second term he distinguished himself by helping to toss a boy so vigorously that the little victim went through the ceiling — a feat for which Charles was given an imposition involving five hundred lines of Virgil. More chivalrous was his stand-up fight in the fives court with a bully whose pleasure in torturing a small boy Charles had interrupted. Fighting was sternly discouraged and punishable, but in this case no punishment was meted out, although the fight was common knowledge and had left its mark in the shape of four black eyes. The bully, it appeared, was already under something more than suspicion, and in company with two other boys he was shortly afterwards expelled for what the newspapers call serious offences.

Holidays in Chesterfield Street were not greatly to be looked forward to, for in the afternoons Charles was turned out into the streets by himself 'for exercise,' and although he was occasionally sent on an errand, perhaps to the Army and Navy Stores, he was generally at a loose end. About once a week he was allowed to go to the Aquarium — where he saw Blondin walk the tightrope and a lady called Zoe shot out of a cannon — or to the Egyptian Hall to see the magic of Maskelyne & Cook, or to St. George's Hall, which offered minstrels or Corney Grain. In his solitary wanderings, the pale, dark-eyed boy in an Eton suit, a top hat and patent leather shoes was several times accosted by strange men who wanted him to go to tea with them or to their rooms, and one of these admirers, an Australian millionaire, was so *épris* that he used to lie in wait for the lad and got so far as calling on my grandparents and offering to 'adopt' him. The boy's mother might have agreed to this course, but his father was unwilling, though it is questionable whether he understood the man's real motives. It suggests a curious innocence or trustfulness on my grandfather's part that he should have allowed his youngest son, of whom he was certainly fond, to be exposed to the dubious adventures and predatory loiterers of the streets of mid-Victorian London.

Returning as a rule to Chesterfield Street in time for tea in the drawing-room, Charles, though naturally a restless and active being, was expected to sit quietly reading Dickens, Scott or Thackeray until it was time to dress for dinner, and he was sometimes offered a bribe of sixpence if he would lie quite still on the hearth-rug for half an hour. In due course his mother would return from driving in the Park or from paying calls in her yellow-wheeled brougham, and the heavy splendour of the bourgeois evening *en famille* began to close in. The meal was heavy, the dining-room sultry with crimson hangings, the proceedings stately, with the surfaces of the old mayoral and shrieval plate agleam, cut glass scintillating, and silver livery-buttons winking as the men-servants moved in the lamplight. As for the knives, their handles were all made of the horns of some rare antelope of which my grandfather had shot many specimens in heaven knows what Asiatic wilderness. Afterwards in the drawing-room, where there prevailed what the advertisements of some digestive medicine used to call a sense of over-fullness after eating, boredom took command of all but my grandfather. That placid man was content, or appeared so, with the latest three-volume novel from Mudies' or a game of bezique or piquet. He was by nature inclined to silence, and from his Scotch mother had inherited that total lack of humour which is so dire and so usual a failing of her race. My grandmother, on the other hand, liked gay conversation at least, and the needlework with which she often occupied herself as she grew older was a poor substitute. This was not a cultured, not a musical, not a merry household, and the children were sent early to bed.

Holidays, however, were not always like this. My grandfather's sister, Catherine, had married George Browne, a farmer — or, as he would have been called in those caste-conscious days, a gentleman farmer — in Lincolnshire. She was his second wife, the first having been a Miss Allenby. Uncle George and aunt Kitty lived at Maidenwell House, near Louth, in an odd style of their own.

Helen Plomer would not go and stay with her sister-in-law, because, she alleged, she had once at Maidenwell found ducks' feathers in her bath water; but, as everybody knows, people often hold such small things against their relations in order to excuse indifference, antipathy or contempt towards them. Uncle George and aunt Kitty, however, were a benevolent couple, and liked nothing better than a houseful of nephews and nieces, and the nephews and nieces enjoyed themselves.

Life at Maidenwell was somewhat patriarchal, and it was a self-contained community, its days punctuated by family prayers at morning and evening, attended of course by the servants.[1] The farm-bailiff, the shepherd, the carpenter, the coachman and the gardeners all enjoyed the use of cottages rent-free, but each was expected to lodge one of the farm-hands and received for this purpose a small subsidy, in addition to his wages and allowances of milk, ham, bacon, corn and other produce of the farm. They were expected, unless ill, to attend church on Sundays.

For the nephews there was rough shooting, and once a year uncle George and aunt Kitty drove with all their guests into Louth to attend the hunt ball. Charles was much impressed by his first, at which he danced with a stately Lady Sophia Allenby. Sometimes he drove to Louth with his uncle George in a conveyance known as the 'minibus.' It was shaped like a matchbox standing on end, there was a seat on the roof for the coachman and a door at the back opening to admit one person to each of the seats on either side, where they sat facing each other. Sometimes, peering out at the rain on the wolds, when the drive was just a drive with no definite object, uncle George would murmur resignedly, 'My dear, this is a wild-goose chase.'

The coachman, a genial soul, was occasionally called in, when

---

[1] Apropos of family prayers, there was in the neighbourhood a dictatorial old lady who, in the hope of reducing what she regarded as an unduly high birth-rate, obliged her maid-servants to sleep in the attics and her men-servants in the basement. After evening prayers she invariably dismissed her retainers with a formula which was apt to cause at least a momentary apprehension to visitors not accustomed to it. 'Now then, skirts up! Trousers down! And a good night to you all!'

the house was full, to help wait at table. Wearing white cotton gloves with loose flaps at the ends of the fingers (since he could never get them properly on to his weather-beaten hands) and sweating freely, he made a most friendly though not a polished footman. Once, when a new local female grandee was being entertained to dinner at Maidenwell for the first time he handed her a jelly on a large dish. Just as she was about to help herself the jelly began to slither dangerously towards the edge of the dish, so in a hearty voice, as he righted the dish, he called out 'Whoa, mare!' which the grandee was for a moment on the verge of interpreting as a veto upon her helping herself. As for aunt Kitty, she was in the habit of wearing blue spectacles, and it is remembered that once when watching a thunderstorm she rather unreasonably complained that the lightning was blue.

Among the visitors to Maidenwell were two nieces of uncle George's, Edythe and Hilda Browne. One spring day Charles was sitting on a haystack with this playful pair when they shoved him off it, an attention he did not take at all well, though there was something about Edythe that impressed him very favourably.

While he was still a schoolboy both his brothers went into the army. William, the eldest, having a not inactive brain, would probably have done better in some other profession, but his career as a soldier proved moderately successful. He served in various wars, collected a number of decorations, and commanded at one time the Royal Irish Fusiliers. He had a literary bent when young, but did not develop it, and the only book he wrote was a manual of infantry training — of which the Library of Congress in Washington once asked me, to my surprise, if I was the author. He was not without curiosity, travelled enterprisingly in Japan, and amused himself in his peaceful later years with a microscope and a garden. His disposition was not naturally sunny and the earlier part of his life not altogether happy, but in his later years he found compensation for a disappointing marriage. His wife, my aunt Florence (born Wildman-Lushington), settled in Los Angeles and married again when she was over seventy. My father never saw much of his brother William and had little in common with him.

Of his brother Durham I have already spoken as my grand-mother's favourite child. He was nearer to my father in age and Charles looked up to him admiringly as a delicate boy will to a healthy one. Durham's body and health were superb and he had a blessedly unspeculative temperament to match. At Cheltenham, at Sandhurst and in the army he excelled at ball games; he swam, shot, played polo and pursued — or rather was pursued by — the opposite sex. He was always in debt, but that did not worry him in the least, for his mother could always be tapped in an extremity and would pop a piece of jewellery to keep him in pocket. In her eyes he could do no wrong. After leaving Cheltenham he went to 'Jimmy's,' a London crammer well known in those days, to prepare for Sand-hurst. His nights were characteristic no doubt of a playboy of the period. Once, when his parents were away and the servants at Chesterfield Street were on board wages, he elected, in company with a male friend, to entertain to dinner under the parental roof a couple of chorus girls. The party went with a swing, but by one of those curious mischances in which life is so prolific, my grandfather had suddenly decided to come up from the country for the night, and the colonel's ears, as he put his latchkey into the front door, were greeted by sounds of unaccountable revelry. As he opened the dining-room door these sounds diminished sharply.

'I am afraid,' he said quietly, with a bow, 'that I haven't the pleasure of these ladies' acquaintance. No doubt they have come to the wrong house — by mistake.'

He then withdrew, and Tamlin the butler hastily shepherded the merrymakers out of the house. My grandfather said little to Durham on the matter beyond pointing out that it was not the thing 'to foul one's own nest.' It is highly improbable that Durham had regarded the entertainment in such an ornithological sense, though it is true that females of easy virtue were then sometimes described as 'soiled doves.' A party in any house whatever, a simple party was to him, and it was nothing more. If any further light on this jovial character were needed, it is shed by an incident that occurred while he was still at the crammer's. He came out of a theatre one night with Lord Sudeley. They took a hansom apiece, put the drivers inside, and, themselves driving, set out for a bet to race from the Marble Arch to Notting Hill Gate. Near Lancaster Gate, however, they were stopped and run in, and the next morning appeared before a magistrate and were fined.

No such gaieties for my father's sister Laura, who was by eight years his senior, and who, though kind and protective towards him, had as a girl a sad and lonely life, which fortunately did not quench her natural vivacity. She was sent to a school for the daughters of officers and returned without pleasure to Chesterfield Street for the holidays, since she had to face being snubbed, ignored, humiliated or ordered about by her mother. Instances of mutual animosity between mother and daughter are not rare — there was a conspicuous instance in London between 1919 and 1939 — and they are apt to arise at least in part from a resemblance between the two characters. It is as if each saw in the other a rival. To call such a relationship unnatural is not reasonable, since we naturally tend to hate those whom, even if it be only in one particular trait, we most resemble. We resent their stealing, or attempting to steal, our thunder, and when the rivals are female the mutual animosity and jealousy may well be sharper. There is no unalterable reason why a woman should love her mother any more than her mother-in-law, and there is no need to draw attention to the miscarriages of happiness caused by misplaced filial piety.

Laura found herself relegated often enough to the company of the servants (in whom she found some degree of sympathy and kindliness), while her mother made much of two other girls of her own age (the daughters of another Anglo-Indian family), taking them out for drives or to parties. Laura found that only one thing was expected of her — to marry as soon as possible a man with money, of at least her own but preferably of a higher social status, and her obligation to do this was dinned into her unceasingly. Prospective suitors seem to have appeared on the scene when she was still remarkably young — she was pretty and sprightly and evidently not without fortune — and since they received every encouragement from her mother, Laura delighted in turning them down, even though her firmness led to stormy scenes. In due course she saw her chance of escape and happiness and decided to take it. Her mother sometimes allowed her to go and stay in other people's houses, being glad to get her out of her sight and hoping she might fall in with a suitable *parti*, and in one of these absences her meeting with a certain young man duly kindled what would once have been described as a mutual flame. He was the only son of a family of rich Quaker merchants, had been educated privately, and was something of an æsthete. His name was Horniman, and the money came from that popular beverage known as Horniman's Pure Tea. (His father gave London the little-known Horniman Museum and Gardens, and his sister was the Miss Horniman who later became famous as the pioneer and patroness of the repertory theatre movement in England and Ireland.)

To Laura the young Horniman proposed, and by Laura he was accepted, though her parents had never set eyes on him. The fact that she had accepted him would no doubt have been enough to set her mother against the proposed match, news of which let loose all Helen's rage. She was ordered to put the matter out of her head at once and hold no further communication with the young man. The precise objections advanced were that his family were not of adequate quality, that they were 'in trade,' and that Laura's intended was 'an atheist and a radical.' All fortunes presumably originate in trade, war, politics or plunder, or some combination of these activities, and it cannot be said that trade is the least noble of them: in any case the colonel owed his prosperity to fortunes made in trade in the previous century. The facts that the young man's character was mild, that he was the only son of a very rich man, and that he and Laura loved each other were not taken into consideration at all. As for the objections to his origins and beliefs, it can only be said that the forces of convention, a grotesque snobbishness and narrow class-prejudice, which had no doubt largely ossified the common sense and humane feelings of my grandparents during their life in the cantonments of Poona, were now erecting themselves as monstrous obstacles to young happiness and independence: equally strong was my grandmother's determination to exercise power over her daughter and make her subservient. Laura, however, was not one of those drooping, docile Victorian daughters: she had a will of her own, and the fact that she was ordered not to speak of the young man or give him any further thought — let alone see him or communicate with him — only heightened her resolve. As stolen fruit, her love must have been the sweeter, and who can now count the wrongs the poor girl had to avenge? — as when once, coming home from school, she had found that her mother, invading the privacy of her room, had made a cruel clean sweep of her treasures and girlish bric-à-brac.

The recalcitrant Laura, though by now almost grown up, was actually imprisoned in her room until she should 'come to her senses,' but these were in fact exactly what she had come to. In default of seeing her lover, she had one immediate wish, and that was to write to him. But how? She was denied not only freedom but writing materials. She managed to obtain these by persuading a housemaid who brought her meals to her room but whose kindness or courage did not extend so far as to provide either a stamp or an undertaking to post the letter when it was written; nor had Laura, in that opulent house, so much as a single penny to buy a stamp with. To obtain it was her immediate problem. Besides resourcefulness, determination, a pink complexion and bright eyes, she had another asset which seemed to her instantly marketable, namely, a magnificent head of fair hair, so long that she could stand on it. At this point such a posture would have done her no good; it was scissors that were needed. She accordingly cut from the middle of her scalp — whence its absence could be easily disguised — a great rope or switch of hair, like the flowing tail of some fabulous golden horse; coiled it up in a wrapping; and contrived to escape from the house for long enough to sell the trophy to the nearest Mayfair posticheur, to visit a post office and buy a stamp out of the proceeds, and to post her letter — then to be back in her room as if nothing had happened.

This was not a spirit to be defeated, and it was ready for the series of pitched battles still to come — the appeals to reason, duty, honour and a non-existent affection; the few but formidable words of the colonel; the rages of the colonel's wife. The direst threat was patterned on an old formula: 'If you marry this man, we shall no longer look upon you as our daughter. You will be disgracing your-self, and we shall never wish to see you again. You will be to us exactly as if you were dead.' To which the answer was the con-temporary equivalent of 'So what?' and a flurry of home truths. Finally it was obvious even to the stubborn father and bitter mother that nothing would move the girl, so they gave in, allowed her to be married from her own home, and accompanied her to St. George's, Hanover Square, and back, Helen in sables and a white fury, Laura radiant with ferocious joy. Unfortunately the constant Maitland was present, and as she was about to drive away for ever, Laura addressed her mother in terms of an uncompromising but not un-justifiable plainness; then, turning to Maitland, she told him with equal directness her wishes for the future, which included the inter-esting hope that he would die of 'some horrible disease.' An unusual wedding-day wish, but out it came: and having spoken her mind and purged it of hatred long unspoken, she went off with a new name to a new life with her radical æsthete, and enjoyed, for the next half-century or so, health, wealth and much happiness.

Many years later, Laura and her husband, going one evening to the play, were a little late and took their seats in the stalls when the theatre was already darkened. In the interval, when the lights went up, she looked about her. So did the handsome bediamonded matron next to her. Their eyes met, and it was her mother. They did not speak, but sat out the evening cheek by jowl yet as separate as strangers.

Much later still, early in the present century, when Laura was the happy mother of several children, her own mother, old and dis-integrating, sought a reconciliation: she wrote and asked Laura to come and see her. Laura made no move to do so, but one afternoon, after the lapse of some weeks, she was trying on a new green velvet dress and much admiring herself in the glass, when she suddenly decided to go and see her mother. Two sentences of the conversa-tion have been recorded.

'I wonder what your children think of me,' said the old woman, who was in bed.

'My children!' cried the unforgiving Laura, full of radiant vitality and again catching sight of her reflection and that of the green velvet dress in a glass. 'My children! Why, they don't even know that you exist!'

Charles, it may be said, to whom his sister had been more of a mother than his mother had been, had no intention at the time of her marriage of cutting her out of his existence. The time came when he, too, was due to leave the parental roof, and when his father asked him what he wanted to become, he said he wished to follow his two brothers into the army. But his father opposed him, telling him he would do better to go into — trade! My grandfather had been impressed by the fortune amassed by his erring brother John Thomas from the backs of sheep, and he had it in mind that his own son should do likewise. Charles, he said, should begin at the bottom and learn the wool trade thoroughly, so the boy was taken from school and sent to Bradford, apprenticed to a firm of wool merchants, lodged with a suitable clergyman, and given a small allowance.

During the first week Charles had to sweep out the warehouse; then he was put on to learn how to sort fleeces; and after a few months he was taken by his employer to attend the wool sales in London. They used to put up at an hotel in Finsbury Pavement, or in rooms in the City Road, and after breakfast they would put on checkered linen coats with brass buttons, known as 'brats,' in order to keep the natural grease in the wool from their clothes, and then sally forth to the Docks to worry the contents of the bales before these were put up for sale at the Wool Exchange in Coleman Street.

My father was always of a sociable disposition and at Bradford he used to play cards and billiards, and fish or shoot with the sons of rich manufacturers, and what with the high standard of living of the gilded youth of Yorkshire, and a somewhat expensive but otherwise highly successful down-to-brass-tacks romance with a gamekeeper's daughter (he was, I am glad to say, always generous to those he loved), the boy's modest allowance was scarcely adequate, so he got a little, really very little, out of his depth. The consequences of this slight extravagance changed the whole course of his life.

He went to his father and laid the facts before him. The colonel listened in silence but was evidently angry. He told his son that he had been 'most dishonourable' to get into debt, that he would talk matters over with his mother, and would let him know what they decided. It is not certain what share my grandmother had in the decision, but it is significant that it was again a sentence of banishment, this time to a remoter region than the Pas-de-Calais. My grandfather said he would pay Charles's debts, but he was to go to South Africa — 'the coming country' and one with great prospects, it was said, in the matter of wool: besides, the climate was good for asthma. Convention had again triumphed: the so lightly erring youngest son was to be packed off to that roomy Eldorado, 'the Colonies,' to sink or swim. So at the age of nineteen, with a letter of credit for a hundred pounds and a letter of introduction to Cecil Rhodes, my father set sail in the s.s. *Athenian* for 'the coming country.' Just before sailing he had paid a visit to Edythe Browne, who was staying with her mother at Buxton, and had told her that he would never marry anyone but her and would come back to her as soon as he was in a position to marry.

3. WANDER-YEARS

CAPETOWN was in those days still Cape Town, and picturesquely exotic. At his hotel Charles was warned not to wander, lest he be waylaid by Malay footpads; but the very regions against which he was warned have long since been respectable suburbs. A little dazzled by the brilliance and strangeness of his surroundings, he made an unsuccessful attempt to enter the wool trade, and then presented his letter to the tycoon.

Cecil Rhodes, though still in his thirties, was in the full flush of his megalomaniac triumph. He had obtained the charter for his company, which, with a capital of a million pounds, and the Dukes of Fife and Abercorn on the board, was to open up a vast *Lebens-raum* for the white man in the interior of Africa; and he was about to become Prime Minister at the Cape. The Chartered Company had an office in Capetown, and it was there that my father saw the man who was of the stuff that dictators are made of. The shy, bright-eyed boy took the chair that was offered, and the heavy purposeful mask, with the slightly hypnotic eyes and cloven chin, leaned towards him. In his high voice Rhodes fired off numerous questions, staring hard at Charles all the time, and no doubt 'sizing him up' in the business man's sense of the phrase. Then he carried him off to lunch with two of his political friends, ignored him during the meal and having made him feel very young and green told him afterwards that such was his nature, finally suggesting that he should join the Cape Mounted Rifles, a then well-known regiment of mounted police consisting largely of more or less 'pukka sahibs.' He was to come and let Rhodes know when he had made up his mind one way or the other.

As he had meant to continue in the wool trade, Charles was in two minds what to do; and in order to reduce them to one he went to the Castle to see an old friend of his father's, General Sir William Cameron, then Acting-Governor. Cameron received him kindly, but was curious to know why he had come to the Cape, thinking perhaps to smell out a misdemeanour. Charles said, truthfully enough, that he suffered from asthma and his father thought the Cape would do it good, besides being 'the coming country.' Cameron, as an old soldier, thought enlistment in the Cape Mounted Rifles would provide 'a splendid opportunity' for the young man to get to know the country: he could always pursue the wool trade, or anything else he fancied, later on.

So my father, anxious perhaps to emulate his brothers and be a soldier, made his way by sea to East London, and thence to Kingwilliamstown, where the regiment had its headquarters. In the uniform, top boots and spurs of a trooper, the young and asthmatic Cockney, who didn't know one end of a horse from the other, went through riding-school (and it was a hard school, in which the inexperienced were told in stentorian voices, among other things less polite, that they resembled baboons riding curry-combs); took many a fall without a murmur; and before long was able to do all the tricks, to ride with a carbine at full gallop, brandish a sword, jump without stirrups, and so on. It was, in fact, a hard life, but he stuck it for nearly a year: then, on the advice of the medical officer, he bought himself out.

Now the wander-years began in earnest. My father had no special bent, so he drifted with all the restlessness of a young asthmatic. At Port Elizabeth he took up with a pleasant and plausible young man, with whom he pooled his small capital to open a café stylishly called the 'Old Madrid.' They engaged an Italian cook and made a roaring success of it, but Charles, suddenly afflicted with asthma, went inland for a change of air, and in his absence his partner decamped with all the funds. If it were possible to divide mankind into those who defraud and those who are defrauded, my father, I am proud to say, would belong to the latter class.

As soon as he got over the first shock of this betrayal he realized that he was on the rocks: but Providence stepped in, taking the shape of an hotel-keeper. This individual had obtained a contract for a banquet which was to be offered to the Governor at the township of Molteno, away up in the mountainous hinterland, on the occasion of the opening of the extension of the railway thence to Bethulie, on the Orange River. My father agreed to take charge of the proceedings, the waiters, the food, the drinks, the cutlery, crockery, linen, flowers, ice — and, of course, the bunting.

All went well. A little after noon on the appointed day a train, much beflagged, drew into Molteno amid the plaudits of the populace. (What a typically nineteenth-century scene!) The Governor emerged, received the local bigwigs, made a speech declaring the extended railway open, and then made a timely move to the banqueting hall. Charles was somewhat taken aback to find that the Governor wasn't the Governor, Sir Henry Loch, after all, but the Acting-Governor — none other than his father's friend and his own acquaintance, Sir William Cameron. The banquet, however, went with a swing, there were more speeches, and His Excellency in due course rose to depart. Charles was congratulating himself on having escaped notice when an A.D.C. arrived and told him that the Governor wanted to see him, and was waiting in his saloon coach —

very much, evidently, as a headmaster awaits a recalcitrant boy in his study.

'What the devil does this mean?' His Excellency demanded — a little ungraciously perhaps, since his enjoyment of the banquet had been largely due to my father's efforts. 'What would your father think of your behaviour?'

Charles gave his reasons for appearing in the role of *maître d'hôtel*.

'Then why on earth didn't you write to me, if you were in need of help, or to Mr. Rhodes? There are certain things that a gentleman doesn't do, and what you've been doing is one of them. I will advance you twenty-five pounds to help you, and I'll write and get it back from your father.'

This was admittedly a kind act and the young man was touched by it, and not altogether unimpressed by the discovery that he had broken a class taboo and committed a social *gaffe* so monstrous that no less a person than the representative of the Queen had felt it incumbent upon him to point it out. His Excellency's behaviour affords a pretty example of caste loyalty, or the herd instinct, but my father was never a man who would have thought useful work of any kind beneath his dignity — particularly if it had to do with food. (In later years he delighted to entertain his family and friends with dishes of his own cooking, and I have never eaten better.) He was honest and trusting and free from meanness, conscious of his background but not in the least 'class-conscious' in the narrow and derogatory sense of the word. Besides, he was on his beam-ends, and had very sensibly jumped at the job of organizing the banquet.

He now took to the land, managed a sheep-farm near Queenstown, attached to himself a delightful Basuto pony, planted nearly a quarter of a million eucalyptus and pine trees, and then went off on a tour of the Winterberg and Tafelberg, making his way by sorting wool-clips. Then he turned tutor; then he went off with a Dutchman, Barend van der Linde, constructing fences; and finally ended up as manager of a native trading station at Driver's Drift, near Lady Frere. This he enjoyed greatly, and he liked and in many ways admired the natives, who were of the Xosa tribe. But one day a swaggering young Xosa offended him; Charles ordered him off, and the Xosa would not budge; whereupon Charles, in one of those sudden rages to which, like his mother, he was liable, seized the nearest thing handy, which happened to be a hatchet, and rushed at the man — intending, I trust, to frighten rather than cleave him to the midriff. The native, whose name was Ulangene, was too quick for him and in self-defence struck him on the head with his knob-kerrie and knocked him out.

The next morning Charles went to discuss the matter with the local chief. They had a formal interview, and the chief told him that he had been in the wrong to lose his temper and take up a hatchet, but that Ulangene was also wrong, had behaved badly in the first place (which was true), and had no right to assault a white man. (Another taboo broken.) The unfortunate Ulangene was ordered by the chief to be flogged then and there with a strip of untanned ox-hide (no light punishment), but he bore my father no ill-will, knowing that he himself had been in the wrong at first, and they became good friends. Ulangene, who was a splendid swimmer, later distinguished himself by saving single-handed a post-cart, containing mailbags and drawn by mules, from being washed away in a flooded river, and Charles successfully exerted himself to get Ulangene an official grant of a sum of money as a reward.

It was time to wander again: after a holiday in Queenstown, Charles had spent all his money and had to cast about for something new. This time he set out on foot, with a billy-can in his hand and a bundle on a stick like Dick Whittington, for a place on the Zwart Kei river where a bridge was being built. When he got there he pretended he was an efficient stonemason, and was set to shape a great block of granite, but the hammer kept slipping off the chisel and soon his knuckles were skinned and bleeding. He stuck to it, however, until the overseer found him out and appointed him store-keeper and clerk to the whole outfit, in which post he continued happily for some time, enjoying bathing in the river or fishing for barbel on the long dazzling Sundays, picnics and excursions, and the happy spirit of camaraderie among the men: but as he had saved some money he grew restless again.

He thought he would like to return to trading with the natives, engaged himself to an old man near Queenstown who was occupied in that way, and served him with great efficiency. But the old man had a daughter who kept house for him, a crabbed virgin with white eyelashes, lustreless eyes of an indeterminate colour set in a dead white face, and sandy hair like veld-grass after a hot summer. She invariably dressed in black merino, in perpetual mourning for a mother long since dead. She never smiled or displayed any emotion except for fleeting moments when talking to her father. Charles was privately warned that she was insanely jealous of his influence with the old man, and finding her presence too sinister to be endurable, he departed.

At this time, under the influence of Rhodes, all fortune-hunters were looking to the north – there was gold on the Rand, there were vast tracts of fertile land to be had from the Chartered Company almost for the asking. Travelling partly by rail, partly on foot, Charles set off in the direction of Kimberley. One day, feeling tired, he made his way to a lonely farmhouse which he had descried in the distance. Here he was offered hospitality by the farmer, a Dutchman of the poorer class. The house, or shack, was built of dried mud and roofed with corrugated iron, the interior being divided in the middle by a calico curtain, on one side of which was an enormous bed and on the other a rough table and some chairs and forms. This dwelling was inhabited by the farmer, his wife, three sons and five daughters, the eldest child being nearly grown up and the youngest still at the breast. At sunset the little clan gathered round the table; the farmer, whose name was Scheepers, read a chapter from a large Bible and offered up a long prayer for his family, himself, and the work of his hands; and a coloured girl then brought in a cauldron of stewed mutton, a dish of stamped boiled maize, and another of sweet potatoes, the meal being completed by a large loaf and copious draughts of sour milk. At bed-time the table was pushed back and a large mattress was spread on the ground and covered with goatskins.

'You can sleep there with the children,' said Scheepers politely, 'but I shall put one of the boys between you and my eldest girl.'

He and his wife then retired to the monumental bed, accompanied by the youngest members of their brood, and Charles tumbled in with the older boys and girls – and the fleas. In the morning, after breakfast and prayers, Charles, being a person of regular habits and anxious to observe the local *convenances*, approached his host, who was smoking an early pipe in the fresh morning air, and enquired the whereabouts of the sanitary arrangements.

'Ah,' said Scheepers in that homely Taal (of which my father already had a working knowledge), and he took his pipe out of his mouth and with a sweeping gesture waved it towards a magnificent landscape of mountains and pastures, 'it is all my land. S—t where you like!'

After this exquisite experience of primitive good manners, my father, who had sixty pounds in hand and was content to drift along, enjoying the sunshine and his by now greatly improved health, found himself not at Kimberley but at the little *dorp* of Aliwal North, a clean town with rivulets running at the sides of its streets. Here he met a lonely young Englishman who was dying of consumption, and gladdened his last days with kind companionship. One night, after Charles had been reading to him, the young man had a violent hæmorrhage. Charles, tenderest of nurses, washed him, dressed him in a clean night-shirt, and gave him some brandy-and-milk. For a few days he seemed better and was able to sit out on the shady verandah, but then he died calmly one night in Charles's arms. Charles had grown fond of him, was much affected by his death, and felt that he could not stay in the town, but as he left it he wondered if he was wise to leave such a peaceful haven for places he knew nothing of and in search of he knew not what.

In the train to Kimberley a fellow-passenger warned him that he would there be robbed of anything he had and might, as a new-comer, be used without knowing it as a go-between for the conveyance of illicitly bought diamonds. The stranger told him of a young man who had been asked at a Kimberley hotel if he would mind taking a note and a parcel to a house about a hundred yards away.

He agreed, and when he got to the house was asked to sit down and wait for an answer. The house was instantly rushed by detectives, he and the householder were arrested, and the parcel was opened and found to contain seven diamonds. In spite of all his protestations of innocence, the young man had been convicted as an accessory to illicit diamond-buying and sent off to a convict settlement for five years. The stranger told Charles that he had no hope of getting work in Kimberley unless he was personally known to one of the 'big diamond men,' and he suggested that the best plan would be to join the Bechuanaland Border Police. Accordingly, after a glimpse of the splendours and miseries of Kimberley, my father made his way to Mafeking to enlist in that corps. Cavalry exercises were no longer mysterious to him, but public school men were here less numerous than they had been in the Cape Mounted Rifles.

It was now towards the end of 1895, and rumours were circulating that the Dutch had been ill-treating the British in Johannesburg, arresting them, it was said, on trumped-up charges and then heavily fining them, and bringing in all sorts of taxation which interfered with their commercial activities, while Dutch citizens were exempt from any such burdens. A deputation had protested to Kruger and had presented him with a petition to grant the British inhabitants of his Republic some share in the management both of their own affairs and those of the State. Kruger was reported to have scoffed at them and told them that if they did not like its laws they could get out of the country, although he knew that they had invested heavily in gold mining particularly, an industry which they were mainly responsible for developing. These rumours gained weight every day and soon it was being said that the British were going to take up arms and force the Dutch to come to terms with them. Presently news came through that Dr. Jameson had come down from Rhodesia with a force of police 'to protect the border' and was encamped at Pitsani.

The Bechuanaland Border Police were paraded and informed that the British at Johannesburg had asked Jameson for armed assistance 'to protect the women and children' in case of more trouble, it being alleged that the Dutch were bent on using armed force in that town. The Bechuanaland Police were to join forces with Jameson at Malmani, just inside the Transvaal.

'I can't order you to go,' said their colonel, 'but I hope you're all willing to go.'

Three cheers rang out, within half an hour everyone was ready, and the column moved out of the town, to the cheers of such of the local inhabitants as were of British extraction. It probably did not occur to any of the mounted policemen, including my father, that there was anything questionable about the adventure for which they had volunteered.

Jameson had successfully cut the telegraph wires to Capetown in order to prevent the expedition being vetoed or postponed by his friend Rhodes, but he was less successful with those to Pretoria, for the trooper sent to cut them was so drunk that he cut and carefully buried strands of wire from a farmer's fence instead. Kruger was therefore kept well informed of what was in the wind.

Just before the column reached Malmani it joined Jameson's column, which consisted mostly of men of the Mashonaland Mounted Police, led by boyish young Guards officers who had been seconded for police work and were lacking in military experience. The whole force amounted only to some hundreds of men. They rode off as fast as was consistent with sparing the horses, and at about five 'o'clock in the afternoon of the 30th December arrived at a trading store, where fresh horses had been provided to replace any that had been unable to stay the pace. After a meal of bully beef, bread and coffee they pushed on, riding all night until they reached another store and went through similar proceedings. After a rest of a couple of hours they pushed on all day and towards sunset reached a point near Krugersdorp where some Dutchmen opened fire on them, which they returned. There were a few casualties, and a man near my father was badly wounded in the thigh.

Jameson now decided to withdraw, and darkness having set in he halted his men and told them to try and get some rest. They fastened the bridles of six or eight horses together and one man was ordered to look after each batch for an hour, the others meanwhile trying to snatch a sleep on the ground between the lines. Shortly before dawn they received the order to fall in and continue on their way, and soon after sunrise they were met by a burst of rifle fire from a rocky outcrop at the end of an open plateau, so they hastily dismounted and advanced on foot in skirmishing order, taking such little cover as they could find. My father took cover behind an ant-hill with one Dick Stone, with whom he had shared a tent at Mafeking, and they fired from behind it at anyone they could see among the rocks some 300 yards off. Suddenly Charles heard a thud and a choking noise and saw that Stone had had half his throat blown away. From this sickening sight his attention was diverted by the appearance on horseback of one of the Guards officers, a Captain Coventry, who was encouraging the men. Suddenly he was hit in the leg, and my father and two other men rushed up to help him from his horse. When they had done so, he gallantly ordered them to separate and return to cover.

Dr. Jameson now came out of a house on the edge of the plateau and with several other men hoisted a borrowed apron by way of a white flag. The order to cease fire was given; some Dutchmen arrived at a gallop; and after a parley terms of surrender were arranged. The men were ordered to find their horses and fall in, and were then disarmed by a large crowd of Dutchmen who surrounded them. They rode off between armed guards to Krugersdorp, where they were halted in the market square and jeered at by Dutch women and children. They then departed for Pretoria, their guards showing great glee – which they expressed by frequently firing their rifles and by singing the *Volkslied*, their national anthem – and often assuring them that they would all be shot when they arrived at the capital. However, they were far too tired, hungry, thirsty and despondent to care, and many, including my father, fell asleep in the saddle, only waking when some inequality in the road had caused some irregular movement of their horses, threatening to unseat them.

At Pretoria they were interned on the racecourse, where they inhabited the grandstand. My father, light-headed from fatigue and hunger, got as tight as an owl on a bottle of sweet Cape wine which he had managed to get from the caretaker, a Dutchman, but he soon recovered. After a few days the men were told that they were to be sent to England, by way of Natal, to stand their trial for entering a friendly State with arms with intent to commit a breach of the peace. They travelled in open trucks to Volksrust, the border town between the South African Republic and the colony of Natal, and there they filed before a General Cox, who was local Commander-in-Chief of the British Forces. My father, on being asked his name and giving it, received from the General a quizzical look in which there was some amusement. This was accounted for some months later, when his eldest brother said he had had a letter from his friend General Cox, saying, 'I have just signed for your scallywag brother and sent him home with the other filibusters.'

At Durban the men received their arrears of pay and a present of ten pounds apiece, thought to have come either from the Chartered Company or from Rhodes personally. The result was that cards were played for high stakes throughout the voyage. My father, entrusted with the winnings of one of his mates, prudently handed them to the purser, with instructions not to give them up on any account until the voyage was over. At Las Palmas an inspector from Scotland Yard came aboard and arrested four men who were wanted for various offences committed in England. The others were told that on arrival there they would be free. Jameson and the officers with him would be tried, but no action would be taken against the rank and file.

They arrived on a Sunday, and my father, who presented a somewhat dilapidated appearance in dirty flannel trousers, his police tunic (somewhat battle-stained) and a grey cap, betook him to his old hotel in Finsbury Pavement. Here he was pursued by reporters, to whom he would not talk, and early the next morning he drove off to the family tailor in Conduit Street to get some clothes. In these, as soon as they were ready, he went to lunch with his father at the United Services Club, where he was greeted with 'What on earth do you think *you're* doing, playing at soldiers! But, by God, my boy, I'm proud of you!' and was proudly introduced to some old military buffers and club cronies of the colonel's, including Lord Napier of Magdala.

Some strenuous night-life began with a rowdy evening at the Pavilion with a mob of similarly repatriated filibusters, and ended with a seductive invitation to her house in Sloane Street by a more or less *grande cocotte*. The lady was the mistress of a successful barrister, temporarily absent in Scotland, and the idea of an adventure with one of the popular heroes of the day, these tanned and sinewy invaders of smutty, wintry London, quite took possession of her. ('You must be one of those delicious men who have been making Oom Paul dance,' was the way she put it.) There were also some cosy suppers with Mabel Love, a successful and pretty musical comedy actress of the day.

Turning aside from these junketings, Charles proposed himself for a visit to the mother of Edythe Browne at Southwell in Nottinghamshire. The little town was all agog at the prospect of a visit from a Jameson Raider and was with some difficulty restrained from providing a civic welcome, complete with band. Charles was treated with affection by Mrs. Browne and with gay good humour by her daughters, but having no money or position or immediate prospects, he felt he had no right to try and manœuvre Edythe into a formal engagement: he left her, however, in no doubt of his hopes and intentions. For the present he was still a mounted policeman from Bechuanaland and in that capacity was shortly recalled to Africa.

Rhodes's *Lebensraum* was now the scene of 'native trouble,' and Charles found himself a mere pawn in the game, attached to the Matabeleland Relief Force under Colonel Plumer (later Field-Marshal Lord Plumer) and occupied with the transport of supplies, a process somewhat impeded by the prevalence of illicit liquor-selling to the native wagon-drivers. He had as his companion another of those rather romantic young Dutchmen with whom from time to time he was associated. This one, called Willy Buissine, came from the Cape – 'the only man I have ever seen,' my father used to say, and one can well believe it, 'who could stand a bottle between his feet and flick it away with the lash of a forty-foot wagon whip.'

Part of the process of 'relieving' the white settlers in Matabeleland was to push forward the building of the railway from Mafeking to Bulawayo, since supplies could only come vast distances by ox-wagon from the south, or by way of Beira, in Portuguese territory, from the east. The engine drivers and firemen on the construction trains used to amuse themselves by throwing pieces of coal at wilde-beests and zebras frisking beside the line. Out beyond the advancing railway my father was able to shoot various sorts and sizes of game, and at his camp on the banks of the Mahalapswe river he had the pleasure of entertaining Prince Alexander of Teck and F. C. Selous, the celebrated hunter.

By the time my father reached Bulawayo the so-called Matabele rebellion was over. He did not wish to continue in the police, obtained a post on the staff of a newspaper, the Pretoria *Press*, and took up his abode in that town with a Mr. and Mrs. Preller. Preller was an official at the High Court, and his wife when a small girl had come from the Cape with the Voortrekkers in 1836. Mrs. Preller used to say she never thought she would like a *rooinek* (= red neck, i.e. Englishman), but, she said, my father was 'like another son' to her. She was so pleased with him that she took him to call on the President of the Republic, Paul Kruger himself. The editor of the *Press* encouraged my father's visits to the Presidency and urged him to gather tit-bits of political gossip. With engaging candour Charles used to tell the President that he had been asked to find out what the Volksraad or Kruger himself were going to do about such and such a matter. Sometimes Kruger would reply, 'I cannot say,' and some-times, 'Tell your editor to wait and see,' but sometimes he spoke plainly and the news went round the world. The old man had a curious habit of pinching my father's leg when his attention was diverted, and then roaring with primitive laughter at the young man's surprised or pained outcry. Kruger's religion, in my father's opinion, was deep and genuine, and he guided his whole life by the Bible, often choosing out for quotation some passage that agreed with intentions he had already formed.

Charles had become secretary of the local swimming club. He had been 'taught' to swim as a small boy by his father's having thrown him out of a boat into the sea. He was a swimmer born and made, and strangely enough his asthma never affected his prowess in the water. He now persuaded the President to attend the club sports. A strip of red baize was laid down at one end of the baths, with an armchair in the middle for the top-hatted and frock-coated old father of his people, and other chairs for members of his Cabinet: he was attended on this occasion by Generals Burger and Joubert, Dr. Leyds, the State Secretary, and one or two others. My father did a high dive and then swam round the bath under the water, picking up as he went twenty-four plates which he gracefully deposited in a pile at the President's feet.

'*Machtig!*' said Kruger. '*De kerel swimmt net als een visch!*' ('Good God! The man swims just like a fish.')

Charles was then tied up in a sack and shoved off the top of the high-diving platform into the water. He had a knife in his hand, ripped open the bag, rose to the surface, and made a bow to the President, who could not think how it was done and had to have it explained to him. He then laughed loudly, saying, '*Maar dit es slim!*' ('Very cunning!')

My father had many good friends at this time, most of them Dutch, and among his acquaintances were Botha and Smuts. But his pleasant existence was interrupted by typhoid fever. When he recovered he went down to the Cape to see his brother Durham, now captain and adjutant of his regiment, which had just arrived there from Jamaica. He drove up to the Royal Hotel in Capetown in a hansom cab, and there was Durham on the verandah among his brother officers. As my father got out of the cab, Durham called out, 'My God, where did you get that hat?' being unfamiliar with the picturesque fashions for males in the far-off South African Republic.

My father was in Pretoria when the South African war broke out, and there was a great exodus of English people to the coast. He did not quite know what to do, and was certainly not in the least interested in fighting the Dutch, of whom he was fond: besides, he had engaged in a business venture which was just developing nicely. Louis Botha offered him a permit to remain in Pretoria if he so wished, but he decided that he had better go, and Botha wrung his hand and wished him good luck. He travelled in a cattle truck with a boy of 15 who had been entrusted to his care, and they saw the Bethulie bridge over the Orange River blown up behind them. It was good-bye to coffee with the President, the sun on the stoep, the bicycle rides and picnics, the high dives and the friendly Dutch girls, good-bye to the weeping Mrs. Preller, good-bye to the Edison Bell phonograph, the leisurely capital of the lost Republic, good-bye to the nineteenth century.

Charles, who was still only in his twenties, evidently took not the slightest interest in the war, but he had taken a great fancy to the boy, and they spent some idyllic weeks together on the Buffalo river near East London, bathing, fishing and idling. He then decided to go to England.

'What on earth have you come home for?' said his astonished father. 'Aren't we fighting for you? It's your duty to go back at once and help.'

So back he went, and was appointed an inspector of transport. Presently he set off with a train of thirty wagons, each drawn by sixteen oxen, from Burghersdorp to Aliwal North. They were loaded with military supplies for the ill-fated General Gatacre. Charles got through, after suffering some losses and casualties at Labuschagne's Nek. After this there were long escorted convoys, sometimes of a hundred and twenty wagons, across the Orange Free State, Charles doing well but having occasional trouble with ignorant but truculent generals, particularly Hector Macdonald. On one occasion the scouts in advance of the column of wagons were fired upon by snipers hidden in a Dutch farmhouse, over which they had hoisted a white flag. My father saw Macdonald turn every living being out of the farm — old women and two babies included — and burn the house to the ground, leaving these people with nothing but the clothes they stood in. The snipers had ridden away from the farm over the crest of a hill behind it just before Macdonald's men had reached it.

'It was a pitiable sight,' said my father, 'but war is no discriminator of persons. The lives of our scouts were taken by treachery and were of equal value with the lives of Dutchmen.'

A thousand head of cattle had now to be taken by him from Bethlehem, in the Orange Free State, to Johannesburg. This convoy was attacked twice on the way, with a loss of seven men and only twenty-three oxen. My father had with him a Captain Luscombe, a regular soldier who was in charge of the escort. Being asked rather patronizingly one day by some other regular officers who the devil was the fellow in civilian clothes with whom he was riding, Luscombe replied, 'Oh, only the brother of the man at Sandhurst who taught you blighters the little soldiering you know.' (An allusion to my uncle William, who had in fact been on the staff at Sandhurst before the war.)

Having handed over his vast herd of cattle at Johannesburg and been complimented by a bigwig on having brought them so far so successfully, Charles went on to Pretoria, now in English hands. There he heard of the death in action of his brother Durham. There is a faded pathos in a telegram (which lies before me as I write) from Durham's commanding officer to my father. It is headed *Z. A. Republiek* and stamped 'Army Telegraphs, 13.ix.00':

'Captain Plomer buried Nooitgedacht. All his things except carbine and pony sent 8th Brigade depot Maritzburg. Wire instructions about horse, etc.'

So perished a healthy, hearty male, leaving 'horse, etc.' It was a blow from which his mother never recovered. Where love for her children was concerned, she had put all her eggs, poor dear, in one basket.

Charles's business venture had luckily not been blasted by the war. It recovered, and having some money in hand, he obtained his release from military service and left for England. It was marriage he had in mind. He had long had it in mind, but there is no matchmaker so powerful as war. He made straight for Southwell.

4. CATHEDRAL TOWN

THE Venerable John Henry Browne, archdeacon of Ely and rector of Cotgrave in Nottinghamshire, was certainly venerable in appearance. His figure was tall and erect, his brow calm and lofty; his features, though not aggressive, were as commanding as they were regular; he had a long upper lip that would have been becoming to a judge; his mouth suggested self-control, laudable prejudice and scholarly precision; and beneath his chin a pair of snowy bands hung like an accent over his flowing black gown. Although only an archdeacon, he was sometimes known as 'the Archduke,' perhaps because of his stately bearing. By some of his descendants it was believed, and by others denied, that he was the natural son of a local peer. What is certain is that his learning and piety were conspicuous, and he would have made an impressive bishop, but at a time when the Tractarian movement was hatching he had already become a hardened Evangelical, and instead of moving with the times was given to public controversy over peculiar dogmas like justification by faith. It cannot in fairness be said that his printed writings, of which there is a considerable collection in the British Museum, make jolly reading; but I have heard his archidiaconal 'charges' extolled as models of their kind.

The Archduke made a respectable marriage and became the father of five sons and three daughters. His sons never went to school: he himself prepared them all for Cambridge, where one became a second wrangler. Another, George Browne of Maidenwell, has already appeared in these pages. He was not the only one who took to farming: there was also Edward, who continued to live at Cotgrave.

Edward Browne was not in the least eccentric. He farmed his land well, lived in some style and had the reputation, like so many Victorian sportsmen, of being the best shot in the county, but was not excessively hearty. In appearance he was sad and supercilious, rather a Dundreary, with drooping eyelids that gave him a look of languor, and a somewhat apostolic beard. In character he was kind, manly and unassuming, and not without a streak of playfulness. He married twice, his second wife being his cousin, Edith Alethea Franklyn, by whom he had five children. When the three who survived were still children, he came in one day wet from the fields, stood steaming before the fire instead of changing his clothes, went into a rapid consumption, and died, still a youngish man.

Edith, his wife and widow, was the youngest daughter of George Franklyn, a member of Parliament, who came on his father's side of a family of rich Bristol tobacco merchants ('Franklyn's Fine Shag, Good to the End') and on his mother's from a pleasant and prolific but rather dim county family, the Wards of Ogbourne St. Andrew in Wiltshire, whose sole claim to fame, I believe, was that they had in the seventeenth century given Ossory a bishop and the University of Dublin at the same time a vice-chancellor. The Franklyns were a very 'Aryan' race, tending to be solid and big-boned, fair-haired and blue-eyed, with ruddy complexions, large appetites, cheerful tempers and no nerves. Very different was George Franklyn's wife, Mary, the seventeenth and last child of the Rev. John Henry Arden of Longcroft Hall in Staffordshire, a dark, elegant and delicate woman, quick-witted, with dark eyes and beautiful hands and feet.

The Ardens of Longcroft, formerly of Park Hall in Warwickshire, have been called the 'oldest' family in England. They claimed descent from one Alwyne, a relation of King Athelstan, and through him from that legendary hero, Guy of Warwick, as well as from the brother of Lady Godiva. At the time of the Conquest they were lording it over the region of Arden, which I suppose roughly corresponded with Warwickshire, and from it they took their name, at first de Arden, one of the earliest English surnames. One of them lost his life in the Wars of the Roses, one was Esquire of the Body to Henry VII, one got into political trouble in Elizabethan times (and so into the *Dictionary of National Biography*), but they never budged — except during a brief contretemps — from Park Hall between the time of Richard II and that of Charles I, when the elder line died out and the younger continued at Longcroft. Shakespeare's mother was Mary Arden, but her kinship with the Ardens of Park Hall, though sometimes taken for granted, has never, I believe, been conclusively proved. The name of Arden certainly had, when William Shakespeare was born, more distinction than his patronymic; and his mother, about whom next to nothing is known, must have been, to produce such a son, one of the half-dozen most remarkable women who have ever lived. It is idle, but tempting, to wonder to what extent his qualities were derived from her, and whether it was she who made him so conscious of the implications of rank, authority and power.

The Ardens took a natural and reasonable pride in their long association with the same countryside and in their tradition as a family rooted in the middle of England, but in later generations they sometimes developed a certain strangeness. In some cases this took the form of an excruciating shyness and agoraphobia and a tendency to hide themselves away from all but their intimates and servants — a consequence, possibly, of centuries of comparative isolation and self-sufficiency. I know someone who went to call on an Arden and found him 'not at home,' but on departing caught sight of a pair of big blue eyes peering out of the shrubbery: for such elusiveness, of course, there may have been more than one reason.

The Mary Arden who married George Franklyn hardly grew up an isolationist, for she had sixteen brothers and sisters, her eldest brother being a major of dragoons when she was still in long clothes. Besides, her mother, known as Madam Arden, had been sociable as well as fecund: as a young woman she used to hold on to a bed-post while two maids tugged at her stay-laces in order to approximate the circumference of her waist to that of her neck; and more than once, when going to a ball, her hair was dressed so high and so elaborately that she had to sit on the floor of the carriage to avoid disarranging it.

Edith Franklyn derived from her mother wit rather than beauty, and her appearance gained more from the quick play of expression, reflecting a warm heart and a lively intelligence, than from an academic cast of face. Educated well in the fashion of the times, she knew several languages, drew with a telling nervous line, and had the great gift of intellectual curiosity, which was sharpened by reading and sojourns abroad with her father in various countries, including Hungary, a country which he particularly liked and in which he had friends, though it was then little visited by the English.

After her husband's death from consumption, Edith Browne (as she had become), comfortably off though not rich, settled at Southwell in Nottinghamshire, in a white Georgian house of moderate size, to bring up her family. Her two eldest sons, Guy and Harold, had died young. There remained Edythe, Hilda and Franklyn. Guy, it may be remarked, was called after Guy of Warwick; Harold, whose other name was Edward, after King Harold; Edythe, though called by her mother's sweet and simple name, was given it with a fancy archaic spelling; and Hilda's other name was Alys. The choice of these names is partly to be ascribed to Edith Browne's wish to commemorate her remote Anglo-Saxon origins on her mother's side, and partly to a fashion of the period. This fashion found one of its quaintest expressions in the poet William Barnes's *Early England and the Saxon-English* (1869) and his *Outline of English Speech-Craft* (1878). That learned and delightful man, it may be recalled, plumped for plain English, though whether he always wrote it is a moot point: for example, of the degrees of comparison he observed that 'these pitch-marks offmark sundry things by their sundry suchnesses.' Barnes would have had us call democracy *folkdom* and botany *wortlore*, a depilatory a *hairbane*, a concert a *gleemote*, an appendix a *hank-matter*, a butler a *winethane*, a perambulator a *push-wainling*, and a globule a *ballkin*. It is true that Mrs. Browne did not boggle at benaming her afterkin after her forekin, but I never heard that she was ready to follow Barnes — whose poetry she admired — to these Nordic extremes of markworthy word-moulding.

In a small cathedral town in the seventies society was still pretty rigidly graded, but the boundaries between castes were slowly, here and there, becoming blurred. Whereas Madam Arden had taken it for granted that the family doctor, when sent for, should go round to the back door like any other tradesman, her grand-daughter Mrs. Browne went no further than writing to her doctor in the third person. Life in Southwell, if not static, was placid, except for an occasional roaring scandal, as when a young woman of the propertied class, returning alone one afternoon from a charitable visit to the sick poor, was raped by a labourer in a convenient meadow. (It was said that as a result of this experience she lost her reason; if so, she can hardly have been richly endowed with that faculty.) Conversation, or rather gossip, was one of the mainstays of life, and the framework of gossip was composed of the niceties of relationships and of social status. Readers of the memoirs of minor royalties of the last century cannot fail to be struck with the fact that, in the stiffly regulated and stylized world they inhabited, the slightest deviation from routine was seized upon as a relief. Their sense of humour fed largely upon trifling unforeseen accidents, slight and unwitting breaches of ceremonial, actions for which there appeared no precedent. Any real display of individuality created amazement, and an elopement or a suicide shook them like a cataclysm. It is perhaps much the same in any formal society; it was certainly much the same at Southwell. Every mannerism of every clergyman who set foot in the minster was noticed and discussed, and at Easthorpe Lodge, where the Brownes lived, amusingly mimicked. There was, for instance, a canon who, while preaching, removed his false teeth, held them at arm's length, gave them a long and quizzical look, and then popped them into place again. And when on fine afternoons a bishop's widow, herself the daughter of an earl, was seen seated, peacefully knitting, on her husband's grave, this custom was widely analysed, and though willingly attributed to conjugal devotion and a sense that in death she and her husband were not divided, was thought by some to show a deficient sense of decorum. The precise relations between curates and spinsters, the gaucheries of the former, the infatuations of the latter, were carefully followed. Indiscreet remarks travelled like wildfire; if social relations were sometimes *en delicatesse*, sometimes *en froideur*, everybody knew why, or pretty soon invented a reason. Amorous advances, matrimonial prospects, conjugal unfaithfulnesses, testamentary expectations or disappointments, the weather, the shortcomings or quaint sayings of servants, the behaviour of children and animals, the absurd pretensions to gentility of successful tradespeople, the rise or fall of fortunes or temperatures, other people's new clothes, arrivals or departures, unusual sermons, clerical or family intrigues — such were some of the main interests of this community.

It would however be wrong to suppose that the people of Southwell were entirely given over to trivialities. In the first place their religion was not merely a matter of assiduous churchgoing. It was 'practical,' as they say, and involved a strong sense of duty on the part of the well-to-do towards the 'deserving' poor. If money was freely subscribed for the conversion of the heathen in hot and distant countries, material comforts — generally accompanied by homilies and often by real sympathy — were as freely provided for the locals who lacked them, unless of course they were judged to drink to excess. Nor was culture absent. Among the clergy particularly there were men of literary culture and taste, derived from the old-fashioned classical education, and educated Southwell had a lively consciousness of its associations with Byron: Edith Browne herself was acquainted with his local friend Miss Pigot, and had often heard her talk of him.

I suppose the widowed Mrs. Browne settled at Southwell because she liked it and because her married life had been lived in Nottinghamshire, where she could keep in touch with her husband's relations and her own acquaintances. I say acquaintances rather than friends, for she was a little stand-offish, not through haughtiness but by nature: it was not for nothing that she was half an Arden. She had a household to order and children to bring up; she did not mind being alone, since she had a taste for reading and music; and although still a youngish woman she had settled down, in the fashion of the time, to the retirement of widowhood. Intellectually she was a cut above her surroundings. Others were observant, she was extremely so; others had a sense of the ridiculous, hers was excruciating; others had done some reading, she was well read; others had travelled, she had lived abroad in countries they knew little of. She did not give herself airs, but lived quietly, comfortably and apparently contentedly, and was devoted to her children, as they were to her.

She did not send the girls to school; they were taught by French and English governesses, whose influence upon them was very much less than her own. If they did not have quite that artificial education which (as Scythrop Glowry remarked) modelled girls into 'mere musical dolls, to be set out for sale in the great toy-shop of society,' it was perhaps because they were too lively. Their mother certainly brought them up to be ornamental rather than useful, with drawing lessons, dancing lessons, music lessons, but no domestic science; I doubt if they could have boiled a kettle, still less an egg. If they wanted to buy anything they merely ordered it and had it put down to their mother's account: they accordingly had no idea of the value of money or of business of any kind. Yet they were brought up to be much more than ornamental. They grew up with a strong sense of their position (involving duties as well as privileges) in a society which appeared secure; with an equally strong sense of religion; with good easy simple manners derived largely from a detailed but almost unconscious knowledge of commonly accepted but none the less complex canons of behaviour; with great kindness and thoughtfulness for other people; with strong conscientiousness and sense of duty (with which no doubt the Evangelical background had something to do) and therefore a great capacity for self-sacrifice; with powers of observing and discriminating; and with great cheerfulness and high spirits.

Their lives had not been wholly circumscribed by going to church and ragging their governesses. As children at Cotgrave they had been taught to ride; as girls at Southwell they were among the first to take to bicycles, and were thought 'fast' for doing so. Edythe wielded a lusty racquet on the tennis lawn, and made many a curate run like a hare after a maliciously placed ball. There were visits to Buxton or Nottingham or to country houses, and once, having reached an age of some discretion, Edythe and her brother Franklyn were allowed to pay a visit to France together. Now it was the custom in the Browne family, as in many other families, to speak French at home before the servants when anything was being discussed that was thought unsuitable for them to hear. This habit, prevalent also among the upper classes in Russia and elsewhere, might be called a breach of good manners, for a sensitive servant might suppose himself or herself to be the topic of conversation and thus feel ill at ease, but its convenience was obvious. As at home, the brother and sister abroad discussed everybody they saw, having the habit of quick and critical observation—but they suddenly realized that they were talking *in French* so that those discussed should not understand. Had their French accent been at all like that commonly achieved by the English they would have been as safe from giving offence as if they had been talking Choctaw, but French governesses and a natural quickness of ear had deprived them of this camouflage: fortunately they resumed their mother tongue before any injury appeared to have been caused.

There were also visits to London, where they stayed either with relations in Oxford Square or Portland Place or in rooms in Cambridge Terrace kept by a retired butler and his wife. That thoroughfare was then extremely respectable, and between it and the Bayswater Road were several nests of hospitable friends and relations. Mrs. Browne, being quite contented with her modest but comfortable place in society and having when young seen not a little of the *beau monde* in London and abroad, now preferred provincial peace and made little effort to put her daughters through the paces of a London season, nor did she trouble to present them, as she had been presented, at Court. They did, however, get carried off to dances or garden parties or to Henley Regatta and other crowded and sparkling diversions, and managed so well to retain their fresh country complexions that their aunt Alice complained to an acquaintance, 'My dear, they keep *pink stuff* in a saucer on their dressing tables'—a remark which was repeated to them and received with joy. This aunt, between whom and their mother there existed one of those tense antipathies which are apt to arise even in the best regulated families, would send them from time to time as a present a large box of costly soaps, scents, toilet waters and other luxuries. These gifts, though not unwelcome, were thought bizarre, and were at first supposed to have been sent in the malicious belief that if the girls were abandoned enough to use 'pink stuff' to heighten their complexions, they would probably welcome elaborate and repeated assortments of toilet accessories. Later, however, there was reason to believe that their generous aunt was in fact somewhat smitten with the chemist who supplied these goods, and that she accordingly wished to please him by the size and frequency of her orders.

Another aunt, Agatha, had married Charles Rumbold, a genial soul with a house in Sussex Square at Brighton, where Edythe used to go and stay with them. It always struck her as remarkable that uncle Charles had a grand piano in his bedroom, and that aunt Agatha wore her clothes until they were in rags, to which, with the utmost nonchalance, she fastened impressive diamond ornaments. The Brighton air agreed very well with Charles James Augustus Rumbold and quickened that blood of nabobs which ran in his veins. He would drive along the front in an open carriage, trolling at the top of his voice and with great gusto the popular songs of the moment, much to the entertainment of the passers-by, whose thronging glances amused his niece, as she sat opposite to him, joining a little shyly in the choruses. When uncle Charles saw her mother he was in the habit of saying, 'Won't you take a cup of cawfee, my dear creature?' (it was always remembered that she much disliked tea) and this phrase became associated with him like a signature tune and grew into one item in a vast repertory of family jokes.

Both in the aristocracy and the upper middle class in Victorian times there was often a very strong sense of kinship between families, of a kind that has now faded. This sense is patent in, for example, that mirror of the times, the fascinating and too little known autobiography of Augustus Hare. It is true that Hare was a toady and a snob, but a great many people, who were neither, carried in their heads an equally detailed who's-who not only of their forebears and near relations but of their most distant collaterals and connexions. It is remarkable how often in all classes, from the aristocracy to the peasantry, a whole group of families would tend to intermarry and overlap. This point may be illustrated by the following bewildering paragraph, drawn from records of the families of Plomer, Browne, Franklyn, Arden, Ward, Blackden and Allenby.

Edythe Browne's father and mother were second cousins. George Franklyn's sister married one of his wife's brothers. Another sister married her first cousin. So did one of his nephews. Two of his nieces married two brothers, themselves the children of first cousins. The son of one of these unions married his first cousin, and their daughter married my brother, who was her third cousin. Edythe Browne's step-sister married the nephew of her aunt by marriage, and one of my great-uncles married the aunt of his sister-in-law's brother's wife, whose nephew later married that brother's first cousin twice removed — but enough!

It seems that this semi-incestuous intermarriage and inbreeding (for which there is of course an excellent precedent in the Ptolemy family) was largely the work of that old matchmaker, propinquity, particularly among villagers and slum-dwellers, who were often interrelated in such a way as to defy elucidation, the law, and the tables of kindred and affinity. It was clearly a working of the herd instinct and among the 'respectable' classes may have been a display, more or less unwitting, of solidarity in a world already threatened and indeed increasingly controlled by new fortunes deriving from the industrial revolution still in progress and by the increasing power, wealth and influence of the smaller urban bourgeoisie.

At Easthorpe Lodge there was a strong awareness of this intermingling of families and with it a perhaps undue respect for class distinctions. Its denizens spoke quite naturally of persons of their own class marrying 'well' or 'beneath' them but never of marrying 'above' them, so perhaps that was hardly considered possible. Such trappings as titles and fortunes (if inherited and not recently acquired), town houses and country places, villas on the Riviera, carriages-and-pairs, plate and jewellery, or the magic of a known name were not nothing to them, for they were human, they were women, and they were living in nineteenth-century England. When Edith Browne's first cousin (like her, the daughter of an Arden-

Franklyn marriage) had married Bass the brewer in the eighteen-thirties, this had been thought by her family an act of condescension, even though he was rich and a member of Parliament. When the son of this union was raised to the peerage, this attitude was naturally not in the least altered. If to be a snob means to be ashamed of socially inferior connexions, to behave with servility to social superiors, and to judge of merit by externals, then the Brownes were not snobs. If they had a respect, possibly excessive, for people's origins and manners — so long as these conformed with their own — one cannot blame birds of a feather for flocking together. They could not help growing up in a world which pretended that its social structure was permanent, and in a class which regarded itself, with some reason, as 'the backbone of England,' for it had produced, even if as a result of privilege, innumerable men and women able and excellent in all walks of life.

The account that has been given of the Brownes is perhaps rather formal and typical, but a formal society aims at producing types. Yet even in societies which have continued formal over long periods of time, such as those of China or Japan, or even in primitive communities ruled by rigid and minute taboos, individuality will out, for there is no such thing as a single life, and each of us is a private as well as a public being, even in a totalitarian State. Mrs. Browne herself, in many ways obedient to convention, was strongly individual, an original even, with a marked indifference to public opinion. Among her children her aesthetic sense came out strongest in her son Franklyn, who had rare linguistic gifts as well as a talent for painting. He went through the routine of preparatory school, public school and Cambridge, to emerge, if not unscathed, still a quiet aesthete with a pretty wit, and, I suspect, little or no ambition: the Arden blood on both sides — through his mother and through the Archduke's wife — was unlikely to animate a pusher or climber. Neither he nor his sister Edythe belonged to that large section of mankind whom Sydney Smith called the Sheep-walkers, 'those who never deviate from the beaten track, who think as their fathers have thought since the Flood, who start from a new idea as they would from guilt.' Edythe, in her twenties, already benefited and suffered from a highly organized nervous system: one must pay the penalties of being more sensitive than the general run of mankind, but if one's sufferings are more acute so are one's pleasures. Her character was formed, she had her standards of taste, but she had developed no strong bent — partly because she had not had to work — and was already aware of the shortcomings of her education. She was eager and curious to live life to the full: how she was to live it would depend upon whom she married.

Mrs. Browne had expected her children to 'marry well,' so, although she was fond of my father, she did not show any special anxiety that he should become the husband of her elder daughter. He was decently bred and kind-hearted but had no 'position' and no money and had led an odd roving life in 'the Colonies,' which she thought, rightly enough, physically and socially unsuitable for Edythe. However, she was not going to try and thwart them if they thought they were going to be happy.

5. LOUIS TRICHARDT

CHARLES PLOMER and Edythe Browne were married in London in June, 1901. In addition to the usual motives, I think Charles wished to carry off with him to his strange new world a living representative of his familiar old world, and one who would compensate him for the want of loving-kindness in his early surroundings; while Edythe for her part was eager to escape from the narrow environment of Southwell and to see something of the world, for she was a young woman of spirit — of more spirit, in fact, than physical toughness. Southwell, by the way, had in time weighed upon the vivacious disposition of her widowed mother, who had found relief in an unconventional attachment, which had set many a spinsterly tongue wagging with the assumption that it signified a double life.

The old colonel was delighted with the marriage, having feared that Charles might take to himself some breezy and uncouth colonial girl. He gave his son five hundred pounds as a wedding present. It would no doubt have been more, had not the colonel, by an unwise investment, recently lost twenty thousand pounds in a single day. As the youngest son of a youngest son, Charles was naturally not insensitive to this loss.

The youngish couple were married by a cousin of my mother's, Edmund Franklyn, who was chaplain to the Savoy Chapel and had built, I think, that neo-Norman church at Tunbridge Wells. After a honeymoon at Brighton they left for Africa, accompanied by a large quantity of furniture. When they arrived at the Cape they were told that the railway line to Pretoria had been cut in many places by guerrillas, and that they would have a better chance of reaching their destination by way of Natal. Delayed by storms, they had a rough passage to Durban and a doubtful prospect when they got there, for in spite of their being provided with a letter from General William Franklyn (who was 'something in the War Office' and later military secretary to Kitchener), asking that they should be allowed through to Pretoria as soon as possible, their journey was of no military urgency and had therefore to be postponed.

They had no very vast sum of money in hand and thought it prudent to move from the best hotel to a boarding-house. Here, at their first meal, a young man sat down opposite to Edythe, removed the yellow kid gloves which he was wearing, and proceeded to clean his nails with a pen-knife. These were not the manners of Southwell but of the great open spaces, and they did not go down at all well, though they made a strong impression and were sometimes held up in after years as a symbol of the deficiencies of white civilisation in South Africa. Durban was crowded with refugees from the Transvaal and the Orange Free State, many of whom were as anxious as Charles to return and had more to return to. His furniture, on which he was having to pay, as week succeeded week, exorbitant war-time charges for storage, was in fact, for want of warehouse room, lying in the open covered with tarpaulins, and as he was assured that there would be no hope of getting it to Pretoria until the war was over, he and his wife decided to sell it. They got very little for it, and were sad to part with it; and Edythe, first buffeted by storms at sea and then trying bravely to adapt herself to her new surroundings, was suddenly taken ill and had to retire to a nursing home for an operation. She was at the beginning of a long test of her fine nerves, her not robust health and her abounding moral toughness.

While she was convalescent her husband received the long-awaited pass for the journey to Pretoria. As soon as the train had passed Ladysmith, new graves were to be seen at each station, and along the line the bloated carcases of horses and cattle, stinking and glittering with flies under the burning sun, were varied by wrecks of trains, twisted rails and other debris of war, and by fortified blockhouses garlanded with barbed wire (that common creeper) and guarded by sweating scarlet soldiers whose khaki uniforms contrasted with the blue distances and the biscuit-coloured landscapes vibrating round them in the heat. When the train came to a stop the air was loud with cicadas trilling like electric bells, or at sunset there was an uncanny silence; a hot puff of wind would rustle the dry leaves of a few eucalyptus trees near the line and a few voices on a lonely platform were thrown into nightmarish relief by the silence of the huge empty landscape on all sides — rocky hills which had been in the news but had no history and grassy plains which not so long before had been alive with immense herds of antelopes and bigger game and were now punctuated, at great intervals, with clusters of whitewashed wooden crosses, far above which the stars, improbably brilliant and numerous, flashed their perpetual indifference.

At Pretoria the newly arrived couple succeeded in finding and furnishing a house. The war had become a process of 'mopping up' guerrilla bands in various parts of the country, and steps were already being taken for the administration of the conquered territories. Charles obtained a minor post in the Treasury, and Edythe grappled with the task of housekeeping, which would not have been easy even if she had been used to it, but was doubly difficult under strange conditions and a war economy, with eggs at seven-and-six a dozen and chickens fifteen shillings apiece. Englishwomen in Pretoria just then were a rarity, and Edythe was much sought after by the officers of the garrison, among whom there were relations and acquaintances. She entertained them with the piano and the fiddle, food, drink and conversation, and then succumbed to a combination of malaria, dysentery and peritonitis. As soon as she was convalescent her friends repaid her hospitality with kind attentions, but her doctor said she must return to England if she wished to live. So off she went with a special pass, in a train preceded by an armoured train, from time to time watching guerrilla warfare through a pair of field-glasses handed to her by a gallant captain.

Without his wife, poor Charles had to wind up the household that had been established by her efforts, and he found that with food at famine prices and the expenses of doctors and nurses and a passage to England, the minute capital on which he had married had almost melted away. A friend of his brother William's, who had been appointed by Lord Milner resident magistrate of the Zoutpansberg district in the Northern Transvaal, now applied for his services as local secretary of the Repatriation Commission which had been set up to restore Dutch prisoners of war to their farms and to devise the best means of advancing them such material aid as would enable them to resume their habitual way of life. Charles accordingly spent six months touring the district, in a cape-cart drawn by six mules, and checking the often grossly exaggerated claims put in by the freed prisoners. This gave him a detailed knowledge of a vast region in many parts of which no white man had ever set foot; he enjoyed some excellent shooting, and received special commendation for the thoroughness of his work. He found, however, an injustice to complain of. While the English administration were, as he afterwards used to say, 'pouring out thousands upon thousands of pounds to the Dutch as a reward for fighting against England,' he himself failed to obtain compensation for the loss of some property in Pretoria which had been looted, in the presence of reliable witnesses, by English soldiers. He saw in this a failure to recognize his services and felt that, while everything was being done to conciliate the Dutch, he, as an Englishman, was ill-used. However, as a reward for his useful work for the Repatriation Commission he was offered, and accepted, a post at Pietersburg under the Department of Native Affairs.

Pietersburg, called after the General Piet Joubert of Majuba fame, was then a small pioneer village: it now has a population of nearly ten thousand people and an important aerodrome. It was no health resort, and the salaries of civil servants were augmented by a 'fever allowance.' For the time being, however, it contained a garrison consisting of detachments of the regular British army, and life was a whirl of dances and dinners, picnics and tennis tournaments, gymkhanas and polo matches, puns and practical jokes, charades and drawing-room ballads. My father succeeded in obtaining and doing up a small house — which, like all the others, had a corrugated iron roof, as if to concentrate the heat upon the inhabitants — and there he was joined, early in 1903, by his wife, who, while alternating garrison gaieties with the struggles of running a house with amiable but untrained native servants, in due course found herself pregnant.

My entry into the world in December 1903 was not well managed. The amenities of Pietersburg did not include the most notable of obstetricians, nor had English girls of the middle class in those days much idea of what to expect or what to do. Much went wrong; it seemed unlikely that either mother or child would survive; and the child, yelling blue murder for months on end, suffered in turn, or simultaneously, from most of the diseases of infancy. Devoted maternal care and some spark of vitality kept it going, but before it was a year old the noisy malarial brat was banished, on medical advice, with its mother to England in order that it might rally its meagre forces.

My father, again alone, had interesting and responsible work to do, in helping to carry out administrative policy among the vast native population of the Zoutpansberg: this included the delimita-

tion of the boundaries of the territories that were being set aside
as native reserves, and involved much travelling and consultation
with the natives themselves. Once a month he went out to collect
the gold which the various local Commissioners had received in
payment of taxes by the natives — two pounds a head as poll-tax,
two pounds for each extra wife, ten shillings for a dog, and so on.
This proceeding was undertaken in a mule-cart escorted by
mounted police, for the vehicle sometimes carried as much as forty
thousand pounds in sovereigns. At one time three highwaymen
were known to have the design of holding up the cavalcade and
escaping with the proceeds over the border into Portuguese East
Africa, but they were forestalled. It was not uncommon to come
upon lions sunning themselves on the lion-coloured roads, but they
never showed themselves partial either to mules or mounted policemen, no doubt because there was plenty of easier and better-
flavoured prey to be had.

In June, 1905, my mother returned, both herself and her child
being improved in health, and life in Pietersburg went along not
unpleasantly until my father had a violent attack of malaria, after
which he was given six months' leave on full pay, and this time the
whole family departed for England. On the daisied lawn at Southwell and on the sands at Scarborough we breathed the benign
English air until it was time to go back.

In May, 1907, my brother John was born at Pietersburg and
despite the attentions of a bibulous midwife he burst into the world
with all the rude health and gaiety that his predecessor had lacked:
in fact he promised to take after his uncle Durham.

My father was now appointed assistant to the Hon. Gideon
Murray (afterwards Lord Elibank) and together they used to
traverse an immense area between the Dwars and Limpopo rivers,
travelling in a covered wagon drawn by eighteen donkeys and
accompanied by eighteen mounted policemen, twelve black and six
white. When the day's work of the two itinerant magistrates and
tax-gatherers was over, they used to amuse themselves by shooting
bush-buck or waterbuck, guinea-fowl or Namaqualand partridges
(those plaintive fliers-in-formation) for the pot. Human interest

was not lacking. Indeed, in the first quarter of the present century a traveller in most parts of what is now the Union of South Africa could be sure of encountering a variety of picturesque characters. Among those with whom my father came in touch was a man who had deserted from one of Her Majesty's ships in the sixties, had taken a wife and had worked his way northwards, trading and hunting, finally acquiring a large tract of land. Now, forty years later, he derived a considerable income from the natives in the form of rent paid by them for land where their forebears had lived for generations before the coming of the white man.

Then there was another Englishman, whom we will call Fitzgilbert, who had 'gone native.' His brother was at this time in command of a crack regiment in England, but he himself had other fish to fry. In fact, for a good many years he had been living in the wilds with a black mistress and had never set eyes on those products of what was once known as 'the march of mind' — the bicycle, the telephone and the sewing machine. His manners were polished, but he was not one of the dinner-jacket type of exiles from civilization: on the contrary, his usual dress was pyjamas, a handsome silk kimono, and a pith helmet. He was hospitable and was always with difficulty restrained from having an ox slaughtered in honour of a visit from my father and Gideon Murray. And he was very fond of his two coloured sons, who were happily named Very Nice and Very Good. 'It was pathetic,' said my father, 'to see how pleased Fitzgilbert was to be able to talk to someone of his own race and class and in his own tongue.' About three years later Fitzgilbert suddenly left for England, married a widow and settled in tamest Devon — but not before sending a legal document to the magistrate nearest his former abode. This was a deed of gift to his ex-mistress of his land, huts, livestock (including three hundred head of fine cattle), and all his other local possessions, besides a provision for the education at a mission school of Very Nice Fitzgilbert and Very Good Fitzgilbert. Mission stations, it may be remarked, were among my father's ports of call, and at that of Waldezia he and Murray used, while taking tea on the verandah with the missionary and his wife, to put down their cups or bread-and-butter in order to take pot-shots at crocodiles in the Levubu river a hundred feet below.

Among the other scattered whites were the nephew of a duke and the son of a Chief Justice of England, both of whom kept trading stations, usually known as 'Kaffir stores.' Another was kept by two educated Greeks. A professional big-game hunter was a Belgian woman. And there was a family with a well-known English name who could not speak a word of English and were reputed to descend from a survivor of the loss of the *Birkenhead*. There was also a little man, pushing, but a good linguist, who managed to get himself appointed to a local magistracy, and thereupon summoned the local native chiefs to an *indaba*, or council, when he took occasion to announce, since the natives always give white men nicknames, that he wished to be known as 'The Great Lion.' They preferred however to speak of him as 'The Little Calf.' (My father's name among the natives was 'Quick-as-Lightning,' for they noticed chiefly his nimble movements and that restless energy which often marks the asthmatic.) Finally, there was Bill Eagle, a half-bred Red Indian, whose one ambition was to shoot a lion. He did indeed succeed in shooting one, but only wounded it, and it clawed him off his horse by the thigh. On the ground he thrust his hand into its mouth and seized and twisted its tongue. The lion shook him as a dog shakes a rat, but he did not let go, and the lion, nearly choked, suddenly got free and bolted into the bush. Unluckily poor Bill Eagle was too badly mauled to recover, and my father had the melancholy duty of reading the burial service over him.

Presently my father was appointed to act as resident magistrate at Louis Trichardt, some eighty miles from Pietersburg. At the foot of the Zoutpansberg mountains, well inside the tropics and highly malarial, the place took its name from the commandant of a number of burghers, who are alleged to have been mostly tiresome, lazy or importunate persons banished by Kruger to found a settlement there. But when my father arrived, the township consisted mostly of derelict or ruined houses, malaria and the Magato and

South African wars having scattered or eliminated most of the settlers.[1]

The district was romantic in a Rider Haggardish way. Diamonds and emeralds, copper and gold were to be found, and although game, with the advance of the white man, was getting scarcer, there were still, besides lions, not a few giraffes and hippopotami, besides wildebeest, eland, sable and tsesebe. Then in the mountains, and almost inaccessible, was a wonderful lake, with weird surroundings and no apparent outlet. It was covered with wild fowl of many kinds, and they were seldom disturbed, for it was reputed to have been the scene in former times of human sacrifices, and was shunned by the natives, who regarded it as bewitched. And lastly, native life was not yet spoiled, and there were to be seen at times spectacular primitive dances *en masse*, carried out with great vigour and much frankly sexual posturing, to the vibrant music of drums and giant xylophones. 'Can the white people dance like mine?' asked a local chief of an itinerant official, but he only received an evasive reply with an allusion to the splendour of the Great White Queen, whom he was perhaps left imagining in the performance of a frantic and provocative *pas seul* in the presence of her enthusiastic subjects.

The only dwelling at Louis Trichardt at all possible for my father and his family was very primitive and barely habitable. It consisted of three rooms with walls of *pisé de terre* faced with corrugated iron, which had also been used for the roof, while the floors were of stamped clay: it had no doubt been built by some wandering Dutchman who had been carried off by war or disease. He had fenced off an acre or so from the open veld and had tried to make some sort of a garden for flowers and vegetables, for which the land was well suited, as a stream flowed through it; he had

---

[1] Long after the Zoutpansberg was in the possession of the Dutch, the natives had maintained themselves in semi-independence. They were Bavenda, supposed to have come from the region of the Great Lakes early in the eighteenth century. They had risen under Malaboch in 1894 and were up in arms again in 1898. After the South African war they were called upon to deliver up their arms in exchange for payment.

planted a few cypresses and indigenous trees, and there was a flourishing banana grove.

It is a little strange to me that my father should have arranged for his wife and her two young children to join him in this outlandish and unhealthy spot, but he knew of other white families who flourished in places just as wild. He was not yet forty, very active and enterprising, and accustomed to a roving open-air life, which had greatly improved his health, and naturally enough he wanted his family with him, but it is doubtful whether either he or my mother understood what they were letting themselves in for. My mother certainly never questioned his decision. Her strong sense of loyalty, apart from any other considerations, would have persuaded her that her place was with her husband; and so, with her two young children and her uncertain health, she made the eighty-mile journey by ox-wagon from Pietersburg to this shack in the blazing wilderness, the more heroic a pioneer because she had been gently nurtured. This was indeed a far cry from Southwell.

Autobiographers' accounts of their earliest memories are often trivial and boring, but the first vision of a man's surroundings to stick in his memory may well afford a clue to his disposition. This was certainly the case with my father, my mother and myself. My father's first memory was that he was ragging with his brother Durham in Kensington Gardens, near the water-garden at Lancaster Gate. Durham picked up a bottle that was lying on the grass, threw it at him, and hit him on the nose — whereupon Charles flew at him in a blind rage but somehow caught a front tooth on a button of Durham's coat, and the tooth was wrenched from its socket. Of these sudden fits of temper I have already given two examples — the occasion when he flew at the sadistic head-master, and that when he made for Ulangene the Xosa with a hatchet. In mature manhood he was liable to furious outbursts of rage, which he sometimes mildly and inadequately explained by saying, almost as if it were a merit, 'I'm very quick-tempered, like my mother,' but which were apt to lead to really tense and frenzied scenes and arguments when he was opposed as unreasonable by members of his family. His opponents — and I have often been one when young — would be left in a state of nervous exhaustion, white, trembling and poisoned with anger, but on him these paroxysms seemed to have a positively tonic effect and to give him new energy. I hardly think that they can be fully explained in psychological terms; I think they were mainly physical and closely connected with his lifelong asthma. The distinguished author of *A Lawyer's Notebook* tells us that it is good for asthmatics to use the telephone in England; the experience of trying to get his doctor's number often so exasperated him that it would produce a flow of adrenalin almost as reviving as the injections he used to get from that doctor. 'Other passions,' he says, 'may be bad for asthmatics, but anger is excellent.'

My mother's first memory was equally characteristic. She was at Cotgrave, and perhaps no more than three or four years old. She was at luncheon with her governess, her parents were away from home, and the footman who was waiting on them had accordingly taken the chance not to put on his livery. The child instantly noticed this and ordered him to go and put it on. There spoke the being who believed all her life long in custom and ceremony, in which alone, according to Yeats, are innocence and beauty born.

As for me, my first memory of any significance is of a brilliant spring morning at Louis Trichardt. It had rained in the night, but now the sky was cloudless and the world of an incomparable freshness and fragrance, exhaled by the sparkling green veld and wafted in the air. I strayed out of the garden and standing on the bank of the stream suddenly saw on the opposite bank, perhaps twelve feet away, two large birds, a kind of wild duck perhaps. One was resting on the ground; the other stood beside it. Their plumage gleamed like many-coloured enamel in the sun against a background of reeds, their eyes glinted like jewels, and they showed no sign of alarm, but watched me as I watched them. My feeling was partly one of delighted discovery (almost comparable, perhaps, to that of a naturalist discovering a rare species), partly of pure delight, both heightened into an ecstasy which could not then and cannot now be put into words, but seemed to have in it a kind of mutual understanding and joy, as if the birds and I knew that we were part of the same life, and that life was splendid. I did not, as a result of this experience, become one of those bird-watchers whom I imagine to disguise themselves as trees, in the manner of Douglas Byng, and plant their feet in the fens of East Anglia or some other damp or precipitous spot in order to spy upon the private lives of birds; but I did take increasing pleasure in the visible world and was indeed trained to do so by my mother, herself richly endowed with what may be called the visual appetite.

After this there came a rush of sensuous experience. Like shots in an exquisite film or phases in a memorable dream, I recall a growing and a shining world that could be touched and heard and smelt as well as seen — the forms and textures of plants, the rasping leaves of the banana, the hostile leaves of the pineapple, the velvety leaves of the cape-gooseberry; the clear yellow flowers and hairy swollen pods of a nameless shrub; the long white thorns like steel nails that stuck out everywhere from the thorn-trees; the intense perfumes of the small aromatic flowers of the veld; the metallic dinning of the cicadas at midday and the imitable colloquies of doves in the afternoon. Then there were insects — the multitudes of flying ants that came fluttering and flickering out after rain and shed their talc-like wings, which they left thickly littered upon the moist earth; the flexible but hard-shelled millipedes that curled up when touched; the striped hornets; the tarantulas that waited, as motionless as ornaments, on a whitewashed wall. At night one could hear lions roaring far off or the nearer howling of jackals, more sad and wonderful than frightening, or the loud choruses of frogs never tired of congratulating the full moon on its brilliance and always using the same formula:

FIRST FROG: *'Le roi*
SECOND FROG: *Est allé.*
THIRD FROG: *Et où?*
ALL: *À Cognac, à Cognac, à Cognac . . .'*

When the veld caught fire one night in a very dry summer, the flames roared and crackled all round the house, than which they mounted higher in their dancing arabesques, while our servants were attacking them with branches: then suddenly a man on horse-back burst magically through the curtains of flame, who had come to see if we were all right.

At night, almost every night, could be heard the far-off singing of natives, monotonous and melancholy but at the same time exciting. With the touch of warm brown skins I was already familiar; a native girl, Maud Dgami, was my first and faithful nursemaid, and I remember the house-boys, their strong and gentle hands, their easy movements, white teeth and wholesome human *parfum de jeunesse*, their clean loose clothes smelling of soap and cotton, the pink palms of their hands, their horny feet; and how once, when the bridge over the stream had been swept away after a cloud-burst, they were called by my father to help him to mend it. I see him now, with the turbulent muddy water swirling round his white thighs and their dark brown thighs, and their naked arms lifting great stones into place, all under a blue-black sky, while pinks in flower on the bank danced in the rain-fresh wind.

I have already remarked that my brother John, who was now more than a year old, was as healthy and jovial an infant as I had been ailing and querulous. Alas, a message reached my father when he was far away tax-collecting urging him to come home at once, as the child was dangerously ill. Riding day and night for thirty-six hours, he arrived to find my mother and a doctor (who had also been summoned from a great distance) exhausted with a long struggle to save the life of John, who was in the throes of diphtheria and malarial fever. He made my mother lie down while he watched by the child's bed. I lay by my mother's side: I remember hearing her weep and seeing through the open window the moon-light glittering on the stream. Just before dawn my father saw the child grow restless; he roused the doctor, who decided that the only hope was to attempt a tracheotomy. The courage of women knows no bounds: my mother held the child in her arms while the doctor cut its throat, but life was extinct before he even had time to insert a tube.

The doctor did his best, but a shack in the tropics is not the best of operating theatres, nor was Louis Trichardt able to provide so common a necessity as a coffin, and old packing-cases had to be knocked together to make one: it was lined with cheap velveteen bought from the local store kept by an Indian. Nor was there a cemetery: a plot of ground had once been surveyed for the purpose, but it had never been enclosed or consecrated, so the body of my brother John was laid in the pagan earth of Africa. My parents later had his grave consecrated and put up a memorial stone of white marble, on which lizards sun themselves.

To go on living in that place must have given my mother a continual sensation of horror. The child's death caused her (as she told me long after) to question for the first time the benevolence, if not the existence, of the God in whom she had been taught to believe, and to whom she had prayed, and taught me to pray, every day. She had now touched a point of human experience at an opposite extreme from that of her almost care-free early years.

Fearing some equally sudden threat to the lives of his wife and surviving child, my father sent them to England. After they had gone he himself was very ill with a tropical disease and was advised to follow them, being once more granted six months' leave for the purpose. So far as we were concerned, that was the last of Louis Trichardt, but our double life, divided between England and Africa, was by no means at an end.

Part II

CHILDHOOD AND ADOLESCENCE

1. NOMADIC

By the time we reached England, there had been several changes among the older generation. Helen Plomer, my father's mother, had just died: her last years had not been happy; she had survived her favourite child and was in any case one of those women who cannot easily bear to grow old. The colonel, his fortune much reduced, had moved to a flat in Kensington, and on most afternoons he might have been seen walking along Kensington Gore, in a top hat and a black coat, lined with beaver and collared with astrakhan, on his daily constitutional to the United Services Club. He politely apologized to my father, because, he said, he would not be able to leave his two surviving sons anything like as well off as he had hoped, but he had been ill-advised in his investments and there was nothing to be done. I remember being taken to lunch with him and insisting afterwards, against my mother's advice, on tasting black coffee with brandy in it. I promptly spat it out again, much to the amusement of the old man, who was indulgent towards me as his 'only' grandchild — for he had never even seen the children of my aunt Laura, whom he had disowned. My father, however, could not endure being estranged from his sister, who had been good to him when he was a child, and without the colonel's knowledge he was again on brotherly terms with her. He had also brought about a reconciliation between her and their brother William, who had followed his father's example of complete aloofness.

My grandfather was insistent on two points. The first was that Charles should take his liver to Sir Patrick Manson, the authority on tropical medicine. This he did, and Manson, after treating him successfully, refused to allow him to return to a fever district and wrote accordingly to the head of my father's department, the Secretary of Native Affairs in Pretoria.

The other thing was that when my parents went back to Africa they should leave me in England, a sacrifice which my mother did not find it easy but thought it prudent to make.

From London we went to stay with her mother, Mrs. Browne. My mother's sister Hilda had married while we were at Louis Trichardt, and her brother Franklyn preferred to live on the Continent, so my grandmother had left Southwell and taken a house at Buxton. The cold winter in that bleak spa set my father up, and in the spring we went to stay at Longcroft, the old seat of the Ardens, which had now passed to my cousin Alwyne Franklyn. Architecturally unremarkable, the house had atmosphere: it had formerly been surrounded by a moat, but this was filled up in the eighteenth century after one of Madam Arden's sons had been drowned in it. We also went to Matlock Bath, which, with its dale scenery and petrifying-wells full of strange encrusted objects — vases and walking sticks, busts and birds'-nests — seemed to me highly romantic. There was a switchback railway on which I rode enthusiastically in charge of my governess, who was splendidly named Miss de Montmorency, but about whose sex I was in some doubt, for the often uttered formula 'Miss de Montmorency' reached my ear as 'Mister Montmorency.'

My aunt Hilda had married a parson's son who kept a preparatory school at Spondon House, near Derby; with her I was left when my parents returned to Africa, and I could not have been in kinder hands. Spondon was then a quiet country village, but has since, I understand, become highly industrialized. As I was only five years old I seldom went to lessons or games with the other boys, and being parted from my parents and without brothers and sisters I found myself in one of those isolated and somewhat anomalous situations which were often to recur in one form or another in my later life. However, I had playmates of my own from outside, with one of whom I invented the sport — soon, alas, repressed — of dropping clods or turves over the high garden wall on to the heads of the passing citizenry: some tantalizing 'near misses' were scored, and one or two direct hits.

My early impressions of life and landscape in Africa were especially strong because it was strange to my blood, which was coming awake in a world unfamiliar to it; my impressions of English life and landscape were equally strong because England was in my bones. My senses recognized what touched them, as a mirror recognizes a face. 'You must have the bird in your heart,' said John Burroughs, 'before you can find it in the bush.' It was not birds that interested me, however, so much as, for instance, the shapes of trees in Locko Park or the smell of ferns and ground-ivy near the hermit's cave at Dale Abbey. I was carried away in contemplation of the summer skies, with their light clouds continually changing shape; of the light and the rain, the fog and the snow; of ditches full of mares'-tails and ragged robins; of lawns netted over with dew and daisies. I wandered between low hedges of the small-leaved, wholesome-smelling box and under lofty hedges of the nipple-fruited yew, inside which were caves of darkness, full of dead twigs furred and powdered with black dust. I noticed the first snowdrops, skeleton leaves, and the ivy on the wall. I loved the richness of early summer, its meadows lavish with rusty sorrel and silky fescue, and I touched the rosy heads of clover and the hard-faced, faintly fetid moon-daisies. I rejoiced in autumn mornings, when, after a blustering night, yellow leaves had been beaten so flat on the asphalt pavements that they seemed to have been painted upon them, and varnished horse-chestnuts lay thick on the ground, waiting only to be picked up. How good the food tasted — the cup of milk, the slice of bread-and-butter, the superb sausages and pork-pies of Derbyshire. As for children's parties, in the Midlands in mid-Edwardian days they were of a lavishness long unknown — veritable feasts of Belshazzar, even if the writing on the wall was still invisible — with their whipped cream and trifles full of cherries, almonds and angelica, their ruby and emerald jellies, their heavily iced cakes black with fruit, their elaborate decorations and fancy dresses. Under the hoarse, incandescent gas-mantles the little girls with sashes tied in a bow behind, dresses of *broderie anglaise*, and neat dancing slippers, and the boys in sailor suits, gazed spellbound at the conjuror or the Punch and Judy show provided for the occasion.

My aunt taught me to collect, name and preserve wild flowers, which sharpened and gratified my eyes and my curiosity and encouraged my natural love of order even more than stamp-collecting would have done, which was a ruling passion among the boys. It was certainly a somewhat Victorian amusement, though none the worse for that, and to a later generation it might seem rather a sissy occupation for a small boy — but then I was rather sissy. I had no taste for mechanical things and had already taken an instinctive dislike to cricket, which seemed to be invested with an irksome appeal to duty rather than pleasure. It had already been raised, though I was too young to perceive it, from a dull game suitable for country bumpkins to a kind of mystic-patriotic cult bound up with a notion of English racial superiority. Of this cult my aunt's husband, the schoolmaster, was a devotee; he supported his trousers round the waist with a silk scarf in the M.C.C. colours and evidently ascribed to the game a peculiar importance.

Among my amusements were drawing and painting — as they are with most children. Now in the hall lay an embellishment not uncommon in those days, that is to say, the skin of a polar bear dressed as a rug. It was mounted on scarlet baize with scalloped edges, and the head had been realistically preserved, with glass eyes that seemed to express some fixed idea, and open jaws showing a fine set of fangs protruding from dry scarlet gums. One summer's morning I was lying on my back in the pleasant white fur, with the back of my head resting on the back of the polar bear's head, when my aunt, who happened to be passing, stopped to talk to me and asked me what I was going to be when I grew up. A little earlier I had had the common ambition to be an engine-driver, but now, oddly enough, and without a moment's hesitation, I said, 'I'm going to be an artist.' My aunt recoiled as if she had been stung, and cast her eyes up to heaven with a look of horror. 'Good heavens,' she exclaimed, 'I hope not!' I was much puzzled: I had apparently said something shocking, but what, I thought, could be more delightful than to be an artist?

Perhaps I was thinking of my uncle Franklyn, whom I much liked and admired, and who was in fact given to painting. Perhaps my aunt was also thinking of him: she was very fond of him, but possibly she thought that his unworldly, unambitious way of life was too 'Bohemian' and ineffectual, and that one such person in a family was enough. Nevertheless, the dear creature who encouraged me to botanize and draw and paint as much as I liked, did impress me as being shocked. She was less of an æsthete than her brother and sister; she had married a man who, whatever his virtues, was the opposite of an æsthete; and she had perhaps been influenced by his hearty attitude to life, which was of a kind by no means rare — particularly among schoolmasters — in the heyday of Edwardian philistinism and in a most conventional environment.

It may be thought that a child of five who 'wants to be an artist' also wants a kick in his little pants, but a child of five does not know very well what he is talking about. In any case this raises the question whether what used to be called 'artistic leanings' in a child should not be welcomed and fostered. In a materialistic society a boy with sensibilities of that kind is apt to find himself destined to be an exile in his own country and a rebel. It may be argued that since an artist, by his very nature, is an originator, a maker of something unfamiliar, he cannot look for early acceptance among the mass of mankind, who are governed by accepted ideas. The artist as protestant may, with luck and toughness enough, become a powerful and useful revolutionary in his own sphere of action; without them he may be involved in an expense of spirit and a waste of effort, leading perhaps to inanition, failure, or, worse still, a compromise with the academic, the vulgar or the banal, against which he has struggled in vain and which prove in the end too strong for him. The artist surely needs a place in society which enables him to work, to drill arduously but joyfully for the oil of his talent until it can flow, to the benefit of his fellow-creatures, in all its natural richness. Perhaps that can only happen in a society animated by a confidence born of something better than mere wealth; in which taste has authority; and which is so constituted that every variety of human ability may have a chance of contributing to the life of the whole. If the artistic child is given his head and nothing comes out of that head, he can find other employment; if on the other hand he is repressed, his natural ability, if strong enough, may benefit by the effort to assert itself. It would be dangerous to lay down any law on these matters.

Whatever I meant when I said I wanted to be an artist (and it is probable that I meant very little, in view of my tender age), I had already entered upon the artist's double life: I might be taken to church or to watch a cricket-match, but I was already a heretic and fantast. One Sunday, when a hymn was being sung in church, my aunt noticed that although I was singing lustily I was not singing the words of the hymn. She told me long afterwards that on bending down to listen, she had discovered that I was singing an improvisation of my own 'all about the flowers.' Two things helped to take me deeper into a world of private fantasy. One was my first visit to a theatre — a production at Nottingham of Maeterlinck's *Blue Bird*, by which I was completely carried away and filled with new emotions. The other was an experience for which I cannot account, though it may have been 'psychic' or atavistic in some undefinable way. It was recurrent, and associated always with a particular garden belonging to some people whom we occasionally visited. In this garden I had the feeling of being *en rapport* with what I could later identify as the eighteenth century. I will not say I saw or imagined but rather that I got to know two distinct characters, a man and a woman with the dress and manners of that period. Their presence, if I may use so strong a word, was associated with music in a minor key from stringed instruments, probably including a harp, and with a strong melancholy, as if I knew that the two persons were obsessed with regret for something irrecoverable, as if I sympathized with them and was afflicted with my inability to do anything to help them — the more so that I did not for a moment suppose them to be aware of my existence. It is possible that the place was haunted by some echo or vibration of a poignant and insoluble situation in the affairs of persons who had lived there long ago, and that this echo or vibration was perceptible to my unhardened sensibility.

As for the outward, everyday aspect of my double life, I began to gain glimpses of social distinctions, politics and taboos. First of all, it became perfectly clear that the world was largely populated by beings called the lower or working classes, and that they were a race apart. Going for walks, one saw them, often roughly dressed, with raucous children who went to 'national' schools, and living in rows of drab cottages with tiny gardens and cinder paths, sometimes edged with bottles or shells, leading up to the front doors; or, driving into Derby, one saw that they lived sometimes more squalidly, in the stink of the gasworks or by some greasy canal: the little girls in shady hats or pinafores and the little boys in caps, celluloid collars, made-up bow ties, Norfolk jackets, shoddy knickerbockers, black woollen stockings and heavy boots, would rush shrieking under the summer sun over roads of soft and pungent asphalt, past the traction engine and the brewer's dray with its gigantic, hairy-hoofed horses, to buy at some little shop pennyworths of sweets with mottoes printed on them, or bottles of tepid, gassy mineral waters with glass marbles imprisoned in their throats. One stared in silence at 'the working classes,' without hostility, but aware of their difference and strangeness. At election time they appeared almost as enemies. One was born, apparently, a little Conservative (just as one was born in the Church of England), and one accordingly wore for the occasion a rosette of blue ribbon; but in the streets there were rowdies with much larger, bright yellow rosettes which showed that they had been born little Radicals, and probably Dissenters as well. One of them went so far as to tear off my blue rosette and throw it in the gutter — a proceeding which surprised but did not in the least anger me.

Sometimes one liked, loved or envied the working classes. The sight of a drunken labourer, from whom one was urged to avert one's gaze, was interesting, for what could be the matter with such a big, strong man that he should move so unsteadily, uttering words that were unfamiliar but merely as sounds were plainly improper? It seemed that he must be unhappy yet somehow inspired, moving on a different plane from other people, and touched with some visionary wisdom. One never saw 'gentlemen' in such a state and did not even know then that they ever entered it. Another labourer, displaying in an alleyway what is not usually displayed in public in this chilly climate, was evidently drawing attention to yet another level of experience, which one knew to be important but which was not discussed, so that one's ignorance was as great as one's curiosity.

Whereas we always spoke of Darby and Spoondon, the working people always pronounced Derby and Spondon as they are spelt. This was said to be due to their ignorance, but that did not explain why one place should have two names. I fancied, therefore, that there were two Derbys and two Spondons within the boundaries of each — and this was not a bad guess, for so there were, one of each for the employers and one for the employed: though I had never heard then of 'the two nations' I had grasped the doubleness of English life. The working people, being a separate caste, had of course their own jokes. What, I wondered, did they mean when they spoke of 'Old Alice who lives in the bacon-box,' or 'The Spondon treacle-well, where they fish for cod'? Perhaps the most striking thing about them was that they generally seemed merry and polite, but this impression was chiefly gained from servants, a gardener, an errand-boy or two, a big benevolent cook, a homely old cottage woman, and especially housemaids — some buxom wench who was always blushing and giggling, wore a brooch lettered *Mabel* or *Mizpah*, and on her day out did her fair hair in a bang and perched on the top of it an enormous lightweight hat, heaped up with pink and red calico roses. If, ragging with Mabel, one pinched one of her breasts, she would only laugh and say, 'Isn't he artful!' That endeared her, but it would never have occurred to me to rag with or pinch the bosom of a middle-class woman in the drawing-room, who would hardly (had I done so to her) have called my behaviour artfulness.

The solitary labourer, the rosy housemaid, the playful dogs in the street — all these had something to do with the business of sex, for which one had not even a name, but which seemed somehow nearer the surface with the working classes, who accordingly began to figure in the curious visions which came into my mind before I composed myself to sleep and in which I imagined myself playing a part. At odd times one played with other children the funny little games that most children play, games inspired largely by curiosity and that unconscious awareness of being a separate person which has so much to do with the way children as well as grown-up people behave; and I again upset my aunt — to me again surprisingly — by inviting her to help me to enact a make-believe wedding ceremony with a little girl of my acquaintance, the vicar's daughter in fact, who had responded to the idea with alacrity.

Enough about me for the present. While life for me, to the then popular tune of *Yip-i-addy-i-ay*, was unfolding every hour, what had been happening to my parents? My father had been posted to Johannesburg and an entirely different branch of the Department of Native Affairs. He now had to deal solely with natives employed in the gold mines or in domestic or commercial service in that city. The natives came to the Rand not because they wanted to but because they had to earn money to pay their taxes, and could not earn it at home. They came from all parts of Southern Africa to seek work, and were then obliged by law to report to a 'Pass Office,' where each new arrival was medically examined and vaccinated; his finger-prints were taken; and he was then provided with a pass, or identity card, containing his name and those of his tribe and local tribal chieftain, together with particulars of his employment. This document was handed to his employer, he himself being given another pass, renewable every month at a cost to him of one shilling. When his contract expired, his pass was signed by the employer, who added particulars of his character, in order that he might look for another job. There were pass offices in every part of Johannesburg (a scattered city) and a large central office, where my father, at the head of a regiment of white clerks, took part in the administration of this somewhat complicated system. At this chief pass office were kept the records and the machinery of registration and tax-gathering, and attached to it were a fingerprint department, a court of law in which breakers of contracts and other minor offenders were tried, a large compound for feeding and housing new arrivals until they found work, and a complaints office, to which employed natives had the right to appeal, and in which efforts were made to settle matters amicably in order not to overburden the court. Many of the complaints were quite frivolous or trivial; some involved accusations of theft, the non-payment of wages, or assault; others were sexual, either against the employer or his family, or against fellow-workers. It was by no means unknown for a native house-boy to complain that when his white employer was out at work in the daytime his employer's wife had been making excessive demands on his virility — a remarkable circumstance in a country where the colour-bar is supposed to be rigid. It will be gathered that my father's work was not lacking in human interest. His liking for the natives increased with his knowledge of them.

Johannesburg had only been in existence for a quarter of a century, but in that time it had grown into a large town with all the material amenities of contemporary life. My parents lived comfortably in a flat overlooking a pleasant park, went to theatres or for drives in the surrounding country, to the races or the club, played golf, tennis and bridge, entertained and were entertained by their friends. Left to themselves, they would not inevitably and perhaps not often have made the same sorts of friends. A divergence in the choice of friends is naturally apt to arise when two people of fairly strongly marked individuality and a limited common experience choose to live together. My father, having gone out young to Africa and lived a free and easy and somewhat unambitious life, had mixed on equal terms with the ordinary people of the country. He had a real affection for the Dutch, from whom he had received much kindness and among whom he had intimates of both sexes. He rather preferred in general, I think, simple and unpretentious and sometimes even decidedly 'common' people, though he always had at the same time friends of origins comparable to his own. In other words, he led a double social life. My mother, on the other hand, had still been living at Southwell when her future husband was for years wandering over the veld. She had grown up in that narrow, sheltered and ceremonious world, he in a wide and casual one. Her ideals of character and behaviour were somewhat rigid and of the high standard to which she was accustomed, and she did not choose, or rather was not by temperament fitted, to adapt herself to lower standards. I have described how, when she first arrived at Durban during the South African war, she had found herself face to face with a young man who cleaned his nails at the dinner table, and had not been amused or indifferent, but disgusted. My father, though he would not himself have departed from the usual canons of decent social behaviour, was not especially fastidious about crudities in others, particularly if he found them good company. Ever since he and his wife had been in Africa together this difference had tended to show itself.

Colonial South Africans born and bred, particularly the women, were apt to show animosity against those whom they called 'home-born,' by which they meant people born and bred in England, to whom, naturally enough, they felt inferior, for of course the English had had advantages denied to colonials; besides, the English, while proud of their empire, spoke disparagingly of its inhabitants, often showing their contempt openly, both in England and in the Colonies. If the English tended to look down on colonials, it was because they found them ignorant and uncouth, and trying to make up for these deficiencies by bumptiousness and petty spite. The 'home-born' Englishman and Englishwoman, finding themselves in any colony, would tend to defend themselves against the strangeness and rawness of their new environment by wrapping themselves, more or less consciously, in a mantle of superiority interwoven with nostalgia. This naturally annoyed the colonial-born, who called them stuck-up, and affected to despise but secretly envied them. This social deadlock, or vicious circle, could only be resolved, and often was resolved, by adaptability, tolerance and good humour on both sides, but all too often it was clear that the 'home-born' had no intention of making a colony their permanent home or that of their children, but only lived for the day when they could return 'home' for good.

Now while my father would not have minded settling in Africa for good or bringing up his children there, as he would almost certainly have done if he had married a colonial, my mother could not help remaining too deeply attached to her native country to think of abandoning it. As a good and loyal wife she had from the earliest days of her marriage tried to adapt herself to her new surroundings, but it was uphill work. At Pietersburg most of the local women, when she tried to be nice to them, thought her condescending. Finding them ill-mannered and untrustworthy, she did not choose to live on terms of intimacy with them, and they attributed her aloofness to an affectation of superiority. They could not forgive her for being better dressed, less self-conscious, more formal, and quieter-voiced: still less could they forgive her and her sister Hilda (who had been out on a visit before her marriage) for winning both the singles and the doubles in the local tennis tournament. I have seen exactly the same sort of conflict between the local Dutch and immigrants who had been born and bred in Holland. Such a conflict was to be found in those days in any colony or 'new' country, but it was probably intensified in South Africa by the fact that the local whites (although lacking all the important attributes of an arstocracy) were the masters of a vast native population five times their own number, who had been slaves and were still virtually serfs. It was therefore galling to the whites to be reminded by the presence among them of persons fresh from Europe that they were not after all the lords of creation. An additional grievance was that the 'home-born' were apt to treat the African native races as human beings.

Johannesburg was in some ways a cosmopolitan place, and my parents had no need to limit their society to colonials, nor did they do so. If my father was the more sociable, my mother had a keener appreciation of quality in people, whatever their race or class. She was far too civilized to harbour any racial prejudice; her prejudice was only against bad manners and the ill-balanced dispositions of which they are an expression. Between her and some of the choicer colonials, whether Dutch or English, there was in certain instances mutual and lasting respect and affection, and her justness and kindness to native servants was repaid with devotion.

The Act of Union in 1910, which was intended to bind the four South African colonies into a single entity, had little or no immediate influence on social and racial problems, but it was naturally of

the greatest interest to my parents, since it must affect the administration of native affairs, which had become my father's profession.
Presently, however, they had a more personal concern to deal with:
my mother was expecting another baby, and in view of previous
trials, she and my father agreed that she had better have it in England. Besides, she wanted to see me.

Her mother had died in her absence; so had the colonel, her
father-in-law; she and her contemporaries were no longer 'the
younger generation,' and their children belonged to the twentieth
century. This twentieth-century child had had the measles. After
her arrival at Spondon, my mother asked me one day what the time
was: I looked across the room at her travelling-clock and could see
neither figures nor hands. It was discovered that ignorance had
allowed me to read in a bright light while I had the measles, and
that this had left me myopic, a circumstance which strongly affected
the course of my life and dashed at once my mother's unaccountable
hope that I might in due course go, by way of Osborne, into the
navy.

I was still only seven, so when we left Spondon I was provided
with a governess, a gay Alsatian girl called Adèle, and we departed
in the spring of 1911 to a house called Lowicks, near Frensham
Ponds, which had been lent to my mother by her sister-in-law.
Among the advantages which had accrued to my aunt Laura
through her obstinacy in marrying the man of her choice were a
town house and a country villa, both built by that remarkable
architect Voysey. These erections combined more than a suggestion of the Pre-Raphaelite tradition and of the *style moderne*, or *art
nouveau*, with even more advanced and enlightened ideas both in
their construction and decoration. The town house was next to the
old Physic Garden on the Chelsea Embankment and had features
which would have impressed even an unobservant child (which I was
not). There was an electric lift; there were bathrooms lined with
bluey-green tiles; there was unstained oak panelling with synchron-
ized electric clocks let into it here and there; there were lofty fire-
places, one of them ornamented with a wide expanse of plain gold
mosaic; in the drawing-room which overlooked the river and its

Whistleresque moods there was a row of richly coloured flower paintings let into a high dado of dove-grey slate; and in every room there was writing paper embossed in black or green with mannered lettering to match that on the front door and in the lift.

Lowicks was equally beguiling and even more idiosyncratic, partly because everything was very high or very low. The roof, for instance, came down steeply almost to the ground; the casement windows were wide and low, and the window-seats very low; but the latches on the doors were very high; so were the backs of the chairs, which, like those at Chelsea, were pierced with heart-shaped openings; on high shelves near the ceiling stood vases of crafty green pottery filled with peacocks' feathers; and the hot-water cans, coal-scuttles, electroliers and so on were made of beaten or hammered brass or copper. It was still, this house, the last word, or at any rate the last but one, in modern taste and comfort.

The spring sunshine lit up the honeycombs on the breakfast-table, the dining-room was redolent with coffee, and through the casement windows could be seen yews trimmed in the shape of peacocks. If we went, as we often did, beyond the garden, we found ourselves in a world of pine trees and ling with dry, sandy paths leading hither and thither. There were no trippers or motor-cars, and it was so quiet that one could hear the just perceptible crackle of the wings of the diverse dragon-flies that haunted the region. My aunt and her husband were probably abroad, motoring in their Rolls through Bosnia or Morocco, a form of travel they had indulged in since the days when it had first become possible for those who were enterprising as well as rich.

In the height of the summer my mother and I moved, for some unknown reason, to Bexhill to await her confinement. The summer of 1911 was excessively hot, and the sun, blazing upon the striped awnings and curiously Mauresque buildings on the sea-front, made them seem almost foreign. More genuinely exotic was the presence of the Maharajah of Cooch Behar, whose retainers went about in splendid costume, in silks and jewels and turbans adorned with aigrettes. Presently he died and members of his suite greatly interested us by sticking cut flowers into the beds in their small front garden and gravely and ceremoniously dancing round them. Many a nose must have been flattened against the windows of the adjacent Chatsworths, Miramars and Fernleas as their occupants strove to get an eyeful of this vision from the Arabian Nights. The death of the potentate is commemorated by a monument on the sea-front.

In August my brother James was born, and as soon as my mother was strong enough to travel, we returned to Africa. In her absence my father had set up in Johannesburg, in a small house near Joubert Park, a joint establishment with an Anglo-Irish major, an old friend from Matabele days. When she returned to Africa with the two children and an English nurse, the major moved out.

At this period Johannesburg (to quote the brilliant Lewis Mariano Nesbitt, who has left in *Gold Fever* the most remarkable account yet written of the place) was 'an ultra modern city on the American plan, where every vice had its panders, and every kind of licentious orgy was perennial.' Standing more than five thousand feet above sea-level in a limpid and rarefied atmosphere, the city is one of the more fantastic results of the Industrial Revolution. Seen from a distance or a height, it differs from others in the prevalence of white peaks which rise abruptly from among the very streets. Composed of quartz dust impregnated with cyanide of potassium, these little alps, the snowy excreta of gold-grubbing, give the urban landscape an odd and dreamlike look. Beneath them man-made shafts extend for three or four miles vertically into the earth, and in these mines, a single one of which may employ ten thousand men, a vast population, mainly black, toils dangerously for gold. But as far as our social lives were concerned, the miners and their 'licentious orgies' were remote. My parents numbered a few mine-managers and their families among their acquaintances, but of the actual lives, so strange and violent in work and pleasure, of the miners themselves, both white and black, we knew little and saw less. Even my father, whose work of course brought him in touch with them, lived on the earth's surface in an utterly different world from theirs.

In 1911 the streets resounded with the clanging and hissing of trams (for me the most romantic of sounds), varied with the clop-clop of horses' hooves. The older residential parts of the town, such as Doornfontein, near which we lived, already had atmosphere; cypress and eucalyptus groves had grown tall and among them could be seen villas built in the nineties by newly rich German Jews, Scotch engineers, quack doctors or successful tarts; they were often rather German in style, with bizarre turrets of hot red or bilious yellow brick and ornamental verandahs of cast iron muffled with flowering creepers, and already had the pathetic glamour of out-moded pretentiousness (like twenty-year-old fashion magazines) and even a touch of mysterious melancholy. In these surroundings, so adaptable is a child, I felt no less at home than I had in the gardens and drawing-rooms of Spondon. I listened with fearful joy to the hailstones drumming on the corrugated-iron roofs in summer thunderstorms, when flashes of lightning, like vast magnesium-flares, made the livid landscape jump. As at Louis Trichardt, the flying ants came out on moist evenings, and the last rays of the sun, as the thunderclouds rumbled away, picked out the yellow fruit of the dark-leaved loquat trees and the bunches of pink, beadlike fruit on the feathery-leaved pepper trees, while a light steam rose from the fresh-smelling earth. Indoors the Zulu house-boys moved about bare-footed, dressed in loose white blouses and shorts piped with crimson — warm-hearted, warm-blooded beings, handsomely made, and perfect in their goodness to this child. But it was time for this child to go to school.

The city was spreading rapidly, not only along the Rand itself, but out on to the surrounding hills, valleys and plateaux, where plea-sant suburban houses in roomy gardens were already half hidden by trees, which grew rapidly, as if to surpass the growth of streets and buildings. On the brow of a hill, on what were then the outskirts of the town, stood St. John's College, which had been founded in the nineties by fathers of the Community of the Resurrection from Mirfield in Yorkshire. They had an admirable purpose — to radiate, in the words of the school motto, *Lux, vita, caritas* on the Transvaal highveld by means of education. They had also brought with them, of course, their High Churchery, which would at once have been evident to a trained eye seeing the school badge, inscribed *Collegium S. Johannis* and adorned with an eagle who was scotching with his claw a snake twined round a chalice, and who bore in his beak, by way of an identity card, a scroll with the words *Quem diligebat.* The site of the school was grandly chosen, it had been nobly and simply designed, and built of rough-hewn local stone, with cloisters, terraces and quadrangles. On one side were the playing-fields of crimson earth, with outcrops of soft shale, and planted round with fir trees and cypress hedges; on the other was an uninhabited valley, beyond which rose a wild hill of considerable size scattered with big quartzy rocks and known as the Kopje.

The fathers themselves were mostly excellent creatures, Englishmen from the older universities who had embraced our national religion in its best shape, Anglo-Catholicism. They were neither cranks nor fanatics, and were mostly more like large good boys than schoolmasters. Their cassocks and birettas lent them an air of distinction and had nothing of that slightly sinister aspect which, to a congenital Protestant, so often makes similar garments on a Roman Catholic priest seem the uniform of obscurantism and bigotry.

As soon as we were dressed of a morning we assembled in the chapel and sang, without musical accompaniment, the simple hymn:

> 'Now that the daylight fills the sky
> We lift our hearts to God on high,'

after which, headed by a long-legged Resurrection father in a flapping cassock, we ran like hares across the main playing field and back to breakfast, which began with maize-meal porridge. It was not at all a bad beginning to the day. Nor were the days bad. Except at midsummer, when there was a thunderstorm almost every afternoon for a month or two, the climate was almost perfect. Not being addicted to cricket and football, I spent many a long afternoon wandering with my schoolfellows on the rocky, solitary Kopje, which had all kinds of enchantments. There were small forts left over from the South African war, and one could pick up old cartridge-cases. On the farther side was a cave which sometimes contained the ashes of recent fires and other signs of life: it was said to be used by some of those native gangsters known as *amaleita*, and this made it agreeably sinister. Lizards and conies lived among the soft feathery red grasses, wild montbretias and red-hot pokers; there were wild fruits to be gathered from low bushes and the flavour of their pink flesh to a young palate was unsurpassed. Here and there stood taller flowering shrubs, their sweet, rank smell drawn out by the heat of the sun and surrounding them where they stood over shadows like pools of Indian ink. If we wandered farther afield, we did not have to go any great distance to find corner-shops, kept by friendly, easygoing Greeks, who sold fruit, sweets, ices and cold drinks. On their walls hung crude coloured prints of national heroes and military exploits : like my mother, they were patriotic exiles, always a little aloof at heart from their surroundings.

When night fell the whole sky seemed to throb and crepitate with stars, among which one instinctively picked out the Southern Cross, as one would the Great Bear in England; and until it was time for prep. we collected glow-worms on the rocky slope below the school, or were playful in other pleasant ways.

It was the custom at St. John's to produce every year a play of Shakespeare's. The father who undertook the coaching always seemed to know and love the play and to be an experienced producer, and when the play was ready it was repeated several times, twice in the great gymnasium before an audience of parents and friends, and once at a distant isolation hospital called the Lazaretto, to which we drove in brakes and from which we came back by moonlight singing in chorus. At the age of nine or ten I had the interesting experience of appearing in *Macbeth* as Lady Macduff's son, who is taunted with being an 'egg':

' "He has killed me, mother: Run away, I pray you!" (*Dies.*)
   [*Exit Lady Macduff, crying* "Murder" *and pursued by the Murderers.*']

I also had some stunning notices for my part in the *Midsummer Night's Dream* — as Titania. That this part should be played by a bright and nimble boy was in the best Shakespearean tradition, and I felt extremely light-footed and ethereal in a robe of white crêpe-de-chine and spangles, though there was an anxious quarter of an hour on the second night when this garment, which I had hitched up for the purpose, suddenly came unhitched while I was making water shortly before the curtain rose: fortunately it was in the winter and there was a portable stove behind the scenes, by the warmth of which it was possible to dry out quickly the evidence of what might have appeared the result of unladylike, unfairylike and indeed far from regal incontinence.

The successive deaths of my grandparents had left my parents much better off, so they moved to another and larger house on a hill-top nearer St. John's, and I became a day-boy. It had a large garden, in which my father took much interest, and he used often to go out very early in the morning, cut the most perfect rose he could see, and bring it to my mother with the dew on it. They entertained not a little, and on their table were now to be seen the colonel's knives and forks with deer-horn handles, his three silver owls with red eyes to contain three different kinds of pepper, and sundry family plate, including the eighteenth-century Lord Mayor's big-bellied soup tureen. I too entertained my friends. It was at this time that I first discovered how pleasant it is to know people of various nationalities, for my schoolfellows were of various origins, including Dutch, Jewish, French and Italian, and there was a burly, gentle German who was perhaps eighteen and was touchingly protective toward me, possibly as a result of playing Bottom to my Titania. He afterwards became a tram-driver. I think he would have pleased Walt Whitman.

Then there were holidays — visits to Pretoria, to old friends on farms, or to Vereeniging to row on the Vaal river. Once a year there was a grand family holiday at the Cape, when we stayed at St. James's on the shores of False Bay. There my father, improving on his own father's system, gently and skilfully taught me to swim, and there he dazzled me with displays of virtuosity in diving and trick swimming. At Simonstown one year, Admiral Bush, a distant relation of my father's, was in command of the Cape station, and he invited us to visit him at Admiralty House (pleasingly built in 1814) and showed us over his flagship. There were visits to Cape Point, and picnics on beaches with scintillating granite boulders and Venus'-ear shells lying here and there like abandoned dishes of violet nacre; to the sandy wastes of Fish Hoek, then 'undeveloped'; to Muizenberg, to watch or join the surf-bathers; or to Capetown itself and the shop in Adderley Street which claimed to sell 'everything from a needle to an anchor' and did sell, among other things, ornaments of crocidolite and dried silver leaves from Table Mountain on which views, emblems or greetings had been painted. Then there was the long train journey back to Johannesburg through the parched Karroo and the grassy, under-populated plains of the Orange Free State, all the melancholy of space and emptiness in unvarying sunshine.

In 1913 a revolutionary strike broke out in Johannesburg: Nesbitt has left a dramatic eye-witness account of it. The rioters were charged by cavalry and fired upon by troops with machine-guns (General Smuts was at this time Minister of Mines, of the Interior, and of Defence) and there were frightful scenes of courage, panic and slaughter. I remember being taken by my father to see the smoking ruins of a newspaper office in the middle of the city; there were heaps of debris in the street, and people were standing about, staring with an air of vacant anxiety at the traces of destruction, as they do nowadays after an air raid. A couple of years later, after the sinking of the *Lusitania*, there were anti-German riots, with looting and arson; and in 1922 another and graver revolutionary strike. Obviously these events were mainly due to political and economic unrest, but allowance must be made for the fact that few of the mixed population of a mining town came into the world with silver spoons in their mouths and kid gloves on their hands, and also for the effects of living at high pressure at a high altitude under an African sun.

Early in 1914 my parents' thoughts were turning to England — my mother's in particular, for I was now ten, and she thought it high time for me to go to an English preparatory school. Reviewing their finances, she and my father came to the conclusion that there was no reason why he should not retire from the South African civil service while he was still in the prime of life, and they considered that by careful management they could live tolerably well in Europe and educate their two sons in the ordinary way. They felt that they could live more pleasantly than in England at some place on the coast of France or the Low Countries — Dieppe, perhaps, St. Malo, or Scheveningen. Wisely, however, they decided to reconnoitre first, and my father, instead of resigning, applied for six months' leave.

I have remarked that their finances were improved: but these were not so good as they might have been, for the simple reason that neither of them really knew anything, except from bitter experience, about the investment of money. There was indeed a streak of unworldliness in both of them, and, as I think I have made clear, they had grown up and were indeed still living in the days of peace and security — not to say securities — when the quiet-living middling gentry gave little thought to money, receiving, as regularly as if by clockwork, the interest on their capital, and thinking no more about it except how they should spend it. It was a complacent world that my grandparents had lived in, and complacency, like other sins, is visited upon the children unto the third and fourth generations, and often further still. In short, though my parents had gained by inheritance, they had lost through ignorance part of what they had gained, and were, through various causes, to lose more.

We returned to England in two batches. My mother and brother went first; my father and I followed about a month later. It was an eventful voyage, because my father left me much to my own devices, and with a companion of my own age I made incursions into the quarters of the Lascar crew, where we were kindly received, and got into various kinds of boyish mischief. The ship's carpenter decided that I was to be a Red Indian at the children's fancy dress party, and having made me a tomahawk and equipped me with a magnificent pair of albatross wings by way of a head-dress, he stained me all over with red ochre. A peculiar interest was taken in me by a young steward, and I doubt if my father would have approved, but no harm was done, and in due course the peak of Teneriffe and at last the docks of Liverpool came into view. So did the *Lusitania*, gliding peacefully in after us from the Atlantic on a sunny May morning.

2. SCHOOLBOY

MY parents were in no great hurry to decide where to settle on the Continent, and we did a round of visits to relations and a motor tour. The next thing was to find a school for me. They equipped themselves therefore with a list, compiled partly from glowing prospectuses supplied by a firm of scholastic agents and partly from private recommendations. When this list had been narrowed down to two or three addresses, my father considerately took me with him to see what I was being let in for. I had little opinion in the matter. I could imagine the kind of school I should have liked, but I hardly supposed that it existed, particularly in England, and after being shown a few sodden playing-fields and draughty gymnasiums by sharp-faced pedagogues or their over-eager wives, I could only resign myself to the thought that my father would choose for me as he thought best.

The choice fell on Beechmont, my mother being pleased that it was on the top of a hill and my father thinking the headmaster sound. An early Victorian country house which had been much and rather freakishly enlarged, Beechmont stood on the North Downs near Sevenoaks and Knole. It was approached by a Gothic nave of tall and blackish monkey-puzzles; stood in 'park-like' grounds, planted here and there with copper beeches, cedars, wellingtonias and rhododendrons, and including some large fields and a wood; and enjoyed what house agents call 'extensive views' over the Weald. I was to become an inmate of this establishment at the beginning of the autumn term.

This was 1914. During the summer it became clear that something was brewing, and my parents put off their search for a dwelling on the Continent. In July we were staying at Burford Priory in Oxfordshire, a specimen of what are sometimes vulgarly called 'show places,' which my aunt Laura and her husband, having abandoned their Voysey villa in Surrey, had bought not long before. This handsome Elizabethan house, which for many years had been a ruin, still had a ruined wing, and the curious late Renaissance chapel was in disrepair. My uncle Horniman rebuilt the wing but did not restore the chapel, for he was some kind of agnostic or indifferentist. The gardens were pleasant and a wood full of moths and ground-ivy sloped down to the Windrush, its banks aromatic with water-mint. After breakfast, on the morning that war was declared, *The Times* was much in demand and members of the house party tried to reassure one another with the wishful catchword that sprang into being everywhere: 'It'll all be over by Christmas.'

My uncle William, who was present, was not of this opinion. He now rejoined the army from which he had retired; and my uncle Franklyn, the least military of men, was soon a rating in the R.N.V.R. His linguistic achievements soon brought him a specialized job, but he was too little interested in his personal advancement to accept, as he was pressed to do, a commission. My father hastened to offer his services to the War Office, where it was thought that his knowledge of French and Afrikaans, which is akin to Flemish, might make him useful as an interpreter or liaison officer. Presently he was ordered to France, but on the point of his departure it was discovered that he was still in the South African civil service, and he was told to report to the High Commissioner, who sent him back post-haste to Africa, where some of the Dutch had taken up arms because the moment seemed to them propitious to try and get rid of the English connexion. He wished to take part in the campaign in German South-West Africa, but was instead given the rank of captain on the staff of the Union Forces and ordered to help in the enrolment and transport of large numbers of native drivers and carriers for the East African campaign. He kept full records of the enlisted men, but the same was not done in

East Africa, and many of the men were lost there and never heard of again. Many others, returning to Durban in the last stages of dysentery and fever, died at sea, into which not only their bodies but their identity discs were dropped. It fell to my father to try and make some amends to these obscure victims of the war, by seeking evidence of their deaths, in order that their next-of-kin might be notified and might receive any allowances due to them. My mother returned to Africa soon after him, taking my still infant brother with her, and they set up house again in Johannesburg.

Innumerable boys, many of them far more vulnerable than I, suffered and were warped at preparatory schools in the last century and this, and made, at least in print, no fuss about it. If I give a few reminiscences of Beechmont it is not from self-pity, but because they are linked with what goes before and after, and because I spent several years in that place. I hope I shall be describing a kind of education which no longer exists, at least with such limitations, and has become a curiosity of social history.

It is obvious that a man of ungenerous character, exercising absolute power over a herd of young boys in an isolated country house, is bound to become a tyrant and to make their lives unpleasant. The headmaster of Beechmont, an old Etonian, Evangelical clergyman and cricketolater, was sour, spiritually withered and unjust. He was the son of another preparatory schoolmaster, likewise a clergyman, and the very man, I believe, whom Mr. Norman Douglas has described in *Looking Back* as 'a pious hog.' His system of education was to inure his charges to Christianity in its drabbest form, to give them a sound training in the classics, and to make them proficient cricketers: a false quantity or a missed catch were to him, it seemed, sins equal to theft, 'impurity' or any other of a long catalogue of transgressions. Apart from cricket, he allowed little or nothing for individual bents or gifts and indeed did his best to repress them, and I feel only obliged to him for his real faculty for teaching the classics and awakening appreciation of the use of words and the poetry of Virgil and Horace. The pleasantest memories of the place are of those rare occasions when the prison-like routine was varied by outdoor activities other than cricket, hockey or football,

such as haymaking in the summer, or, in the hard winter of
1916–17, skating on a pond in the Weald every afternoon for a
fortnight, and the exhilaration of tobogganing on the snow-muffled
slopes of Knole Park in a tingling, frosty silence. There was
something to be said, too, for cross-country runs, though I was
handicapped, not in running but in jumping, by a slight osseous
deformity of one foot.

It was, I think, in 1916 that another preparatory school, disturbed by the war, amalgamated with Beechmont, arriving from
Thanet with its entire personnel. At first the two herds kept apart
and would not mix; then there were scraps between individuals,
in one of which I was worsted. Then a curious thing happened.
Two or three Beechmont boys evolved a fantasy which implied that
a master from Thanet had made passes at them in such a way as
to suggest a contemplated *attentat aux mœurs*. There is every
reason to believe that, whatever may have been in his mind, the
master in question was perfectly innocent in his behaviour. In
complete contrast to the headmaster of Beechmont, he was a kind,
sleepy, fatherly sort of being, who, in a paternal way, would
occasionally and quite openly put his arm round a boy's shoulder
while correcting a mistake in class or looking at a stamp album out
of school hours. False accusations on these lines by boys are of
course not uncommon (this one was dismissed as absurd) and are
akin to those made by solitary virgins in railway carriages against
male strangers — less frequently nowadays, I dare say, since virgins
are fewer and carriages more crowded. They are the result of
more or less unconscious wishful thinking and of the herm-
aphroditic nature of boys before the male element in them asserts
itself. I have already indicated how once or twice in what I may
call my Titania period I had aroused a protective feeling — and in
one case rather more — in young or adult males. In my Beechmont days, before I reached the age of puberty, I was twice the
subject of phases of devotion, half amorous, half maternal, by
young but adult women. In both cases they were deprived by the
war and other circumstances of coeval male society; both were
persons of strong natural feeling, and propinquity and chance made

them fasten on me. In the later of the two instances I grew very romantic and kidded myself that my feelings were those of an adult. Love moves on many mysterious planes, and when it entangles the young and immature they can be expected even less than adults to behave reasonably.

Boys herded together in isolation and not imaginatively treated are even more of a problem than men in the same situation, for men can at least be expected — though the expectation is apt to be disappointed — to display some sense of balance. Boys can be disgustingly barbarous — lazy, dirty, cruel, silly and scatological — but there is no reason why they should be. The main argument advanced against libertarian ideas of education is that it is unfair to let boys, or girls either, have too easy and pleasant a time, since they will find the world later on a hard place where they cannot have their own way, and will suffer accordingly; and that character is only developed by having to resist pressure and overcome difficulties, and by learning to do without things much desired. There is something in this argument, but it scarcely justifies a system of education like that at Beechmont. Every boy is a mass of physical, mental and emotional potentialities, and some scope must be allowed for the most vigorous of these to develop naturally, if only in a sublimated form. This is precisely where Beechmontism failed. Take, for example, the matter of religion. Whereas at St. John's the religious instinct was given full play, so that a boy could become genuinely religious and enjoy it, without becoming mawkish or goody-goody, at Beechmont religion was repulsively dull, colourless and hypocritical, and contributed not a little to instilling in most of the boys superfluous feelings of sin and guilt, and in some a morbid longing for spiritual light and grace: it is not surprising, therefore, that one boy set out to invent a new religion, complete with creed and ritual, and for this purpose convoked a little synod in a bramble thicket. It smacked, I remember, of pantheism.

At St. John's the Kopje was a paradise of which the boys had the freedom; at Beechmont the leafy environs, including the wood, were permanently out of bounds. To put harmless and pleasant places a few yards away under a taboo for no good reason is to invite any but priggish and timorous boys to enter them, just as in an adult community the multiplication of petty rules and regulations brings them and their propagators into contempt with spirited persons (who will certainly defy them) and tends to turn the rest into ciphers by persuading them that obedience is a virtue in itself. A harsh and narrow government provokes conspiracy: we boys therefore conspired to break bounds and sexual and other taboos, to smoke, and so on. No appeal was made to our reasoning powers or our sense of responsibility; conformity meant dullness, nonconformity meant impositions, beatings, petty persecution, or at worst expulsion; obviously nonconformity was the more attractive, since it had the spice of danger.

Perhaps the most interesting of our conspiracies arose from the sympathy some of us felt for the Sinn Fein movement and Sir Roger Casement. None of us was Irish, and we had no wish to injure our country, but that adventurous upsurgence against a repressive authority (associated vaguely and by no means erroneously in our minds with our headmaster, with Kipling, cricket, Sabbatarianism and all that bag of tricks) excited us very much and we formed elaborate plots, with a whole apparatus of codes, invisible ink, and so on, which in fact came to nothing. I think it is no exaggeration to say that we were as much stirred by the events in Ireland in 1916 as many young men were twenty years later by the events in Spain.

Little or no scope, as I have said, was given to our creative faculties. There was, it is true, a carpenter's shop, presided over once a week by a dreary old faggot called Cronk, and there was also a dancing class, at which we galumphed without conviction in that curiously flat proceeding, the barn dance, or, with more spirit, in the lancers or Sir Roger. But amateurish tendencies towards acting, gardening, modelling, botanizing, bug-hunting, bird-watching, chemistry, astronomy, mechanics, music or drawing received only the most perfunctory encouragement or none at all. It was probably considered (if indeed any consideration was given to the matter) that these activities would do far less to fit boys for adult life than would the composition of Latin verses, practice in wicket-keeping, and the study of Hebrew mythology. Is there any reason why boys should not be taught, let us say, the elements of gardening and cooking, and the construction and functioning of the human body with which each of them is equipped? Is there not rather every reason why they should be enabled to learn these things, as well as being trained, by Latin or what not, to be methodical and judicious?

The holidays of children whose parents live abroad often tend to sharpen their wits more than would be the case if they spent their holidays in their own homes: a good example of this was Saki, the development of whose mind and character was clearly much affected by the aunts who housed him while his father was absent in India and Burma. My holidays were more varied, being spent partly with aunts but more with various schoolfellows, and all under the not very heavy shadow of the war. The winter of 1914 I spent partly at my aunt Laura's house on the Chelsea Embankment. One day she gave an entertainment for some wounded soldiers, and a rather angular woman sang drawing-room ballads with somewhat forced gaiety, accompanying herself on a guitar, to which a bunch of long coloured ribbons had been attached, perhaps to lend a festive air to the instrument. The soldiers listened politely. One of them greatly impressed me, for he had lost his arms and legs and was blind. What was left of him lay in a kind of shallow basket on wheels, smiling and smoking a cigarette. This was fascinating, because he belonged to a species of humanity, the mutilated, of which I had no knowledge but which evidently must have a different character from the rest of mankind. Even the blind or the deaf, or the deaf and dumb, or cripples, draw the solemn gaze of a child, who rightly sees them as persons apart: but here was a blind man without limbs, smiling and smoking and chatting; it was as impressive as meeting a Royalty or a Red Indian. It occurs to me now that an interesting novel might be written, tracing the effects upon a man or woman of losing one or more limbs or senses. Such losses often appear to lead to a concentration of energy in the remainder of the organism and to have a tonic effect on the personality; in other cases the character may change for the worse. A German doctor who lost a limb in the first World War and was a military surgeon in the second has observed that the man who has undergone amputation is generally 'a diligent person, free of that exaggerated urge to assert himself which is characteristic of so many people who suffer from a physical disability.' He also remarks that the astonishingly low death-rate among people who have lost a limb by amputation is probably due largely to their inner bearing as well as to directly physical causes.

In gazing at that smiling torso in my aunt's drawing-room I was too interested in his behaviour to think at all clearly of the causes of his mutilation. The war did not come home to me at all sharply and directly, though the war atmosphere became increasingly obtrusive, and, without my knowing it, the cumulative effect of chance incidents and anecdotes was a reinforcement of my innate pacifism. On still days at Beechmont, when we were bent over Xenophon or quadratic equations, the windows would be rattled by a sudden crescendo of the interminable thunder of the guns in Flanders, and a wandering breeze would stir the war-map on the wall, where little flags on pins marked the graph of the western front, and to the east, the progress of what the newspapers called 'the Russian steam-roller.' People made jokes about the Kaiser or 'Little Willie,' there would be heroic drawings in the papers by Bernard Partridge or Louis Raemakers; somebody had seen somebody who had seen the Russians go through or a Zeppelin brought down; a harmless old gentleman in Sevenoaks was wrongly suspected of being a German spy; and there were continual reminders that it was a long way to Tipperary. Gradually confusion began to dawn. At one moment we might be listening in the chapel to the Sermon on the Mount; at another we might be watching bayonet-practice in a park, where overgrown errand-boys in khaki were being taught by a sergeant to stab sacks filled with straw and daubed with a rough likeness of the Kaiser. Ours too in due course, we knew, 'but to do and die,' but it was not at all clear for what reasons. Vague feelings of resentment arose even in a young breast against those who, in comfort and security, expressed themselves on the rightness and justice of that war and even of all wars; so did feelings of pity for its victims, pity that was heightened from time to time during the holidays, when one visited wounded soldiers in hospital or helped to serve unwounded ones in canteens, gazing through a mist of steam from tea-urns and the smoke of Wood-bines, for fresh supplies of which they stretched out their clumsy innocent hands while their thick coarse uniforms, soaked with the sweat of route-marches, gave off a rank, sour, khaki odour.

Holidays, on the whole, were less positive reminders of the war. At a country house in Lincolnshire one seemed almost to be living in the eighteenth century, everything was so peaceful. The prim-roses came out in the Long Walk; the keeper added a stoat and a jay to his 'larder,' where the outlines of tiny skulls, as delicate as eggshells, showed through rotting or withered tissue; the engravings of Hogarth's *Marriage à la Mode* over the staircase became slightly more foxed with damp; new issues of *Punch* and *Country Life* appeared promptly on a table in the hall. At a gentleman-com-muter's house in Sevenoaks or a widow's seaside villa in Devon-shire one was chiefly aware of cosy domesticity. The Christmas of 1915 I spent with my aunt Hilda. What had once been Spondon House School had twice moved, first to Deal, and then, as a result of the war, to Kenfield Hall, near Canterbury, a beautiful Queen Anne house with a pinetum, where the trees let fall, not without danger to those who walked beneath them, a collection of astonishing objects, suggestive of hand-grenades, Negro carvings or wooden rissoles. On this occasion a notable event was the appear-ance of a guest, a distant relation, who although a permanent civil servant and obvious *Grossstadtmensch*, appeared dressed very much 'for the moors' in the shaggiest of tweeds and attracted some atten-tion by his assumed rusticity. Some years later he retired and bought a house in the country where he is said to have acted to perfection the part of a Victorian squire, greeting the yokels with kindly condescension and apparently acknowledging salutes which it had not always occurred to them to give. The great-nephew of a duke, he was evidently trying to revert to genteel feudalism on the land at a time when that form of life was on its last legs: such is the power of heredity. This is, I think, the only instance I have to give in these pages of a really determined attempt by one of the stranded gentry to revert to the lost world from which they derived. It was as if some dinosaur, having been domesticated and taught to pull its weight between the shafts, should return to its ancestral swamp and jungle, only to find the one drained and the other cleared.

Bob Synge, a fellow-conspirator and the only close friend I made at Beechmont, lived in Radnorshire, and there I went to stay with him and his family one summer, and fell in love at first sight with what has later come to be regarded as the Kilvert country. Near at hand was that curious neo-baronial edifice, Maesllwch Castle, and not far off were the pleasant sleepy towns of Hay and Hereford. The garden at Cwmbach sloped to the fields, and the fields to the Wye, beyond which the Black Mountain rose and varied in the varying light: it was as good as an African mountain, but softer in its moods. Away up on the wild moors we wandered, lay in the bracken, or bathed naked in some icy pool, breaking the silence and the reflection of a mountain ash, or explored dingles loud with the isolated sounds of water descending an irregular stairway of rocks in cascades, rapids, runnels, jets and gushes, fanning as it fell the cool green plumes of ferns. Bob was a promising being, but died soon after he had gone to a public school.

As I went every summer to Burford, I got to know it well. It was not then as arty as it became later, though there was no knowing when some elderly publisher who had been famous in the nineties might not be staying at one of the inns, or an obscure poetess with beads as big as cherries and a Katherine Mansfield fringe at some ancient cottage, or an academic painter with ample private means inhabiting one of the handsome seventeenth-century burgess's houses. Or it might fall to me to show some much-laddered bluestocking over the house and garden, where she would contrast strongly with one of the strapping lady gardeners shoving a barrow-load of dung. However, a deep peace had settled over the place for the duration of the war, and the silence quickened that awareness of the past created by so many and such choice ancient shapes and surfaces. I read all I could of local history and that of the Priory particularly, and when I went up alone to bed and the moon shone in upon the waxed oak staircase, or when I walked alone in the dark wood, my thoughts were often so fixed on the past that it seemed more real than the present. I was inclined to dwell, perhaps morbidly, on the discovery of the corpse of a murdered man in the Priory grounds in April 1697. The lady of the house, left a widow by John Lenthall (son of the Speaker of the Long Parliament), had married her cousin, the Earl of Abercorn. The murdered man was one of the trustees of her sons by her first marriage, and gossip held that Lord Abercorn had quarrelled with the man over some matter concerning the Lenthall boys; he was tried for the murder, but acquitted. In the owl-haunted twilight I seemed to see the crime enacted: it took shape in my mind like a memorable scene in a play. An inflammable imagination was also affected at this time by a reading of Havelock Ellis's *Psychology of Sex*. Rather stimulating reading for a boy, it provided startling information about the private behaviour of many adults and showed, like no other book, how this behaviour realized the fantasies of children.

There was not much entertaining, but sometimes Hamo Thornycroft the sculptor came to stay, or Walter Raleigh would come over from Oxford, and lifting a huge stone ball off one of the garden terraces would playfully invite me to join him in using it as a football. Except at meals, I saw little of my uncle Horniman, who spent much time in his study, planning the preservation or restoration of the architectural beauties of the town, of which, as of its ancient grammar school, he was a benefactor. Tall and unathletic, with a droopy moustache, he was not what is called a good mixer and had a manner which was often taken, or mistaken, for superciliousness; but he had a sense of social responsibility, had sat on the London County Council and in Parliament once as a Liberal member for Chelsea, and certainly used his inherited money largely for the public benefit. He had travelled much and had an enquiring and well-stored but uncreative mind. In early life his interests had been mainly æsthetic and if he had not been born rich he might have developed them in some way in order to make a livelihood. Since those days Liberals have often been sneered at for complacency and one thing and another, but they were born into an easy world. and if they did not always realize how far removed was their way of life from that of the great mass of mankind, they were anxious to do good in the world and to help it to share their own by no means unenlightened views.

Thirty years earlier, in the winter of 1885–86, my uncle Horniman had been a fellow-student with Vincent van Gogh at the Académie des Beaux Arts at Antwerp. That was not an easy time in van Gogh's difficult life and he was under-nourished, over-working and *farouche*. He looked and dressed like a peasant (said my uncle, who kindly noted down his recollections for me) and 'gave the idea of red earth' with his short hair, wiry red beard, and sabots. His eyes were 'green-blue,' and his face was very lined. He used to crouch over his drawing-board making strange faces and noises, was 'subject to violent passion,' and seldom spoke.

'He worked very rapidly in charcoal, looking steadfastly at the plaster cast of an antique figure and then at a great pace making a strong black drawing of, say, a landscape with peasant figures in a storm. The visiting master used to be very annoyed, but I think recognized his talent. We thought him mad and were in awe of him — his work was so strange that in those days, when even Whistler was hardly accepted, few conceived that a new school was already in being.'

For the painting of van Gogh my uncle never acquired a taste. To-day, when it has become hackneyed, it is perhaps in danger of being underestimated, but great as his achievement was in painting, van Gogh is perhaps even greater as a writer: this is to be seen in his letters, which body him forth as a great exemplar of the single-mindedness of the artist — the protestant artist. My uncle was, I suppose, at Antwerp for pleasure and education, van Gogh was helping to make a revolution; my uncle drew the plaster casts, van Gogh drew peasants in a storm; both did what they could to enrich the world, but the contrast between their opportunities and methods could hardly have been more extreme, and this very contrast affords a vivid illustration of that nineteenth-century social and economic pattern — or, as some would say, chaos — which persisted well into our own time.

There was one inhabitant of Burford during the war who, like van Gogh, had a red beard, but it was the well-combed beard of a dandy. Monsieur Bizet, a youngish professor from the University of Brussels and a relation of the composer, was a polished and affable being, a refugee with his mother and sister, and the three of them found temporary sanctuary in Burford. My aunt kindly arranged for me to improve my knowledge of French with him. In conversation his maxim was '*Toujours répondez par une phrase complète*,' so one could not get away with punctuating his elegant discourse with an occasional '*Oui*,' or '*Non*.' His eloquence, his beard, his dandified bearing, and his patent-leather shoes tempted a fellow-pupil and myself to the mischief of leading him unawares into the soggiest culs-de-sac in the water-meadows, or to cross slippery planks over ditches, or to struggle through thistles and nettles, but he was never resentful or more than momentarily put out.

In the middle of the war my father made another attempt to be sent to France. The War Office had asked the South African Government to recruit and equip a native labour corps for service at ports and rail-heads in France. My father had much to do with the raising of this corps and managed to obtain permission to go with it to Europe, but at the last moment he was told that it was essential for him to remain in South Africa as its records officer. He established his office in a house at Rosebank, near Capetown, which bore the name of Charlie's Hope: this was naturally considered funny, as his own name was Charles. There he was kept busy for the rest of the war.

The move to Capetown had meant getting rid of the house in Johannesburg, and it was decided that my mother should return to England to see to my transition from Beechmont to Rugby, which would soon be due. Bringing my young brother with her, she had a somewhat tense and roundabout voyage, for a German raider, the

Möewe, was at large and was in fact sighted, and there were submarines about as well.

She settled first at Tunbridge Wells and then at Eastbourne, and of course I spent my holidays with her. I still have a secret passion for Tunbridge Wells, most particularly for the Common and the High Rocks, which are to me two of the most adventurous places in England. At Eastbourne, where I conceived an almost equal passion for the South Downs, then free from trippers and litter, we lived (since the war and other factors had again much reduced my parents' income) in a boarding-house in Spencer Road. Its only denizen on the brighter side of forty was a schoolmaster with loco-motor ataxia who was said to be unmercifully ragged by his pupils. There were two more or less nondescript unattached women whose relations were strained: they were not on speaking terms, and communicated with one another by leaving haughty notes under an embroidered 'runner' on the top of the piano in the drawing-room. There was a kind, ancient and plain old maid whose well-meant visits to wounded soldiers in hospital were scarcely a success, for when they saw her coming they unanimously pretended to be asleep and snored like grampuses, a ruse which did not deceive but saddened her. And there was an elderly retired captain of marines, courtly but gaga, and wretched in his dignity and loneliness. Almost blind, he would sit in the window, half veiled in shabby lace curtains, reading the newspaper through a large magnifying-glass held up to his eye, and grunting, as well he might, at what he read. Sometimes he could be seen in profile, looking out of the window towards the privet hedge and the trees in Devonshire Park, which were not much to look at anyway and can have been to him no more than a murky blur. The story was that on retiring from the service he had taken a lump sum in lieu of a pension and had squandered it, leaving himself penniless: he was now grudgingly maintained by two sisters, who paid for his board and lodging and allowed him exactly sixpence a week as pocket-money. Never have I seen a man more solitary and wretched; he appeared quite friendless and without hope, but he never complained, was dignified and courteous, and kept his short white beard in trim and his nails clean. My mother, a compassionate woman, treated him with unobtrusive civility and consideration, listening with as much attention to what he had to say as if he were a diplomat of repute. It was almost more than she could bear when he spent his weekly income on sweets for my brother, and he too, though only a child, sensitively tried to dodge acceptance of this kindness. It is terrible to think of all the depressed men and women of the middle classes, middle-aged or elderly, who have eked out more or less barren and forlorn existences in lodgings all over England since the great nineteenth-century illusion of peace, plenty and progress began to dissolve.

In Blackwater Road was a villa containing some distant relations of my mother's, an aged brother and sister known as uncle Walter and aunt Ada, who, on the other hand, lived very snugly and had never done a stroke of work in their lives. Aunt Ada (who once offered me a copy of *Punch* and then said gravely, 'But perhaps you would rather not be seen carrying it on a Sunday') sat in a room like a museum, full of Victorian objects and souvenirs, where tea was served with elaborate ritual by notably well-nourished servants. She had snowy white hair like swansdown, which her maid washed every morning, and would not accept money from her bank unless it was new. Even then coins had to be scrubbed by a servant with a nailbrush, in hot water to which washing soda had been added, before she would touch them. That was what was known as a sheltered life: it was led within earshot of the perennial cannonade across the Channel.

By the time I went to Rugby in 1917 the war was no longer being regarded quite so light-heartedly as in the songs:

> 'Hats off to Tommy Atkins
> Taking his chance,
> On duty with the Blankshires
> Somewhere in France,'

and

> 'Three cheers for little Belgium,
> So small and yet so true.'

The lengthening casualty lists, the air raids, the success of the German submarine warfare and the shortage of food were not making for optimism. Wherever you went, the war was with you.

I wanted to go on the modern side at Rugby, but having taken Greek in the common entrance examination, I had been posted to the classical. A fearful confusion resulted, and I sought the guidance of a porter, an individual who, as I learnt later, had the occasional duty of preparing boys for birching, when he told them, "Tain't the hagony, it's the disgrice' — not realizing that the disgrace of flogging attaches to those who order or sanction it. I began to get used to the routine, and the elaborate system of taboos, both official and unofficial, by which the life of the boys was governed but which nevertheless allowed a dizzy freedom by comparison with Beechmont. I do not know if the system of fagging at Rugby was peculiar to that school. A prefect or somebody would bawl for a fag, all the little boys would scuttle down passages or stairs to answer the call, and the last to arrive would be given a task. This seemed to me so silly that I soon ceased bothering to leave my study: I am only energetic when interested, and might have answered a fag-call by a boy whom I specially wished to please, and should then have taken care to arrive last.

During that war, schoolmasters were often either dotards or weaklings, but at Rugby there were, at any rate, Dr. David and Mr. B. The latter taught French and taught it well, by a method of his own aiming at fluency rather than precision. In my first term, insignificant and bewildered, I was amazed to receive from Mr. B. an invitation to a tea-party to be given in honour of my birthday. His handsome head, with a wing of grey hair brushed back on either side, was full of ideas, and there was intelligence (and a degree of cynicism) in every line of his face as well. I could not understand how such a brilliant and pleasant person as he seemed to me could ever have become a master at a public school, a man so full of curiosity and up-to-date knowledge. He had asked to meet me three of the brightest of my contemporaries and we used afterwards to meet at his house quite often. He encouraged us to think, and we prepared and read papers on subjects that interested us.

Dr. David, later Bishop of Liverpool, was the headmaster and also my housemaster. A tall, dark man with a rugged face, he differed greatly from the smoother type of ecclesiastic and looked as if he had come to grips with things. I think of him with respect, and with gratitude for having treated me as an individual and not just as one of six hundred Rugbeians. He lent me books by Turgeniev from his own shelves, and when my existence began to be affected by special circumstances he gave them the most careful and sympathetic consideration.

I cannot remember ever having played games at Rugby. Certainly I had already spent a good part of several years of my life in keeping balls out of goals or away from wickets or propelling them towards those structures, though I never cared twopence about either process. Darwin, who in his youth had a passion for shooting, put on record his discovery that the pleasure of observing and reasoning was much higher than that of sport. I had already begun to use my eyes, but my powers of reasoning only developed much later. If I did not play games, I was by no means immobile in my spare time. I did a good deal of running and also took part in the Officers' Training Corps, which, being in those days a preparation for the trenches, was taken seriously. I led indeed an active life indoors and out, but was unable to sustain it. I was soundish in wind and limb and had nothing much wrong with me but the weakness of my sight, but I was beginning to outgrow my strength and the food was inadequate. We were allowed, I think, an extra half-hour in bed in the mornings to help to make up for the shortage of food, but under-nourishment, puberty and too much book-work by artificial light, began to tell on me, and every time I saw the oculist in Harley Street he found my sight growing weaker. Dr. David accordingly allowed me to give up some of my form-work and to resign from the Corps.

Having time on my hands, I got a bicycle and went out, not always alone, into the surrounding country. During the war the countryside, in the absence of people and traffic, was peaceful as it never was again, even in the following war. Its peacefulness was not free from melancholy and tension, for war, like a cancer, gnaws all the time, even if painlessly, at the back of the mind, but the quietness of Newbold-on-Avon or Hillmorton or Dunchurch or Ashby St. Ledgers or Stoneleigh or Kenilworth in the summer days of 1918 was almost bewitched. In the presence of the past one felt like a revenant, not a sightseer. When the wind suddenly caught the willows of a water-meadow in a silver net, tugging them sideways against a stormy background, rustling the ivy on a ruin, and shifting the fragrance of meadow-sweet or water-mint, or when a shaft of late sunlight slanted upon some tomb or memorial urn in a silent, musty church, surrounding with its radiance the kneeling alabaster children of some Jacobean squire, all rendered headless by Puritan zeal—at such times the atmosphere seemed that of an earlier age. Fresh and tranquil, the landscape was full of ancient peace, like the landscapes of Constable and Cotman; leaning against an old oaken pew and looking at the trunks of those young persons in ruff and doublet or deep-folded gown, one could well suppose that only a few years had passed since Cromwell's men had beheaded them. But if in the stillness, the magic suspense of that war-time countryside the sense of the past was strongly evoked, incongruities were present: the telegraph wires did not cease to hum; on my way to the fields I might have to pass through the industrial squalor of New Bilton and might later catch sight, in the blue and bosky distance, of the smoking chimneys of Coventry; and a long procession of army lorries, like migrating monsters, would sometimes appear on the high roads. In a lane I met a German prisoner driving a farm-cart and sucking a straw, somebody's blue-eyed boy,

'And his teeth made for laughing round an apple.'

With him I exchanged on more than one occasion a few phrases of classroom German, wondering if the adjectives were agreeing with the nouns and feeling pleasure, not the less keen because it was secret, at a human contact which seemed to make the war a half-forgotten bad dream.

I made some study of local history, finding the school library helpful, and even compiled a little monograph about a hamlet on the Avon, including in it an account of a murder that happened there long ago: a certain Theodosius Boughton was poisoned with laurel water by a Captain Donnellan, his sister's lover. How much more real it was to me than everyday life at school! With the sense of the past there grew an enthusiasm for country churches, fanned by the worthy Bloxam, who had so neatly classified their architectural styles. Instinctively I preferred the round arch to the pointed, the affinities of my nature being more with the Romanesque kind of civilization than with the Gothic, more southern than northern. It was a relief to get away from the hideousness of Rugby Chapel and the striped brickwork of Butter-field's quadrangle and to see and touch the bold and simple Norman semicircle, yellowed and slightly distorted by age, of the chancel arch at Stoneleigh. The sight of such a structure gave me a sheer excitement, and in the summer holidays that year, when I was ill in London with the Spanish influenza, an image of a Norman arch haunted me in delirium and seemed to recall me to life. None of your Gothic rhapsodies for me, your ogees and crockets and heaven-ward soarings.

At school the taste for reading and writing was beginning to form. One of my masters, 'Tiger' Hastings, commended my essays but found fault with a tendency I had to use long Johnsonian words of Latin derivation. 'Good English,' he said, 'is written with Anglo-Saxon monosyllables.' The use of the last word rather weakened a pronouncement which may have had some value as a corrective, but was obviously absurd as an opinion, though it might have gratified William Barnes. A language so rich as ours deserves better use than a style which steals its thunder from the spelling-book. We were 'taught' English with texts from William Morris, Tennyson (I was quite bowled over by *Maud*), Stevenson and Belloc, and in our spare time those of us who were so inclined read the latest volume of *Georgian Poetry*, still no doubt too daring and uncanonical for the class-room. In the school library, however, I routed out a little edition of *The Marriage of Heaven and Hell*, and doors opened into a new world.

Presently other doors opened. The oculist was so unwilling for me to do even a modicum of book-work that it became pointless to remain at school. Dr. David wrote me the kindest and most encouraging of letters, suggesting that I might be able to do something good in life which would not fit in with an ordinary career. The oculist recommended a life in the open air, at least until such time as my short-sight ceased to be progressive, so my mother sent me to a farm in Berkshire, between Newbury and Lambourne. Here I was most kindly treated, and the farmer's wife was a reader of Swinburne. I was not of much use on the farm, though I worked hard at threshing time and there were energetic occasions like that on which I drove two recalcitrant heifers on a frosty morning all the way back from Newbury market. I contrived to visit all the local churches, one of which was unexpectedly embellished with a number of carved and painted elephants' heads. The incumbent who had placed them there had bought them abroad at an international exhibition, and when asked why he had put them up in his church used to reply that the elephant being a symbol of wisdom, a quality notably lacking in his parishioners, it was a comfort to him to address his sermons to the sagacious-looking elephants' heads suspended above their own: this might well be described as preaching over the heads of the congregation.

Shy and gawky, I was not much at ease with the locals. There was a dear old labourer I used sometimes to work with, but I could at first scarcely understand a word of his broad local speech. It seemed very strange to me that there should be such great differences in background and education between two fellow-countrymen, albeit of different generations, standing side by side on the same soil. I had never ceased to feel attracted (as I had been from my earliest years, at Louis Trichardt, for instance, and at Spondon) by working people, their physical dignity, good sense and free and natural manners, and I liked to associate with them. When there was a shoot I used to go sometimes with the guns and sometimes with the beaters, and the reward of this double life was getting to know a man of about thirty, who later seemed to me not unlike some gamekeeper or other out of the novels of D. H. Lawrence. Instead of treating me like 'a young gentleman' he treated me as a boy who did not want to feel lonely and needed the affection of an older man. I responded with gratitude and something like hero-worship, and he might have become an even more important influence in my life than he was, but suddenly the war came to an end; on Armistice Day the Kaiser was burnt in effigy in the streets of Newbury; and presently my mother decided that the best thing to do would be to return with her sons to Africa as soon as possible. She had felt in particular the strain of taking decisions by herself and missed discussing family plans with my father, nor indeed was she pleased to have been so long separated from him. The war had been a greater affliction to her spirit than it was to persons less imaginative and vulnerable, and I dare say she hankered, if not for South African society, at least for the African sun. I was not whisked away like a piece of luggage. Treating me as a more reasoning being than I had yet become, she explained to me the arguments for and against my going with her, and then gave me the choice. As any enterprising boy would have done, I plumped for Africa.

3. HIGH ALTITUDES

The ship was crowded, mainly with people who had been waiting for the end of the war to return to their homes, families or vested interests in South Africa. As happens on ships and in prisons, they quickly revealed mutual attractions, antipathies or indifference and stood forth clearly, a society constituted by chance and existing briefly in isolation and idleness, with each individual, like a moth under a magnifying-glass, to be seen in greater detail than, as it were, by the naked eye.

Usually seated together on deck were two semi-millionaires from the Rand. Slightly too well-dressed, they stuck together, talking, one gathered, much about money and a little about politics. 'The knights,' said somebody, 'are so exclusive' — an observation that might have annoyed one of them, for he was a baronet of very recent creation and a man not without self-importance. Two of the female passengers, if one chose to compare them, afforded a striking contrast and symbolized two very different kinds of society. One was Lady Buxton, the Governor-General's wife, whose quiet dignity, simplicity of manner, and good humour tinged with sadness were not merely charming but fitting to one who presides but does not struggle, and who assumes without fuss a share of the burden of authority in a vast and powerful empire — a perfect embodiment of what is meant, in the best sense, by a ruling class. The other was a Johannesburg Jewess, who was travelling with her husband. She was in her forties, tallish, with an excellent figure expensively corseted, and a slightly too splendid collection of smart new clothes. In an evening dress of Venetian-red lace, with stockings and very high-heeled satin shoes to match, she would appear on deck after dinner, her big eyes flashing under heavily darkened lids, and would raise, in a carefully manicured hand weighted with two or three large diamonds, a long cigarette-holder to a mouth made up to match her dress. Everybody stared at her and commented upon her, but hardly anybody seemed to talk to her, and her husband, obese and silent, was generally in the smoking room with a cigar. There was something faintly ridiculous about her (even in the most distinguished women, says somebody in Balzac, there lurks *un fameux singe*), but there was also something distressing in her decorated solitude. Her restless glances made it seem that her clothes and jewels had not given her confidence; her very vitality made her seem ill at ease; she seemed worldly but without a world of her own, as if she enjoyed all the good things of life but none of the best things; and by over-stressing her appearance, as Jews so often do, she only drew attention to her anomalous place even in this mixed company. In her mobile eyes one could read, as in dark crystals, the torments, past and future, of her race.

I spent much time with a Portuguese girl who was returning to the Cape after being 'finished' in England. I heard later that her family were reputed to have an emphatic 'touch of the tar-brush,' and this made me look back even more romantically on the memory of her slightly frizzy hair, dark eyes and primrose skin. Around us the usual shipboard pairings-off took place, quickening as we approached the equator and mostly tending to cool as we left it behind and drew nearer to the responsibilities, ties and separations waiting beyond the horizon. All this was vivid to a schoolboy escaping from murky wartime winters in England: so were our ports of call. One day Ascension Island sprang from the sea like an old coloured print, with its rufous rocky foreground, a few white buildings, on one of which a magenta bougainvillaea had spread like a stain, and the Green Mountain towering in the background. The island was then officially known as 'H.M.S. Ascension' and 'manned' by a naval staff and a few jet-black Kru boys to do the heavier work. There were said to be only two white women 'aboard' the island, naval officers' wives, between whom there was keen competition in the matter of queening it over the males and over each other. Turtles were abundant, but too rich a diet, one would suppose, in that climate.

I had been sharing a cabin with a landowner from St. Helena, who kindly ordered his carriage to meet us when we went ashore on his native island. We drove with him through Jamestown in some state, in the wake of Lady Buxton and the local Governor, on a tour of the interior. It was not at all the horrid rock which history books had led one to imagine. There were flowers and pretty people everywhere: wisps of tropical mist ran past like long scarves of grey chiffon in mysterious levitation, and the sun came out on groups of peasants working without haste and without rest in a steeply sloping sisal-field; on the winding upland roads donkeys trotted past with loads of melons or brushwood on their backs; young girls offered for sale necklaces of dyed Job's-tears; at Long-wood the fresh Atlantic breeze blew through the empty rooms with their austere remains of decoration in the Empire style, and glancing through the windows one could see rows of blue agapan-thus lilies wagging and nodding like the heads of people in a crowd. A smell of wood-smoke from a hut in a ravine, flowering creepers, flying mists and steamy fragrance — a lovely place of exile, but not for a self-made militarist emperor.

At Capetown my father was on the quay to meet us, sunburnt in a bleached khaki uniform, and we drove up to the International Hotel, a long low building with a wide verandah behind hibiscus hedges, and with more abundant food than we had seen for a long time. We felt, rather mistakenly, that the war had only been a rumour here — except that it had brought the Spanish influenza in the previous year. At the height of the epidemic the main street of the city had been empty at noon, except for a wagon laden with uncoffined corpses. The coloured people had died in thousands, and many had been buried in huge common graves.

The physical pleasure of being in Capetown was intense. Drunk with warmth, like a bee in spring, I wandered in the streets or in the resinous stony pinewoods on the slopes of Table Mountain, or under the heavy-shadowed oaks planted in the seventeenth century by Simon van der Stel, or into the Michaelis gallery of minor Dutch masters — clean, cool pictures of an honest, domesticated civilization. Or we visited my father's friends — the cultivated woman with a collection of fans and a bishop to lunch, the rich couple with a house built in imitation of the old Dutch colonial style, the English colonel with a fruit farm. Presently we moved out to the salty air and white sands (as Kipling observed) of Muizenberg.

I did not at this time find my father particularly sympathetic. We had no recent memories in common; I was beginning to grow up, and that does not always make for easiness between a son and his father; my character and tastes had begun to form and were somewhat at variance with his. He was sociable, and had a taste for good living, old furniture and china and gardens, but little or none for literature and painting. If he did nothing to encourage me in my preferences it was partly because he was not equipped to do so. I think he unconsciously saw me in the light of his first arrival at the Cape more than thirty years earlier. One day at lunch he made a scene because I washed some grapes in a finger-bowl before eating them: I think the objection he advanced was that such niceness was out of place in one who had to make his way in the world. It was almost as if I were on my way to join the long disbanded Cape Mounted Rifles, where such sissy behaviour would be impossible. I think my father, now close on fifty, was beginning to 'glamourize' his youth and to see it largely in terms of a shaggier virility than with his asthma, his nerves and his kind-heartedness he had in fact exhibited. I replied that I was not going to eat dirty grapes to please him or anybody else, and took some more, which I also washed, with studied and I expect irritating deliberation, before eating them. Naturally too docile, I had always had a core of independence, which was now very gradually, too gradually, beginning to harden and expand.

That trivial incident was merely a sign of protest against a conviction I had formed that my father was trying to subdue me into following a pattern of life that would not suit me. I suppose nearly all parents do this with their children to some extent. They try, generally with the best intentions, to make their children grow up in their own image, not always allowing enough for changed times and fashions and differences in character. My brother was too young to be a confidant, I had no sister, and, having been jerked suddenly into what was by now practically a strange environment, I had no friends of my own age. I was aware that my father was trying to make me grow up into one sort of person, rather hearty, and my mother into another sort, more civilized, and that I had embryonic plans of my own to become different to either variety. The fact that both my parents were apt to speak their minds and display their emotions much more freely than most English people drove me into a certain reserve and even secretiveness, but any momentary ill-feeling soon blew over, and in many ways they both treated me as parents should treat a child — that is to say, as a separate being. To take a small example, nothing could have been more sensible than their attitude to smoking. As I was only fifteen, they might with some reason have forbidden me to smoke, in which case I should possibly have smoked much in secret. But they willingly let me smoke, merely observing that it was not thought to be good for growing boys to smoke to excess. This appeal to reason worked well, and until I was grown up I smoked very little.

From Muizenberg, as my father had some weeks' leave, we moved, before returning to Johannesburg, to the delicious country town of Ceres, which, as befitted its name, was steeped in peace and plenty. Lost on an inland plateau at the end of a branch railway, this place is famous for a lavish variety of wild flowers, notably some spectacular heaths and proteas. The streets are shaded with avenues of trees and there is a pleasant and pervasive odour, faintly acrid, of silver-poplar leaves rotting on the river bank. I used to go out and paint the landscape in water-colours in the company of an eccentric Englishwoman with red hair, turquoise earrings, a flat face like a Kalmuck's and a lively intelligence. Some years later she was shot as a spy in Italy.

To arrive in Johannesburg, in the thin bright air of the high-veld, five thousand feet above the sea, is always exhilarating. It was especially so in 1919, when the world was supposed to have been changed by the war and there was an atmosphere of renewed effort and hope. Peace was supposed to have returned for good, but my father, though out of uniform, was to be occupied for many months more in tidying up the affairs of the native labourers who had returned or failed to return from France. With the passing of time, and after so many nomadic years, he had developed a strong taste for settled domestic surroundings and would now have liked to take a house again. My mother, on the other hand, hated housekeeping, with which she had had such hard struggles in earlier years. We therefore went to live in a boarding-house in the 'best' part of the town. It was obvious that I should have to go to school, as I was still too young to do anything else, and the obvious school was St. John's, to which I now returned as a day-boy. In spite of having been there, and of having been happy there before, I had been so conditioned by my schooling in England that I returned almost as a stranger. 'Look who's here,' I heard one boy say to another on the very first day, as he nudged his companion to look at me, 'the Emperor of China.'

The buildings and the trees had grown. There was a handsome new chapel, a swimming bath, and a new quadrangle, or at least two sides of it, with cloisters: the place had quite lost the primitive, pioneering air which had formerly given it such charm. Father A. was now the headmaster — before long he was to startle everybody by forsaking the celibate Community of the Resurrection for the connubial bed. Father B. had returned from France, where he had been a chaplain to the forces, with a wound and a decoration, and looked more like an eagle than ever. Father C. had become a bishop. Father D. had vanished. And Father E., with his skimpy apostolic beard, was still shambling about in cassock and biretta, a football in one hand and a bunch of keys in the other, still smiling and nodding gently and resignedly at me because I would not play games. Pink and white cosmos still waved below the terrace, on windy days red dust-devils still raced across the playing fields, a play of Shakespeare's was still produced every year — but somehow the spell had broken. Villas were encroaching on the Kopje, so what was the good of climbing it? I felt no incentive to work perhaps because my body was busy with adolescence, because I was not in harmony with my surroundings, because there was nobody to direct my mind, because the future was indistinct. Feeling myself now like a foreigner among my schoolfellows, I could not become as I had been earlier, part of the school. I ragged about, idled and dreamed, neither head nor heart was fixed on definite objects, and I was driven in upon myself.

In the holidays I pursued culture by choice and society under parental pressure. Society meant mostly tennis or dancing, but nature did not intend me to be either a tennis-player or a dancing man, so such pleasure as I took in these activities was not the result of marked accomplishment. However, I now for the first time got to know something about bourgeois girls and young women — the dumb *ingénue*, the congenital tart, the tomboy, the clinging goose, the sinewy sports-girl, the prim prig, the maternally-inspired social climber fresh from a Swiss finishing-school, the calculating teaser, the nubile monkey, and even a nymphomaniac. The last-named was in fact in her thirties and married to a most respectable husband. Women told each other that no man was safe alone with her, 'even for a moment': how right they were; her strategy was decidedly offensive and she aimed at taking her objective by storm and by surprise simultaneously. In appearance she was attractive, and even without knowing of her proclivities one might have guessed that she was dangerous. As lean and supple as a cat, she dressed very well but very plainly, generally in neat tweeds, as it were *en chasseresse*. Her dark hair, done in a modest and even severe style, set off an always colourless face, an 'interesting pallor' in which a pair of restless dark eyes, not large, glittered feverishly and observantly: but it was the mouth that chiefly caught one's attention, the thin, unappeasable, relentless mouth of a monomaniac, and one could fancy that it resembled the mouth, seen under a microscope, of some rare parasite. And were there no nice, ordinary girls? Oh, yes. Aren't there always? And there was an intellectual, a finely-bred Jewess, with a delicate profile like an ancient Egyptian queen, and the quiet manners of conscious superiority.

I did not as a rule take much to those whom I partnered on the tennis court or steered round the dance floor — nor they, I dare say, to me. 'William is so critical,' somebody said to my mother, and the observation was just. An adolescent *déraciné* (so far as I had had any roots), I was in a state of physical and emotional turmoil, and the society in which I moved was equally wanting in naturalness and glamour; on the whole it was boring and second-rate. Nobody was making anything except money or plans to make more money, most people climbed and pushed in pursuit of illusory worldly gains, and, so far as the women went, their chief happiness was for themselves and their offspring to attend entertainments given by the Governor-General, who was at this time a royal prince. Imagine him standing to receive his guests at a dance. His consort stands by his side; she has bobbed hair (very modern and daring), a face unmarked by thought, and a great many very large diamonds scintillating on the upper half of her person — some of them came out of African earth and have returned to flash above it. Royal liveries of scarlet hover in the background, and among some of the guests approaching to be announced and received an anxious debate is to be heard on the theme 'Does one or does one not remove one's gloves before shaking the hand of Royalty?' This strange scene is, so to speak, the crowning ornament of a materialistic city, under which black men and white are grubbing for gold.

Since all societies are mixed, even Johannesburg contained its saints and simpletons, its persons of taste or creative solitaries.

There was, for instance, the Orpheus Café, where Greeks with Turkish coffee and Turkish delight beside them, played the guitar and sang the folk-songs of their native land. There were at least three Jews with a knowledge of painting. One possessed a Courbet, another several Matisses (he was later to open an imposing gallery in Mayfair, and later still to take his own life), a third was himself a painter of talent. This last had also, one might say, talent as a character. Slight in stature, with a Byzantine face under a heavy black fringe and gifted with a wonderful gaiety and childlike zest for life, he made his own world and lived in it. He was as good a friend to me as a nomad who brings one dates and water in a desert. His work and his talk and the vivid environment which, like a bower-bird, he had created for himself refreshed my eyes and spirit and easily lured me away from the tennis parties and coming-out dances.

At one time he went to live in a vacant barrack of a native compound on a gold-mine, the machinery of which thundered in the background as he showed me his drawings. These had caught in a flowing line the shapely sadness and exiled vigour of naked black miners. Sweating and half-choked underground, they loved when above the surface of the earth to dress themselves in gaudy finery and would wander about playing mouth-organs or zithers, or wrapped in cherry-coloured blankets would sit smoking or singing mournfully in the sun. Sometimes on Sunday mornings they were allowed to indulge in their tribal dances, and nothing could be more splendid than the strength, freedom and precision of their movements and the barbaric music of the drums and primitive xylophones that accompanied them. But a deep melancholy pervaded the proceedings, and I was gradually becoming aware of the reasons for it. They have been well put by Nesbitt, in the book to which I have already alluded, *Gold Fever*:

'The natives, whose own social and economic systems have been trampled under foot by the invaders, are debarred from any real participation in the benefits of that civilization to the introduction of which those invaders point as the justification for their acts.

While the natives are kept down by the legal imposition of inferior status, and by the denial of their right to undertake and be paid for skilled work, they can never taste the fruit of Western progress. At the mines they are, in fact, kept herded like cattle in compounds, from which it is extremely difficult for any of them to go out, even for a few hours. They are kept in close confinement, overworked, underpaid, and denied even such rights as are indispensable for the maintenance of their dignity as human beings. As for progress, that is quite out of the question for the native. His deprivation of all chance of profiting by it is ensured by the administration of laws made by those who are devoted to progress, for themselves.'

I had not at this time come across any such clear expression of these facts, but I was beginning to perceive them, by sympathy rather than argument, for myself.

I had so much to learn, so much to read. In the matter of books I was certainly not starved. A sensitive Dutchman (who later made a name in London by his light touch as a painter of landscape) lent me Proust — and there were not many people in South Africa reading Proust in 1920. An English South African lent me Joyce's *Ulysses*. To read these books then, at the age of sixteen, was to be carried away and to return to earth with an immensely enriched perception of the nature of life and the possibilities of language. There was an excellent municipal library, which would have done credit to a European capital, and it enabled me to read a vast amount and variety, my preferences being for English poetry from Chaucer to Eliot, Russian novels, and the best and newest contemporary prose and verse, which included the writings of D. H. Lawrence. That writer has rather gone out of fashion, and to-day it is not sufficiently understood what freshness, life and clarity, what a revolutionary newness of vision he brought, however fanciful his doctrines, to replace the increasing staleness, thinness and banality of the English novel of his time.

The impressions of what I read (without guidance, and almost without discussion) were as various as they were keen. In a turmoil of imaginative and sensory experience I would hide myself in the eucalyptus forest known as the Sachsenwald, and in that dry, balsamic air would compose immature verses; or I would go home and draw (I remember that I drew over and over again a profile that I first got to know ten years later); or I would practise physical culture — muscle control, and so on — with a professional who made my growing body more resilient and better able to enjoy the mere acts of breathing and walking in the electric air under the clean African sky: so that when we went down to the Natal coast for holidays, and a tepid wind blew in from the Indian Ocean and rustled the stiff leaves of the sugar-cane, and walking through an orange grove one encountered a thin Indian girl dressed in a magenta sari, with big humid eyes and garnet studs in her nostrils, this different world seemed to invite one on to others more remote and exotic. I was hungry for life, and the appetite seemed insatiable. Not that the coast was all glamour. When the wind blew from the direction of Park Rynie, it brought with it the effluvia of a whaling station, compared with which burning rubber smells as good as mignonette; and an acquaintance who went for a swim rose indignantly from under the water wrapped in a clinging pelisse of decomposing blubber. We were also a little disturbed, when staying at a primitive hotel in an idyllic solitude, by the private life of its owner, who at dead of night chased his wife round the garden, firing a revolver as he ran, and only desisting when she took refuge in a place meant for less dramatic activities. However, the Plomer family did not actually come under fire, and the fish at breakfast the next morning was quite excellent.

Sometimes my father would ask me if I had made up my mind what I wanted to do in life. There are times when an adolescent feels he could do almost anything, when the whole of life seems to boil in his veins. 'If we are all a part of God,' said Firbank's Mrs. Cresswell, 'then God must indeed be horrible': be that as it may, every man and every woman contains the whole of humanity. The idiot and the blockhead carry within them the unfertilized seeds of all the qualities that might go to make an Admirable Crichton; the senile stockbroker with hardened arteries, the withered virgin alone with her cats, the blind masseur, the worn-out housewife, the brutalized Nazi, might have been all things to all men. A Shakespeare or a Goethe contains inarticulate multitudes and gives them voices, but Tom, Dick and Harry only ripen in their breasts the simpler, commoner impulses of mankind. Each of these three probably has it in him to become a passable soldier, mechanic, gardener, small shopkeeper, athlete, clerk, waiter, husband, father, good man or criminal, but the workings of fate and of hormones only allow him to become some of these things, perhaps even only one of them. My father, if circumstances had allowed, might have made good as a regular soldier, or a professional swimmer, or a wool merchant, or, if he had become the 'adopted son' of an Australian millionaire, as goodness knows what. I once heard my mother say that if she could have had her life over again she would certainly have been an actress; but she had religious feeling, energy and modesty enough to have made her a good wife for a parson, and worldly wisdom, tact and poise enough to have made her an excellent wife for a diplomat; yet her line was cast in other places, and if, like most people, she sometimes thought of what she might have done, she made the best of what she had to do. As for me, I have managed to earn a living as a farmer, shopkeeper and schoolmaster, but there were other things I might have done as well or better: I could perhaps have become an actor or a doctor. All through adolescence I was, like most people, aware of pent-up potentialities, but apart from purely physical and emotional ways of expression my strongest bents were for writing and drawing. If I had been strongly encouraged or taught to draw when young, or if I had grown up in a world where painting was the main interest, I might well have made it my profession. But at sixteen I felt that I must renounce either writing or painting, and deliberately preferred, or rather was impelled, to write. My father had little or no interest in this decision until some years later, when I proved that I was at least publishable. He did not regard writing either with hope or approval as an eventual means of my making a living, but he did not try to prevent me from preparing myself for it as best I could.

My irregular education had provided me so far with a little Latin and less Greek, rather more French, a smattering of German, a passion for English, and no mathematics or 'science,' for neither of which I was in any way gifted, though I had been obliged to waste much time on these subjects. It had also (and here I count the influence of my mother as the chief part of my education) sharpened my curiosity, my powers of seeing, enjoying and discriminating, and my dismay at the want of justice for the larger and more vulnerable part of mankind, unprotected by money or power. Both my father and mother, even at the cost of encroachments on their never more than moderate capital, and indeed at whatever sacrifice, had stuck to their resolve to give both their sons the most liberal education they could. They now most generously offered me the chance of going to Oxford as I should have done if I had stayed at Rugby. I refused the offer, which was attractive, for two reasons: first, it would have meant an undue strain on their resources, and probably on my not yet stabilized eyesight as well; secondly, I rather fancied a more erratic course. I see now that Oxford might well have given me a valuable intellectual training and discipline; the chance of working out in conversation with people of my own sort many ideas that I have had to grapple with by myself; the chance of making good friends; and the chance of beginning early in England to play a part, however slight, in the life of my time, among my own compatriots and contemporaries. I see also the narrowing effects it might have had, for I have known prigs, pedants and flashy intellectuals turned out by our older universities. I see also the advantages I had by not going to Oxford, for I learnt much from early and close contacts with those who may be called ordinary people, and the faculties of my university were those of solitude, remoteness, self-reliance and frugality. It certainly never occurred to any of us that I might go to a local university, probably because in the world from which my parents came the word 'university' could only mean either Oxford or Cambridge. There was little point in my remaining at St. John's, especially as the oculist was still in favour of my fastening my eyes upon the great open spaces rather than upon books, so my parents set themselves to discussing how this could best be arranged.

In the year 1820 there had been a considerable immigration of odds and ends into South Africa from the United Kingdom. A century later an organization was founded, under the title of the 1820 Memorial Settlers' Association, to attract a new influx of white settlers, of what its founders considered a desirable type, into the Union. The real pioneering days were over, railways and been built, the land taken up, and the natives thoroughly exploited, and if the new settlers were to establish themselves and not become a burden on the country it was judged essential that each should have a capital of at least two or three thousand pounds. The plan was that each settler should be expertly advised by the Association as to what kind of farming to take up, and that he should then be placed on a suitable farm or farms for two or three years to learn the rudiments. During this period he would offer his hosts his services in exchange for board, lodging and tuition, and when qualified to set up on his own would be again advised by the Association on the choice and purchase of land and on cognate matters. The scheme was quite well thought out, and when advertisements began to appear in *The Times* and elsewhere they found a ready response. The aftermath of the first World War had left many youngish and enterprising English people high and dry or at a loose end, and many of them were not satisfied with the prospect of peddling vacuum-cleaners in the London suburbs or running chicken-farms in messy Metroland. South Africa once more appeared to many—including retired soldiers or civil servants from India and other parts of the Empire, scions of the stranded gentry both married and single, and well-to-do parents with high-spirited sons — a 'coming country.' My parents thought that the scheme might well provide a niche for me, either for good or at least until my tendency to progressive myopia had been checked. 'There is no reason,' they justly said, 'why you should not write or do whatever you want to do later on.' There would be no difficulty about my candidature, for I was a palpably 'desirable' type — that is to say, I was not some hunted and penniless Polish Jew, or a talented mulatto, and so far had shown no signs of any ambition to sell hooch clandestinely to the natives — and if I decided in due course to set up as a farmer on my own, my parents were still in a position to launch me with something more than a mortgage. Therefore I became an 1820 Memorial Settler, in my own interest and not in that of any fantasy like a 'White South Africa.'

Matters were promptly arranged, and my father took a more special interest in them because he remembered how much he had enjoyed his own early years in Africa, travelling from farm to hospitable farm, sorting wool-clips, planting trees, making friends and fences, jogging about on a Basuto pony, going for picnics with the girls on Sundays. It was no doubt these memories that made him think that the eastern part of the Cape Province, the scene of many of his early activities, would be a suitable region for me: it was as if he was going to re-live part of his life in that of his son. A farm was chosen, my boxes were packed, and in the middle of the winter of 1921 (that is to say in June), at the age of seventeen, I found myself bound for far-off Molteno — the little *dorp* where, it may be recalled, my father had been taken to task, some thirty years earlier, for breaking the laws of caste by organizing an official banquet.

No banquet awaited me, but a cold bedroom in a small hotel and the glowing hospitality at their rectory of an old English clergyman and his wife, while I waited a couple of days for my farmer to come in from the country and fetch me. It was all rather like what the Middle West might have been at the end of the last century. Molteno, a one-horse town, had its main street, its railway and police stations, its hotel, a few shops with chickens pecking about on the threshold, a Dutch Reformed church, a Wesleyan Methodist chapel, and much smaller, an Anglican church. The streets were few, wide, dusty and drowsy; an occasional ox-wagon creaked past; everybody knew everybody else's business, and small scandals took on colossal proportions; Europe seemed a conception as remote and unreal as heaven or hell; and the cats, asleep on window-sills or hearth-rugs, looked as tranquil and detached as so many images of Buddha. In due course a buggy appeared at the door, my luggage was strapped on behind, and off I drove in an icy wind, seated beside my unknown farmer, to an unknown new life as a farmer's boy.

The arrangement for training a prospective 'Memorial Settler' placed him in a somewhat anomalous position vis-à-vis the farmer with whom he was to dwell, for he was neither precisely a guest nor an employee. The arrangement was, in practice, obviously open to abuses and in order to work well required at least good sense and good will on both sides. An idle or frivolous apprentice-settler would not be worth his keep, whereas one too young and docile might be exploited or even harshly treated by the farmer under whose roof he found himself. I came to hear of instances where little or no consideration was shown either on one side or on both, and of one case where the pupil-settler was so oppressed by the loneliness of his surroundings and the unkindness of the farmer-tutor and his wife, that he hanged himself in a barn. For myself, I was lucky; I tried to make myself useful and was treated always with friendly consideration.

As we drove out of Molteno in the direction of Dordrecht we found ourselves on a third-rate road, in places no more than a stony track, devoid of traffic, and with wide treeless prairies or occasional cultivated lands on either side, backed by the bare rocky mountains of the Stormberg, then turning blue and violet as the westering wintry light gave way to advancing shadow. Once or twice in the course of our fourteen-mile drive I caught sight of some distant clump of trees and the walls of a farmhouse, and at last, as the light was beginning to fail, we came to a great amphitheatre enclosed by mountains, at the foot of one of which stood the homestead that was our destination. It bore the Brontë-esque name of Marsh Moor, which was appropriate enough to its wild character.

As one turned off the road there was a short approach to the house. On the right were flat arable lands and on the left kraals, or enclosures, with stone walls about five feet high, some roomy stone sheep-sheds, a barn, a wagon-house and other farm buildings. Behind the kraals was a row of circular huts where the native labourers and their families lived, and behind the huts a plantation of conifers. The house itself was little more than a cottage. It was of one story, had a thatched roof, no stoep or verandah, and a central living room, out of which doors led to three bedrooms, a kitchen, and a small unkempt garden, where in the summer lilies and parsnips jockeyed for position. Beyond the house was a dam overhung by one enormous willow, and beyond the dam loomed the rocky spur of a mountain. The farm had first, I think, been won from the wilderness by the occupant's father. It was of a couple of thousand acres, half flat and half mountainous, and supported a great many sheep and some cattle.

Soon after I arrived there was a blizzard and a heavy fall of snow (the Stormberg is more than five thousand feet above sea level, and so cold that maize, for example, cannot be successfully grown there). It was the lambing season, and I at once began to learn the arts of midwifery among the ewes and the curious variations among them of the maternal instinct. Many an evening have I spent in stone sheds by lantern-light, obliging a reluctant udder to accept the blind mouth of an unwanted lamb, or dressing a live lamb in the skin of a dead one in order to persuade the bereaved ewe to bring up the changeling as her own offspring — exercises in patience. Persons unfamiliar with the ways of sheep think of them as merely silly and timid and as being all alike. The widow of Thomas Hardy once told me that her husband, leaning with her on a gate leading into a field full of sheep, drew her notice to the fact (which every shepherd knows) that they all had different faces. Indeed there are as many variations of character among them as among horses, cats or dogs, and they are capable of exhibiting, among other qualities, affection, cunning and wilfulness. 'The rage of the sheep' is a ludicrous-sounding phrase, but it does not seem so when one has seen a man charged and knocked over by a full-grown Merino ram with great voluted horns, testicles like a bull's, and the light of battle in its eyes. After the snow had thawed I was sent one morning on horseback to an outpost of the farm to count a flock of some thousand-odd sheep grazing on a mountain in charge of a shrewd and wizened old Xosa shepherd. The usual medium of communication with the natives thereabouts was Afrikaans, of which I then knew very little, and I had never counted sheep in my life, even imaginary ones as a soporific, so the proceedings were liable to more than one technical hitch. However, the great flock was driven, according to custom, towards a fence (from which I stood at a distance of some twenty yards, perched on a rock) and was then chivvied past by the shepherd. Sometimes they ran past in ones or twos, sometimes in dozens, and sometimes, having run past, they felt misgivings and bolted or straggled back again in twos or threes or disorderly dozens: so it was no wonder that, not being in any case a ready reckoner, I had to count them three times and arrived at three markedly different totals. However, practice soon made me perfect.

Merino sheep are bred not for mutton but wool, of which they carry a surprising quantity, beautiful in its density, texture and length, and pearly or creamy in its lustre, which can only be seen when it is shorn or when the surface of the growing fleece is parted with the fingers. At shearing-time, when the tawny mountain-sides were softened into summer green, we worked, glistening with sweat and the natural oil in the wool, from daylight to dark, the muscular native shearers looking like heroic bronzes in their gleaming nakedness as they bent over the task and then gathered up the heavy white fleeces and shook them out flat on the sorting-table, where I sorted them, packed them and sewed up the bales, learning thoroughly what is meant by the poetry of manual labour — a phrase just enough, since it implies skill, rhythm and exhilaration.

My chief joy at Marsh Moor was health. The dry, temperate climate, the superb mountain air, the long days out of doors, the brilliant cloudless nights, the sweet sleep and wholesome food, youth, freedom from care — these were great advantages. It was a nineteenth-century way of living, for there was no motor-car, no wireless-set and no telephone. Indeed, life there was extremely simple. We rose early and went to bed early by candlelight, too pleasantly tired to do anything but sleep. We lived mostly on wholemeal bread and wholemeal porridge of our own growing and grinding, mutton, milk and butter also from the farm, and coffee; a bath was taken at night once a week, the water being heated in empty paraffin tins on the kitchen stove ; and once a week the post was fetched from Molteno. I thus learnt the unimportance, at least in a good climate, of material comforts. I learnt to thatch, to make or repair fences, to cover roofs with corrugated iron, to sow broadcast, to do simple blacksmith's or carpenter's jobs, to cut up a sheep as deftly as any butcher could, and to make bread, and I used with my own hands to make up to sixty pounds of butter every week. As for sheep, I learnt all about them, in theory and in practice, their diet and their diseases, their points and prospects, and we used to dock the tails of a couple of hundred lambs and castrate them before breakfast and think nothing of it. Not the least of my pleasures was to wander in the mountains, where the solitude was complete and the wild flowers unknown to me — tree-heaths, curious liliaceous plants, and canary-yellow dwarf arums with mottled leaves and a wicked-looking puce finger pointing rigidly upwards in the sheath of each flower — and I discovered some unknown caves adorned with spirited and elegant Bushman paintings, ritual and hunting scenes carried out in black, white and red and yellow ochres. So I lacked neither a garden nor a picture gallery.

Had I not been so busy, the solitude might all the same have driven me mad, or at least peculiar, for apart from the farmer and his wife there was almost no society. Once a week he drove to Molteno to buy provisions, collect the letters and do business. Occasionally I went with him, but generally I had more important things to do, and in any case there was little inducement, for the sleepy *dorp* had few amenities. I did not even bother to go there to get my hair cut, but ordered a pair of clippers and with these and a couple of looking-glasses learnt to do it myself. A mile away from Marsh Moor was a farm belonging to some pleasant relations of my farmer's, and we saw them now and again. There were other farms here and there, three, five or ten miles away, but their denizens were Dutch, and my farmer and his wife, who were colonials of English descent, were not on terms of intimacy with any of them. Very occasionally we had visitors. A Dutch mounted-policeman would call on his rounds, or somebody would come to buy sheep, or a relation or two of the farmer's would come for a short stay. Once two carpenters came for a couple of weeks, an Englishman and a young Dutchman, the latter full of life and mischief and bearing the Horatian name of Posthumus. Another time several men came to do some repairs to the house. They were spoken of as the Hottentots, or Totties, but called themselves the *Bruyn Mense*, or brown people, though in fact they were pale buff or primrose colour, with a strong strain of Malay in them. Their manners were simple and winning, and in their clear soft voices they talked the Taal very distinctly. It was a pleasure to converse with them and they made that often uncouthly-spoken language beautiful to hear and easier to pick up.

Best of all was a grand old Scotch wanderer, who, born a gentleman, had come to Africa when young, had served in the South African war, but had otherwise led a drifting life — rather like my father's when he was young, only begun earlier and continued permanently — gathering no moss and obviously enjoying himself. With the air of a *grand seigneur* and the most natural and pleasant manners, he got a living as a journeyman blacksmith and he stayed at Marsh Moor in that capacity, mending farm implements and making various things of wrought iron. He was a fine figure of a man with flowing golden moustaches and a ruddy face, a cheerful, sceptical sensualist with wonderful stories of his earlier days, when the country was freer and wilder and fuller of odd characters comparable to himself. In spite of his rough life he had retained many of the little as well as the stronger prejudices of his class: 'I do *wish* they wouldn't say "serviettes," ' I remember him saying. While I kept the forge going for him he built up for me out of his past a world of legend, and I grew fond of him as one might of a benevolent uncle. But he left abruptly after giving offence by exhibiting an entire lack of colour prejudice.

Everything comes back to that in South Africa, and at Marsh Moor the colour bar was stronger than the iron he had hammered and tempered in the smithy. I remember that when I first arrived I made a gaffe by suggesting that I should learn to milk the cows: no white man, I was instantly informed, ever milked a cow. If the Xosa farm servants, who worked faithfully and well, lived at a very low standard and were paid a mere pittance, that was because it was the custom. They were not treated in the least harshly, but there were no signs of the human touch in their employer's attitude towards them; there was nothing of the paternal care that had been sometimes shown by benevolent owners long before in the days of slavery. They were there, they were necessary, they must do what was expected of them, and that was all there was to be said: but to me their strength and grace, their melancholy songs and cheerful banter, were a continual consolation and allurement — which I needed, for I was young and lonely: how lonely, I realized when my farmer and his wife went away and I never saw a white face for a fortnight. There was I, at seventeen, responsible for that enormous farm, shouldering willy-nilly the white man's so-called burden.

The Eastern Province is not without its literary associations, and the knowledge that two distinguished writers had grappled successfully among such rocky peaks as those of the Stormberg with the solitude of intellectual exile gave me comfort. One was Olive Schreiner, who had died at the Cape only a few months before my arrival at Marsh Moor and had been buried on the top of a mountain not very far away, as distance is reckoned in those parts. Though I never saw her, I had met people who had known her, including one old woman who had known her when they were girls together. She told me that Olive once lost a post as governess through replying to a homily from her female employer with a scornful 'God, indeed!' I had with me *The Story of an African Farm*, and I was aware of its author both as one who had given lasting shape to forms of life hitherto unperceived or unrecorded (the proper function of a writer) and as one who therefore, though dead, was still living. Such is the power of the written word that she was in fact a closer companion to me than those beings with whom my life was passed. Later I was to read, with increasing sympathy and admiration, all her published writings and most, I think, of what has been written about her. It is high time that some competent person wrote the life of this dynamic being, a creative artist at odds with her environment, a force and influence in England in her prime, and a writer of permanent value. In Europe she dazzled some of her contemporaries and impressed others, but can hardly be said to have struck new roots or been made fruitful in this continent; then she returned to South Africa — 'a whole nation,' she had called it, 'of *lower* middle class Philistines' — where she left her bones. Hers was a heroic life of struggle — physical, intellectual, emotional, social and artistic; she was hounded from place to place by asthma, and animated by a rare passion for truth and justice. In South Africa such intelligence and sensibility have never been matched before or since her time.

Then there was Thomas Pringle, a lively Scotch cripple, who had come out to Africa at the age of thirty, with the blessing of Scott, as one of the original 1820 settlers, and who wrote, among other things, a poem which Coleridge enthusiastically pronounced to be among the two or three most perfect lyrics in our language. Pringle was only in Africa six years, but it was long enough for him to leave a record of his sojourn there in prose and verse (both at times very good), to champion the natives and the freedom of the press, and to defy with real courage the tyrannical government of Lord Charles Somerset. Africa, as a place to abide in, defeated him as it later defeated Olive Schreiner, but both were spiritually and artistically victorious. Returning to England he became less active in literature than in philanthropy. He did what he could to encourage the talent of the youthful Ruskin, who afterwards wrote patronizingly of him in *Praeterita*, but his chief activity was as secretary of the Anti-Slavery Society. Pringle was that rarity, a transparently good man; he was the first poet of his briefly adopted country, and if his subject-matter was on the whole more original than his approach to it, he managed to strike some bell-like notes; he fought against injustice; but he was no prophet, and went so far as to believe that 'the dragon Slavery' having been destroyed, 'its odious brood, the prejudices of caste and colour, must ere long also expire.' Alas, the odious brood is not only still with us but has multiplied.

At Marsh Moor there was scarcely any time for writing, but I once sent some verses to Harold Monro, the leading poetic impresario of his day. He wrote me an encouraging letter in reply, of which he reminded me when I met him years later. I was also heartened by a schoolfellow in England with whom I used to correspond. There was likewise little time for reading, and in any case I had few books with me. Among them were Shakespeare, Blake, Rimbaud, a selection of van Gogh's letters, and two or three volumes of stories by Maupassant and Bunin, and I used to get various periodicals, ranging from *John o' London's Weekly* to the *Nouvelle Revue Française*, both of which I think of with gratitude. Although I intended to be a writer I felt very much my youthful want of experience and, to speak paradoxically, the constriction of the great open spaces. I felt strongly the lack of congenial and coeval society. I was too much alone with my turbulent thoughts and there was nobody to tell them to. It may be true that it is only by being alone that a man (even an adolescent man) can find himself, but it is not by being alone that he can find his proper level. I was observing and dreaming rather than reasoning, and one of my dreams (though by no means one of the most persistent) was that I was going to be a farmer and about how I should live then. There was much that I liked in my surroundings and the life I was leading — or at least in its possibilities — and in fact I was quite seriously, though dispassionately, preparing to set myself up as a sheep-breeder there in the Stormberg. I kept a big notebook in which I wrote useful prescriptions for the diseases of sheep, the measurements of cow-sheds, and particulars about silage, fertilizers, and other recondite matters. I did not quite see how I could start a farm on my own at eighteen and was wondering whether I might not spend a year or so on a fruit farm in the Western Province in case I should prefer growing peaches to breeding sheep, when a perfectly different project was suddenly put before me.

4. THE PLACE OF THORNS

By 1922 my father had wound up the affairs of the natives who had been recruited for labour during the war, and had returned to the native affairs of peace-time, but there were rumours of an impending drastic retrenchment in the civil service, and he began to wonder whether, if he were retired, it would be better to return to England or remain in Africa. He and my mother were inclined to go and see for themselves what England was like in the nineteen-twenties, but they hesitated to do so because of the expense of the journey. They flattered me by asking my opinion in the matter, and I advised them to make the journey, which they accordingly did, taking my brother with them in order to leave him at a preparatory school. Johannesburg, just as they were leaving, was in the grip of a revolutionary strike; their train was fired at soon after they had left the station and they lay on the floor while bullets cracked and whistled through the windows. There were some extraordinary incidents during the strike, and I heard from an eye-witness of a man who went quietly out of his house to see what was happening and was overpowered in the street by three women who detached themselves from a crowd of rioters. They did not know him and could have had no grievance against him, but being carried away by sadistic hysteria they mauled him horribly and stabbed him with hatpins in his vital parts. The victim and his assailants were all of the white race.

When my parents came back, my father was made inspector of native affairs and devoted his attention to the welfare of the natives working on the mines. This task was congenial to him, but the rumours of retrenchment persisted. It was a fashionable policy at that time in various countries and in establishments both civil and military and was no doubt an outcome of the reaction from artificial prosperity during the war and of the need to reduce staffs swollen by war-time needs. Presently a large number of civil servants, most or all of whom were of British origins, were put on pension in the name of economy, but the places of many of them, instead of being abolished, were promptly filled by men of Dutch extraction. This was an inevitable result of the growing power and influence of the Dutch, who had been gradually taking over more and more of the administration of the country, in which after all they had been long settled and had done much, if not most, of the basic pioneering. But the retrenched Englishmen could not help feeling a slight sense of grievance. My father, for example, had given his best energies to the country's service; he was only just fifty and active for his age, and would willingly have continued to do so. Although he had always been inclined to like the Dutch and had often stoutly defended them against their traducers, he now felt, I think, a little less cordial towards them. His pension was very small — about one-seventh of that with which his father had retired from the Indian army — and the sudden obligation to begin life anew caused him anxiety.

'They are at once the gentlest and the most determined of peoples,' said Olive Schreiner of the Dutch. True enough, but not one of her pithier sayings: she should have known better than to generalize, for the same might be said of the English, the Chinese, the Greeks, and so on. A race, like an individual, leads a double life: those who are made to suffer by a nation's ambition may feel that they have reason for calling it aggressive and unprincipled, while those who have enjoyed its kindness may call it civilized and lovable. Like other races, the South African Dutch have too often been judged by the less amiable traits of individuals. Their enemies have often called them dirty, lazy, ignorant and unscrupulous, and have blamed them for narrowmindedness, racial prejudice, political intransigence and religious bigotry. In the Stormberg I have heard a poor Dutch *bywoner* spoken of as a degraded outcast for having taken his gun out to get something for the pot (round which his numerous and hungry children were sitting) and for having then cheerfully described the successful slaughter of several partridges simultaneously as they were running along the ground. I have myself seen a bed-bug ardently pursuing a member of its species round a hat upon the head of a Dutchman in broad daylight. I would not quote these trifles as triumphant vindications of sportsmanship and hygiene, but both these men were physically vigorous, gentle in manner, and animated in conversation, and they appeared to be leading harmless and contented lives; to be hungry at times is common to all of us and to be generally verminous is habitual with many estimable members of the human race. The South African Dutch, like other peoples, have their faults and weaknesses, some of which are often obvious; but as I have never, to my knowledge, had a personal enemy among them, I shall not enlarge on their shortcomings, the greatest of which, to my mind, are their short-sighted views and unjust treatment of the indigenous inhabitants of the country. I have, on the other hand, had close Dutch friends and have been grateful for their imagination, tolerance, good humour, beauty and generosity. As a race the South African Dutch may well produce men of distinction, and not solely in the sphere of politics and war.

Their visit to England had not convinced my parents that they would be wise to return there for good, and they were now faced with the problem of beginning a new life on a much diminished income. If they had only had themselves to think about, they would no doubt have returned to Europe, but they put the interests of their children first. Their chief wishes at this time were to provide for my brother's education and to give me a good start in life, and in order to do these things it seemed necessary to try and make some money. Probably the only one of us who had any ability in this direction was my father. He had been thinking of his early experiences in trading with the natives, when he had seen Europeans — including quite unbusinesslike 'pukka sahibs' — making an adequate and honest living without undue exertion; he had also been wondering how my newly acquired knowledge of farming could be turned to account, for it was still thought advisable to keep my eyes off books for a time. He now thought of a plan, which was to take over a native trading station, or 'Kaffir store,' with some land attached, where I could live with him and my mother, our combined energies being given to a happy blend of agriculture and commerce. The main flaw in this plan was that it did not allow for the amount of continuous hard work it would involve.

Having made enquiries of an old colleague in Natal he received a letter with details of a place which seemed promising. The letter he at once sent on to me, with the suggestion that if I liked the idea I should meet him in Natal; we could then go on together and see the place for ourselves. The first and most startling fact was that the place was described as 'one of the oldest trading sites in Zululand.' Zululand! This was enough to quicken my interest, and raising my eyes from the letter to the bare and ochreous mountain over against the house at Marsh Moor I at once saw a vision of a softer, warmer landscape, of sub-tropical verdure and a more generous soil than that of what Pringle had called 'Stormberg's rugged fells.' Entumeni, said the letter, was in a fairly densely populated native reserve. And the Zulus, I said to myself, thinking of those I had known, are by common repute the finest of the Bantu tribes. Entumeni, the letter went on, was some dozen miles west of Eshowe, on the main road to Nkandhla and the middle drift of the Tugela river; it was about fifteen hundred feet above sea level; the climate was very healthy, and the place was in 'a fine mist and rain belt'; there were a hundred acres of land and the soil was good; there was permanent water from a spring, and several acres of natural forest on the site; there was a fair-sized house of wood and iron, besides the store and various out-buildings; there were grazing rights in the reserve for a hundred head of cattle; the place was not freehold — there was a ninety-nine years' lease, of which about fifteen years had run, with a virtual right of conversion to freehold at the expiration of the lease. Fifteen from ninety-nine, I said to myself, is eighty-four, so I shall be a hundred and two when the lease runs out. Then my imagination began to play with the words 'Zululand,' 'Zulus' and 'natural forest.' Providence, it will be gathered, had not really designed me to speculate on the possibilities of commerce and agriculture but on the magic of words. I wrote at once to my father and agreed to visit with him this earthly paradise. Sanguine is not the word.

We travelled up the Natal coast from Durban to Eshowe (the capital of Zululand) by train through the sugar plantations. The platforms of the little stations were thronged with Indians, and sometimes through a clearing in an orange grove one caught sight of one of their white temples, small but ornate. After we had crossed the swirling Tugela the landscape became flatter, more open and less populous, and then the train wound up the serpentine line through the fertile hills to Eshowe, embowered in leaves. Eshowe, by the way, is a word of three syllables, with each 'e' as in 'end' and the accented 'o' as in 'show': the name is onomatopoetic and represents the prevalent sound of the wind in the leaves. A conspiracy of leaves surrounded the hotel where we spent the night. They were as dense as in a tropical scene by the Douanier Rousseau. The verandahs were tunnels of ferns, creepers and flowering plants, and an immense avocado tree near at hand was covered with heavy and innumerable fruit. All night long the wind was sighing, and continuous dulcifying rain made a melancholy solitude, pattering among stiff or flexible foliage and dripping and dropping into overflowing cisterns. In the morning the spring sun came out, and in its heat steam and fragrance rose together from thickets and flower-beds, and we climbed into a rickety flivver with a young Norwegian, the son of the non-resident lessee, and drove out to Entumeni with chains on the wheels, churning at times through deep clay, red and gluey, up gradients of an alarming steepness.

Whether because Entumeni bewitched us, or because my father had already made up his mind, or because I was bowled over by the contrast between Zululand and the austerity of the Stormberg, someone described us, after we had returned to Johannesburg, as 'the two enthusiasts.' We both had something intense and impulsive in our temperaments. My mother, like us, was prepared to throw all her energies into an undertaking that seemed worth while, but with characteristic scepticism and common sense, born of bitter experience, she opposed our rhapsodizing with a few practical questions. Was the road good? No. Was the house habitable? Barely. Had we seen the books? No; the sub-tenants said that the books had been sent away for audit. (A wry smile from my mother.) Did I think the land likely to be productive? Possibly, but it was completely different from the hardy, heathy country I was used to and certainly was unfit for sheep-breeding, the only branch of farming I had thoroughly learnt. Was there any white society? We had heard that there was a mission station a mile or so away, and that a few white farmers had settled here and there outside the native reserve. Did we know what we were letting ourselves in for? No, but if we couldn't make a success of it, that wouldn't be for want of trying. My mother sighed: hers was in some ways a hard life. She folded up her needlework and quietly put it away, with a peculiar air of finality. Her friends and my father's were, if anything, even more sceptical. How could we possibly expect to make a success of it? Were we not used to a civilized existence? Could we speak Zulu? Did we know the first thing about the trade? Could we stand the exertion, the isolation, the lack of all amenities, the inevitable loss?

Enterprising perhaps, those Plomers, was the general opinion, but foolhardy.

The first thing we did was to clinch the bargain. The second was, for us, even more extraordinary: we bought a large, new and handsome American touring car, 'cherry-black' like the highwayman's horse in Harrison Ainsworth's song. None of us had ever taken the slightest interest in machinery (except my brother, who was at school in England), and hitherto, when in need of a car, we had hired one with a chauffeur. I learnt to drive, we made all our preparations, and off we went with a pilot by way of Durban. It was the rainy summer season, but there was only one contretemps. North of Durban, about half-way to the Zululand border, we came, late one afternoon, to a place where the road forded a stream. It had been raining heavily in the hills, the stream was swollen, and we stopped to see if it was safe to cross. Our pilot judged it so and we were in a hurry to get on, but, in the very act of our crossing, the volume of water suddenly increased visibly, and the laden car, suddenly awash and half afloat, wobbled as if about to overturn. There was, as they say, no time to be lost, so we three males jumped into the water, which was nearly up to our necks, and with some effort shoved the car out on to drier land: my mother, who for some minutes had been in great danger of being swept away inside the car and drowned, had sat as calmly as if at a tea-party. She and my father, though both at times extremely emotional about trifles, were both admirably phlegmatic in their behaviour at moments of real danger or crisis.

Our pilot discovered that the carburettor and other intestines were flooded and also that we were short of oil. The district was fairly populous, we were on a main road, and it seemed likely that with luck a fresh supply could be got fairly easily. An inconspicuous Indian of middle age was watching us from a polite distance. My father accordingly asked him, quite civilly, but with the slightly *herrenvölkisch* air of a white man addressing a coolie, to fetch us some oil. The Indian then gravely turned and summoned with an imperious wave of his hand another of his race who was approaching in the middle distance and passed on the request as an order. The humour of this small incident was that the first Indian, as we learnt later, was a very prosperous sugar-planter and far richer than we had ever been.

Even more important than oil was the need of dry clothes and a shelter for the night. Luckily there was a small wayside hotel at no great distance, so we squelched off towards it, with the water running out of our boots as fast as they were refilled by the torrential rain that had come on once more. 'Hotel' is perhaps rather an imposing word for the simple bungalow which stood back from the road in a grove of eucalyptus trees. There were no residents or casual visitors, but there was alcohol, dispensed by the proprietor and his wife, a picturesque and affable pair. The man had evidently come out from England in the South African war, some twenty years before, had remained in 'the coming country,' and had apparently modelled his appearance on that of, perhaps, his former sergeant. With his white gym. shoes, his big chest outlined by a tight white sweater, his red face and long moustaches waxed to a lethal sharpness, he had the air of being about to take a class in physical training, and one almost waited for him to shout 'Knees—bend! Up—down! Up—down!' His wife could only have obeyed such an order with difficulty, for she was notably plump, with a gold tooth, fluffy hair like gold wire, very high heels, and a white satin blouse enclosing, with every appearance of tension, an ample bust: she had the air of a retired barmaid and spoke with a Midland accent that took me back to Spondon. This happy and hospitable pair carried the white man's burden with cheerful insouciance, which even the downpour outside could not damp, for it had brought a windfall in the shape of ourselves. After supper the lady entertained us with popular songs at her upright cottage piano, but every now and then, while singing

> 'I'm for ever blowing bubbles,
>   Pretty bubbles in the sky,
>   They fly so high,
>   They nearly reach the sky,
>   Then like my dreams they fade and die——'

she struck a curiously muffled chord, which she excused on the grounds that the piano was little in use and had been affected by the rainy season. It had indeed, for when she looked inside the instrument she gave a girlish shriek on discovering that inside it was a frog. Heaven alone knows how it got there, but it can hardly have been there very long, for it was still alive, though somewhat bruised by her spirited and not wholly successful arpeggios, and wearing, I thought, a rather hurt expression. Lying in a small room, a trifle uneasy about a large and motionless black spider on the white-washed wall, and reflecting that it was still a long way to Entumeni, I fell asleep to the sound of rain drenching the eucalyptus trees and drumming on the corrugated-iron roof.

It was perfectly fine by the time we got to Entumeni and began to take possession of what really seemed the African equivalent of a battered Irish cabin. There was no fence round the garden, and gaunt cows were scratching their pelvises against the trunks of some handsome tree-ferns, planted evidently to form an avenue; famished-looking chickens, light-headed from hunger and wearing disillu-sioned expressions, tottered feebly in and out of the house in search of food; and everything looked rubbishy and unkempt. We took over, by agreement, some cattle, a white horse of middle age and little character, several donkeys, and the forlorn birds already mentioned. In fact we took over the whole place as a going concern — going downhill, it almost appeared, at no mean pace, like the Gadarene swine. The interior of the store, which was the *raison d'être* of the whole outfit, was discouraging. It was lofty but dark and musty and cluttered with old, outmoded and unsaleable goods. Having seen, without regret, the last of the outgoing denizens, we set to work to reduce dirt and chaos to cleanliness and order. We fenced the garden, we painted the house and built on to it a pillared con-crete verandah, we improved the outbuildings or built new ones, we hacked away undergrowth and grubbed up rank and sinewy weeds, we provided proper quarters for the servants, who had in any case to be trained, we struggled with the store, with the house, and with the hundred acres. Entumeni (a locative form, like Eshowe) means 'the place of thorns,' and thorny were those early days — more formidable in some respects than the existence at Louis Trichardt years before.

The donkeys made straight for mud-holes in an adjacent valley, sank in them up to the eyes and were only extricated with difficulty and ropes and some expense of time and labour, and then in most cases too late; the horse, which nobody had the time, the need or the inclination to ride, ate, as they say, its head off, without, strangely enough, any marked effect on its physique or spirits; the cows either strayed into other people's fields (the native fields were unfenced and cattle were watched by herd-boys) and gobbled up the contents, which then had to be paid for, or they behaved oddly, bellowing like fog-horns in the middle of the night for no discoverable reason, or contracting rare diseases with disquieting symptoms; the chickens, unaccustomed to a balanced diet, collapsed from surfeit, or grew strong enough to deposit their in any case undersized eggs in the 'natural forest' (also known to us as the Virgin Bush), where nobody had time to look for them, or, if there had been time, any earthly chance of finding them. Altogether it seemed to me that there was much to be said for wool-gathering in the Stormberg.

Had we been less preoccupied we might have taken much delight in the surrounding landscape, as indeed we came to do. Open, fertile, and undulating, with clusters of dome-shaped native huts, groves and thickets and streams, and patches of cultivated land here and there, haunted by exotic birds like toucans, hoopoes and humming birds and by small mammals like the galago, and with a rich and varied flora, it invited inquisitive saunters which we were quite unable to take. From the very first we were pleased with the climate, which never ran to extremes, and particularly with the heavy but not wetting mist which in the summer, after a hot day, would often rush upon us from the south and steep everything in an opaque and silvery silence.

My mother was fully occupied in the house, and although she had never liked housekeeping and was less physically strong than she had been, she worked like a slave to provide decent food and drink, clean linen and other domestic comforts, so that we were able to live very well. I struggled with the outdoor work, the perverse livestock, the neglected garden, and parts of the hundred acres — except, of course, the Bush, of which I allowed the virginity to remain almost intact, weary-boned, I struggled at night with Bishop Colenso's Zulu dictionary and grammar, and whenever I had a chance in the daytime I went to the store to try and get the hang of things. My father's energy, early experience and love of order were soon improving matters, and we had hired a white assistant who was supposed to know the ropes, but as he was not especially cherished either by us or by the natives, we arranged to manage without him. It thereupon became clear that there was more than enough to keep two men busy and that trade was more likely to be lucrative than agriculture, so we got rid of the horse and the surviving donkeys, kept only a few milch cows, and ate such of the chickens as had managed to regain their embonpoint.

For months on end we worked unremittingly to make a success of what we had undertaken, to win the confidence of the natives by honest dealing, to meet their needs and tastes, and to keep everything ship-shape. The result was that whole families waited on us daily, and the place became a kind of club or assembly room. Even so, we ran it for a year or more at a loss, but this gradually diminished and turned into a useful profit. The Zulus brought us their handiwork or their money, their labour or their produce — maize, millet, chickens, eggs, vegetables, hides, skins, and so on — and could obtain in exchange an extraordinary variety of merchandise, ranging from ploughs, lanterns, textiles, parasols and musical instruments, by way of many kinds of food and clothing, to aphrodisiacs, love-philtres and *cache-sexes* — the last named in suitably assorted sizes. At first we were much encumbered by an accumulation of unwanted or demoded goods, but as we got rid of them we replaced them with better stuff, and I would make an occasional journey to Durban and go round the great and fascinating warehouses of the wholesalers, buying imitation jewellery from Czechoslovakia, textiles from Manchester, bales of American military clothing left over from the World War, tinned beef from the Argentine, pen-knives, mouth-organs and jew's harps from Germany, silk handkerchiefs from Japan, kettles from Birmingham, and heaven knows what besides.

The natives were mostly quite primitive, but some had been superficially 'Europeanized' by the missions or by spells of work in Durban or Johannesburg, and some were betwixt and between. The most primitive were generally the most dignified and the most suspicious. If one played them a Zulu record on the gramophone their astonishment and pleasure knew no bounds and were continually renewed. Occasionally they would recoil from the machine in terror; sometimes they would peer round it as if they expected to surprise some cunning midget vocalizing behind it; often they would exclaim that it was bewitched. Their physical beauty was conspicuous, for many of them went about all but stark-naked, and their mere presence was to me deeply and agreeably disturbing. Well-developed young girls would long remain unselfconsciously chatting, with their prominent upper charms almost under one's nose, or they would playfully divert themselves and each other by removing their scanty coverings in order to reflect their nether charms in a pier-glass just inside the door: some were more modest but not less attractive. The young bucks, descendants of Chaka's braves, ornamented with a few beads and little else, and moving with superb grace, erectness and ease, were often models of bodily perfection. They used to remind me of Herman Melville's comparison of the Marquesans with the inhabitants of New York. 'Stripped of the cunning artifices of the tailor, and standing forth in the garb of Eden — what a sorry set of round-shouldered, spindle-shanked, crane-necked varlets would civilized men appear!'

What was particularly interesting about these primitive Zulus was their extreme conventionality in matters of custom, conversation, and personal adornment. We sold or bartered, among all the other things, large quantities of beads of various colours, which they were very fond of making up into ornaments to wear, but there were certain kinds, or rather colours, among the old stock we had taken over which no girl would have accepted as a gift. To wear the wrong nuance of pink or blue would have made the Zulu debutante as freakish as an English girl who should go about to-day in, say, a hobble-skirt, a big hat decorated with ostrich feathers, and a braided bolero trimmed with bugles. Convention imposed certain taboos in ordinary conversation — as it does with us, but not for the same reasons — yet I never expect to hear better talkers. Their voices are euphonious and finely produced, and they know all the arts of conversation — the skilful maintenance of tension in leading up to a point, the graphic description, the harangue, the formal speech, the quick exchange of repartee, the dry and ironical comment, the perfect metaphor, mimicry, and so on. It was as the result of trying to find convincing answers to their awkward leading questions that Bishop Colenso startled the mid-Victorian world, and more particularly his archbishop, by plunging into the heresy of common sense. So exalted did he become by his studies of the Zulu language that he claimed that it could be used to express the most subtle philosophical or scientific ideas. Although no linguist, I myself found it, perhaps from necessity, easy to learn, pleasant to use, and in some directions surprisingly rich.

The more or less christianized natives were inclined to give themselves airs, especially the women, many of whom had acquired names like Tryphena and Sophonisba. I suppose they had got it into their heads that they were 'saved' and were therefore a cut above their less enlightened sisters. They tended to adopt European-style clothes, to wear boots and shoes, drink tea, do crochet, sing hymns, use strongly scented soap and air their modest accomplishments in reading and writing. An undoubted tendency to pertness in their intercourse with the whites has provoked a thousand tirades against the folly of allowing or encouraging them to ape their alleged betters, but there is no doubt that they enjoy switching over to a new set of conventions and even, when they can run to it, purchasing a harmonium. In between the naked primitives, daubed with fat and stained with ochre, and the sometimes stuck-up would-be petty bourgeoisie turned out by the mission stations, were the nondescripts who tried to make the best of both worlds — charming backsliders who would take off and roll up their trousers and carry them on their heads when undertaking a long walk; or demi-mondaines, christened but not yet confirmed, who would go straight from church to a wild party, and were more able perhaps to 'enkindle wantonness' by enclosing their ripe curves in a loose-fitting calico pinafore than were their equally sexy sisters in nothing but a girdle and apron of blue and white beads. It was not uncommon to see a 'saved' tart in a print dress but with the lobes of her ears distended in the primitive style to admit decorative circular plugs as big as the top of a teacup.

The Prince Imperial was said to have ridden right past the front door of Entumeni to his rendezvous with death, and there were local place-names which commemorated English officers who had taken part in the Zulu war, but such white neighbours as we had were of a different kidney. Once a week either my father or I would drive to Eshowe to do business and buy food, and we made acquaintances there — the local magistrate, a parson, and so on — with whom we exchanged occasional brief visits. Our nearest and most congenial neighbour was a stately old Lutheran missionary, a Norwegian, and what used to be called 'a gentleman of the old school' — in other words, a distinguished survivor from Victorian times, educated, courtly and benevolent, and clad always in a frock coat. His mission station — the first, I think, ever established in Zululand — had already an air of antiquity. He was a widower, but was helped in his labours and in his domestic life by two or three Norwegian spinsters or widows and by native converts. They lived far out of the world, but were none the worse for it. Of most of our other white neighbours, who were few and scattered, it cannot be said that their characters were liberal, their treatment of the natives good, or their behaviour to one another polished. Some of them oppressed and cheated the natives as a matter of course, were at times cruel to them, and would even boast of it to one another but not — after one attempt — to us.

Some of them disliked us very much and their dislike was mixed with envy; but if they disliked us, they detested one another. The worst of them would assassinate each other's livestock, remove their neighbours' landmarks, and take away the characters of their supposed friends: one man drove a long way to call upon another merely in order to fling a dead dog in his face — it was no lap-dog, so the gesture must have cost him an effort. We did not need these people in any way, either for our livelihood or for social intercourse, but when we first arrived they hoped to become parasitic upon us, imagining that we should be naive enough to grant them credit. Some of them came to call and were entertained to tea on the verandah. We could not help noticing that either the tea or the unwonted strain of polite conversation appeared to have a laxative or at least a diuretic effect upon them and more particularly upon their wives; after fidgeting they would excuse themselves and make for a little edifice not far from the back of the house. We had built it ourselves in the interests of hygiene and called it the Pagoda, but in fact it was purely functional in style — of plain brick, whitewashed within, and having a concrete floor. We were at first puzzled by the repeated pilgrimages to this place of convenience, but presently it appeared that it had become the talk of the countryside and that our visitors — who were not 'poor whites' but tolerably well-to-do farmers — wished not to use it but to see its splendours for themselves. It was perhaps partly on account of the harmless, necessary Pagoda that they spoke derisively of us among themselves as 'the Royal Family'; it was also partly because we kept aloof from them and had in general a higher standard of living; but I think the chief reason was our unforgivable car.

The car was indeed large, black and glossy, and had a contented purr when in motion, but we only regarded it, like the Pagoda, as a necessity. After my father had been driving it on and off for more than a year, I discovered by chance that he believed that it went by steam. His conviction was that the petrol, which he knew to be highly inflammable, was ignited and then, on the principle of a spirit lamp, boiled the water in the radiator, which then gave off steam to provide the motive power. I thought this by no means illogical though I knew it to be incorrect ; I also thought it very distinguished and endearing of him to be so indifferent to the banalities of a mechanical age. In view of his quite unmechanical mind, it is hardly surprising that the car once broke down with a horrid grinding noise when he was at the wheel, and great was the joy of our neighbours to see the hated symbol of our superiority stranded on the road miles from anywhere for several days. To the more primitive natives, again quite logically, cars were objects of terror. I must admit I used to drive very fast, but that was for my own pleasure and not because it gratified me to see, as I occasionally did, some frantic woman — with a coiffure as tall as Madam Arden's and a pot-bellied baby strapped to her back— throw up her lean hands with a gesture of '*Chacun pour soi!*' and then scramble madly up a steep bank by the roadside, her pendulous breasts flying over her shoulders like the ends of a scarf, long before I was anywhere near her. However, I did once make use of the car to remove a sick French *réligieuse* from the trackless hinterland and nearly lost my life from sunstroke in doing so.

One of our diversions in Entumeni days was the visit to Zululand of the Prince of Wales, and we were invited to stay at the residency at Eshowe by the magistrate and his wife, who were among our friends. It happened that the Prince's secretary, Sir Godfrey Thomas, had married a cousin of my mother's, and the settlers round Entumeni were further acidulated when they got to hear of this fortuitous connexion. Apart from Prince and Princess Arthur of Connaught, whose guest I had occasionally been in Johannesburg, I had never had more than rare glimpses of royal personages, but I share to the full the popular interest in them. I do not see how anybody interested in the power of heredity and in the variations of human nature can fail to pay some attention to them; even though they are politically less important than formerly, and are expected to be 'democratic,' they are still a species apart, differently conditioned, thinking differently, and looking at life with different eyes. Upon them the light of fatality is fastened like a spotlight, so that they excite a special curiosity and a special admiration, dislike or sympathy. I remember in London, about 1917, seeing the Crown Prince of Serbia (who, as King Alexander of Yugoslavia, was assassinated at Marseilles) and being strangely saddened by his grave, pale face, his pince-nez, his erect bearing and preoccupied air. It was not less saddening when the royal train drew into Eshowe in the late afternoon sun, and a slight, hatless young man emerged from it, discarding a cigarette only just lighted, then fidgeting his tie with lean, boyish fingers. He looked strained, like an athlete too long keyed up to the top of his form, this errant servant of staring mobs and shaker of innumerable public hands. One had only to see him to understand that the immense volume of cant continually poured forth about this 'Prince Charming' who was 'the Empire's best ambassador' was based upon a reality — that he was young, that he did his duty with energy, and that he had for most people an appealing charm. It is a pity that the revulsion against him (a typical *volte-face* of an ungrateful mob) was so strong at the time of his abdication. It was perfectly obvious that the British puritanical instinct which causes pleasure, especially that of other people, to be regarded as sinful and therefore hated and feared, could not forgive him for finding and sticking to private happiness, and so rose up and swept him away. The political and constitutional reasons for the abdication seem to me less important than they were made out to be.

The whites in Eshowe, as elsewhere, ran after the Prince, staring and jabbering excitedly as if trying to round up a rare animal. The chief event was a gathering of the Zulu clans for a war-dance *en masse*, a fine barbaric spectacle which at moments got a little out of hand. Owing to some fault in stage-management, the assembled natives largely failed either to perceive or to show interest in their sovereign's heir, and their attention was diverted by the presence of a descendant of their own former rulers. In the evening there was a small European dance for the Prince, at which my admiration was evoked by my mother, who was able to step out of the tough obscurity of Entumeni and without effort look as if she were in the heart of European civilization — if it ever had a heart.

We were not dinner-jacket backwoodsmen, but the fact that we were able to live virtually in the orderly way to which we had been accustomed was chiefly due to my mother's hard work. To be able to sit down to a proper meal at the end of a hard day, with decent linen and silver on the table, and to see from where I sat a cabinet containing some good miniatures, the candlestick which Byron had given Miss Pigot at Southwell, and books in sober old bindings — Shakespeare, Milton, Pope — did not make me feel rooted at Entumeni, but it did make me feel that wherever I was I should continue to draw gratefully from my roots any good sap that might nourish my fibres. All the same, I was suddenly struck by the incongruity of some of our possessions. We were only keepers of a 'Kaffir store' in Zululand, without any visible prospect of ever being able to live anywhere in more than a modest and simple way, and it seemed absurd that we should have with us, for instance, a quantity of plate (including a bag of crested livery-buttons) and an enormous coverlet, with sumptuous Stuart embroidery, which had come down to us from the Ardens. My parents had preserved such inherited objects for their children, but their children had to live in an austerer and an unsettled world, so I prevailed upon them to send to England for sale whatever was superfluous.

As we grew more used to our task and the natives more used to us, we prospered, thanks chiefly to extremely hard work by my father, and after a time we took on a native assistant. He was a Christian and had some education, and the primitives resented his superiority as much as our white neighbours resented whatever advantages we had enjoyed, so he had to go. I was sorry, for he had been a good companion to me. He had some concern about the hopeless position and prospects of his race, political, social and economic. I used to encourage him in this and urged him to try and work for their betterment. We used to have long talks on the subject, and I asked him to write down some of his ideas. The result was not altogether satisfactory, but he made some good points, and I feel justified in giving some quotations, because they are of some human and anthropological interest and are symptomatic of the dawning restlessness of a primitive people in a most uneasy state of transition.

Lucas (for such was his name) began his observations by looking back to the times when the white man was unknown. Although in those days, he wrote, 'kings and headmen were killing and troubling their own blood,' the people had many cattle and goats, 'which were their beauty and bank.' They did not look forward or 'trouble themselves to find new things,' and were on the whole satisfied with their position. Then the Europeans arrived, 'full of experience and curiosity.'

'One here and there tried to civilize the natives. To make the natives understand that a man is a man without depending on the people, they put Government taxes on them. Somehow these are still increasing . . . Even now the natives are still wandering in the wilderness . . . They are waiting for God Almighty to come down from Heaven and do something for them which will never happen.'

Lucas lamented that his people were too resigned to their position, too easy-going and pleasure-loving; they were 'fast asleep.' 'Let us all stand up on both feet,' he wrote, 'and see what will happen to-morrow.' By this he did not mean political insurgence, which he knew would be hopeless for a long time to come, but work and self-reliance, in which he had been taught to believe. In conversation he often lamented to me the lack of unity among his people and their habit of envying, decrying, and pulling down any one of their number who sought to lead or unite them. He had strong views on the desirability of domestic steadiness and concord and he drew up a set of rules to be observed by man and wife.

'It is disgraceful to see a man and his wife keep their lives like dogs biting each other . . . A husband must do things, pleasant things, for his wife in order to keep love going. There must be no disturbance of any sort, otherwise love gets cold . . . The wife must know and keep her house, her husband and her children . . . A good clever wife must learn her husband, she must know what things please him and what things annoy him, and she must do those things that please him.'

In spite of this ideal of the submissive wife, Lucas (perhaps as a result of his mission training and the example of white people) did not hold with the old Zulu tradition of despising women; and he advocated temperance and conjugal fidelity in the male. After a homily about the ravages of *utshwala*, the native liquor, upon domestic harmony, he remarked that 'a man might have a private wife somewhere,' but 'private wife and private husband, those two things do not help the house, they are always making the trouble.' He deprecated the old Zulu custom by which a man roams or idles, 'doing his glories,' while his woman works in the fields. Even more, he disapproved of the custom by which a bridegroom pays a sort of inverted dowry, called *ilobolo*, to his father-in-law. In consequence, he wrote 'a man is always thinking what he paid for his wife, so he has a good mind that she must work in order to repay him.'

Lucas drew up a list of wedding expenses likely to confront a prospective bridegroom. £10 had to be paid to the prospective bride's father 'to open his mouth to talk,' besides a horse, six head of cattle, a blanket and a great coat; £6 were needed for the bridegroom's wedding get-up; 14s. 6d. for the marriage licence; 10s. to 'a reverend gentleman'; 4s. in connexion with the slaughter of an ox to be provided by the bridegroom for the wedding feast; a sack of millet and a sack of maize for the brewing of the wedding *utshwala*; a goat (or 10s.) as a post-nuptial present for the father-in-law; and a more mysterious 10s. 'for the girls who help the bridegroom after the wedding day' (I trust he meant 'who help the bride'). According to Lucas's calculations, the bridegroom would have to pay, in cash and in kind, £85 6s. 6d. for the pleasure of getting married, and would thus be only able to contribute to the new household 'a small empty wooden box without anything inside.' It will be seen that a Zulu father regards not only his livestock but his daughters as his 'beauty and bank.'

'Suppose you don't pay *ilobolo*,' Lucas wrote, 'have you got a hope to get a wife? No, never in this world . . . If Christians do not leave this custom, what is the good of Christianity to them? . . . I am writing all this in order to make all our Christian people thinkable.'

An ambitious undertaking. Having indulged in this diatribe against *ilobolo*, and also in some temperance propaganda (which did, however, include leave to 'drink when you feel like drinking'), Lucas gave some account of the love life of the unmarried Zulu:

'When we are young men we always have the competition of girls, counting the number of girls we are in love with, and running up and down the country trying to increase the number. By the time we want to get married we simply marry the girl we were not intended to marry . . . I think we can call that sort of marriage with beautiful short words — LOOK FORWARD FOR THE TROUBLE

. . . What would you think of a man who took a nest home without a bird inside, fearing that the bird would fly out when there was no bird? Let us not look at the nests, how beautifully they are made. The main and important thing is inside.'

He concludes this part of his essay with some advice on the choice of a husband or wife, and sagely remarks that 'of course it is very difficult for a human being to know very well somebody's heart and his general mannerism.'

On the subject of education, he regretted that too many of his people wished to be teachers instead of learning some useful work. 'Young ladies and young men are all running for teaching, which will never improve our race. If we follow each other like sheep how will we make our country better? It will be like this generations and generations.' Besides, 'when a teacher teaches, he follows the scheme of work and syllabus. His mind is tied up in a bag. He doesn't worry about little lives.' Finally, Lucas looks with envy and admiration to the achievements of the negroes in the United States and wishes that his own people could be like them, for 'we are the only people in the whole world who have not done even a little work. Let us all move and work for Africa: it is very poor now, it must not be poor for ever.'

5. LOOK ELSEWHERE FOR YOUR BEDTIME STORY

WITH the departure of Lucas, it became necessary to find someone else to lend us a hand, and my parents rather surprisingly decided to send for my brother from England. He had been at a preparatory school in Northamptonshire (the fourth metamorphosis of the school originally set up at Spondon by my aunt's husband) and was now just at the age to go to a public school, but my father was of the opinion that he would do better to come and learn to make his life in

Africa. I think my father, as he saw Entumeni developing, looked forward to a time when it would become an enterprise on a larger scale, and he sometimes liked to imagine that both his sons, as they grew up, would take it over and expand it, perhaps running in conjunction with it a farm and a hotel; but in the meantime he was beginning to realize that the life was too much of a strain for my mother, and that although I had put my back into the work I had not put my heart into it as well.

A more startling transition for a boy of thirteen than that from a preparatory school in the English midlands to 'the place of thorns' can hardly be imagined, but my brother, who from early childhood had been of a cheerful, sensible and independent disposition, managed it very well. As I was eight years older than him, we were not exactly companions, though we were on affectionate brotherly terms. Unlike me, he never really took to the natives, though he treated them with civility and good humour, and during his holidays (for he was sent to school at Durban) made himself very useful in our daily work.

Lucas had left his essay with me. In it he made the following complaint:

'Our paper, *Ilanga*, is not taken into sufficient consideration. The man who founded it and built up a school for boys on the mountains at Ohlange, has done a great work, and we natives do not appreciate it. We don't put our hands in order to help him.'

It is possible that Lucas had made these remarks to please me, because he knew that I was a correspondent of the man in question and had from time to time contributed anonymously to *Ilanga*, which was the only Zulu newspaper. John Dube, who had founded and edited it, was indeed a remarkable man, the nearest the Zulus had produced to a Booker Washington. He invited me to visit him, and I did so. He sent a boy with a white horse to meet me at Phoenix and I ambled up to Ohlange through a rather Indian landscape. Dube was a most amiable host; he had the natural dignity of his race and was serious without being dull or pompous, and we sat up late talking. The next morning he showed me his school and then took me to visit a Tolstoyan settlement in the neighbourhood, one of two founded by Gandhi in his African days. Gandhi's son Manilal, who was about my own age and had, I think, been born there, received me with great courtesy; he was graceful, gentle, mentally very alert, and of finely-bred appearance. We found him superintending the production of an Indian newspaper, which had for years been printed there. It was a strange meeting this, between the son of a great man who had been kicked, stoned and imprisoned for defending his own people in this harsh and radiant country, a representative of a recently barbaric race who was seeking to better his oppressed and disoriented people by helping to adapt them to a 'Western' civilization of a sort, and myself, a mere youth, but a member of the ruling race who was there to show that he regarded it as a misruling race.

Had I yet done anything more concrete to show what I thought of a country run in such a way as to pander to race prejudice? I was not the kind of person who takes to political action or propaganda; my business in life was to write, and I conceived of writing as a making of images — anything I had to say must be said in the line and colour of the written word. In spite of the unending work at Entumeni I had managed to find time both to read and write. I occasionally ordered books from England, we subscribed to various papers (including the *New Statesman*, to which I presently became an occasional contributor — literary not political), and I used to receive *Querschnitt*, that brilliantly edited German magazine which reflected so vividly the somewhat feverish outlook of the advanced and smart rather than solemn European intelligentsia of the early nineteen-twenties, and which was more strikingly illustrated than any other paper I have ever seen. I wrote a few sketches of local life and an article on the beautiful Dutch place-names of South Africa, and these items were printed in a Johannesburg newspaper. I wrote indifferent verse and had also begun that commonplace task, the writing of a novel; but it was not an altogether commonplace novel, as will presently appear.

In forming my ideas about the world and my standards of behaviour I had been much influenced by my mother. Not an intellectual in the strict sense of the word, she was highly intelligent, observant and imaginative. She had the divine gift of curiosity, particularly about the manners and motives of human beings of all kinds, compassion for their sufferings and a longing that they should be more just to one another. As I became more thoughtful and we discussed many things together, she would apologize for the inadequacy of her education, but I never heard her speak a word against her mother, who was responsible for it, on this or any other account. She was in fact the most loyal of women and held it a great lapse when people abused their own nearest kin to others. I remember occasions on which members of her own sex revolted her by pouring out undesired confidences in heart-to-heart talks of the kind that inferior women love. One of these individuals attempted to obtain sympathy by a detailed account of the private mis-demeanours of her husband, and another by speaking disparagingly of her own offspring. It was perhaps a kind of loyalty that helped to keep my mother a good Christian. I had been through a phase of emotional Anglo-Catholicism, very much as I had fancied myself at times to be a pantheist or a Buddhist, but was now, if anything, a determinist. When an Anglican priest, a congenial acquaintance, sometimes on Sundays made the journey out from Eshowe with a portable altar in order to fortify us with the sacrament I could not but join in the proceedings, if only to avoid hurting anybody's feelings. All the same, I was beginning to feel an increasing distaste for many of the manifestations and results of Christianity. It appeared that Christian civilization had not only failed to prevent but had made possible what seemed to me then the greatest imagin-able horror, that is to say, the war of 1914–18 ; and that, through the workings of puritanism, whether of the Catholic or Protestant variety, it had built up a false conception of life and by imposing this conception had widely distorted human nature. My mother was not in the least bigoted, saw the force of my objections and to some extent admitted their validity, but she argued that, whatever the shortcomings of Christians and whatever the harm they had done, their creed was a force which had made far more for good in the world than for evil, and that any force which tended to make men less inhumane towards one another was deserving at least of tolerance.

Her loyalty also showed itself in her patriotism. She was aware of the failings of her country and its people, but she could never bear to hear English men and women run it down to outsiders (as they have very often done, even if with conscious superiority), still less to hear it run down by foreigners or colonials, and in any of these cases she would defend it vehemently and convincingly, leaving her interlocutors not a leg to stand on. If I twitted her with having grown up in the heyday of imperialism and with being a jingo, she would argue that there were plenty of people in the world who envied, abused and sought to harm England, and would declare that she would continue to stick up for her country. What was even more admirable was her conviction that narrow patriotism and exclusive racialism or nationalism, both in politics and economics, had led up to the World War and would lead up to another unless some form of internationalism could be brought into being that would enable men to put their energies and apply their science to something better than murdering one another wholesale. She saw clearly that the League of Nations must fail unless there was a change of heart. So great was her detestation of war that she used to note down sayings that had a bearing on the subject — for instance, *Dulce bellum inexpertis* from Erasmus, or that saying from Euripides, 'Alas, that facts have not a voice for men, so that subtle words might be as nothing.' [1] She confirmed me, in fact, in a hankering for an internationalized and peaceful world, and still before me as I write there stands a framed sheet of paper, bearing in the handwriting of Hardy the following lines :

> ' When shall the saner, softer polities
>   Whereof we dream, have sway in each proud land,
>   And Patriotism, grown godlike, scorn to stand
>   Bondslave to realms, but circle earth and seas?'

Any of the saner polities, as we envisaged them at Entumeni, would

[1] "φεῦ, φεῦ, τὸ μὴ τὰ πραγματ' ἀνθρώποις ἔχειν φωνήν, ἵν' ἦσαν μηδὲν οἱ δεινοὶ λόγοι . . ."

necessarily provide for the abolition of the colour bar. This was really the theme of the novel which I had begun to write.

I was not devoid of talent of a sort, but I was young (I began the book when I was nineteen); I had been largely deprived by circumstances of the direct influence, correction and guidance of my intellectual equals and superiors; I was full of youthful priggishness, of the conceit of the solitary and the false confidence of inexperience; and, in the matter of writing a novel, I was attempting to reach by a short cut what can only become even visible by taking an arduous road. I finished the book when I was twenty-one, and sent the manuscript to Leonard and Virginia Woolf at the Hogarth Press. It was written with a hard pencil on thin paper, and they must have had a strong curiosity to read it at all. They not only read it but expressed a lively interest in it and accepted it for publication, which led to much rejoicing at Entumeni. *Turbott Wolfe* bears the date 1925, but in fact, owing to a printers' strike — not caused, I hasten to say, by their having to cope with this particular volume — it did not appear until the following spring.

I shall now give some account of the book and of its reception, but the reader shall be spared a synopsis of the plot, partly because it is not impressive and partly because of all bores the outliner of plots is almost the greatest. It will be enough to say that Turbott Wolfe himself was an improbable and ineffectual Englishman who made a sojourn in an imaginary African country (not wholly far-fetched) where he became a negrophilist and encouraged miscegenation. There was not much of a story, but the story was not the point.

After a suitable lapse of time a man ought to be able to criticize his own work with some detachment, so let me see what I can do. My impulse was to present, in a fictional form, partly satirical, partly lyrical, partly fantastic, some of my own impressions of life in Africa and to externalize the turmoil of feelings they had aroused in me. I had no intention of drawing a self-portrait or of giving a naturalistic account of African life. Somebody called the book 'expressionist,' and like many first books it exaggerated the literary faults and excesses of its period. To speak of it as a novel is perhaps a misnomer: it was a violent ejaculation, a protest, a nightmare, a phantasmagoria — which the dictionary defines as 'a shifting scene of real or imagined figures.' Judged as a novel it is very deficient. By realistic standards, the story or plot is exiguous and somewhat absurd, and it was not even well constructed. The main characters are neither well drawn nor convincing, the development is episodic, and the whole proceeding is crude and immature, and disfigured by an unpleasant superficial smartness or vulgar cleverness. Nevertheless, the book is not wholly without merit. If it was crude, it had vitality; some of the minor characters are noted with skill and true feeling, and there are scenes, passages and phrases which are at least not banal. In my opinion its justification was that of an original sketch-book, an outburst of poetic frenzy on the part of a solitary and emotional youth who had not reduced his thoughts to order but had reacted convulsively to his surroundings; and also (in the words of, surprisingly, a South African critic writing fifteen years after its appearance) as a picture of a world 'dominated by race fear and race hatred' and 'a revelation of savagery in a vaunted civilization.'

Although I had foreseen that I might *épater le bourgeois*, I was pleasantly surprised by the stormy reactions that *Turbott Wolfe* immediately provoked. Leading South African newspapers devoted long leading articles to vituperation, which served very well as advertisement and was in a small way as much of a tribute as the scurrilous attacks that have been made in other times and places upon original artists. Not wholly unlike hysterical Nazis decrying 'degenerate' art, the book's detractors borrowed their vocabulary from the back-yard: they said it was nasty, that it was garbage, that it was pornographic, and that it ought to be burnt — a form of tribute which has been paid to greater writers for holding up a mirror to catch a society in attitudes which, when reflected, make nonsense of its self-esteem. 'Gone are the days,' wailed some puzzled and toothless old journalist, 'of *Jock of the Bushveld* and Rider Haggard!' (So might our grandmothers, confronted, let us say, with the paintings of Max Ernst, have exclaimed, 'Gone are the days of Marcus Stone!') Another, slightly more eloquent, said that my world — by which he meant the world of the book — was one 'of shattered perspectives and perverse stimuli, of lascivious gods and outer darkness.' Of course it was, so I took this not as a reproof but as an approach (albeit somewhat rhetorical) to an attempt at evaluation. Most delicious of all was the *Zululand Times*, which complained that the book was 'not cricket': such is the absurdity into which the mind sinks when bewitched by what a great Victorian called 'the superstition of games.' The book was in the meantime much discussed, and I heard of two instances of men coming to blows over it in public places — for it had its champions.

I took the violence of these various reactions as evidence that the book was not without power, and it was perfectly plain that it had particularly stung the whites in that part of their psychological being where guilt and fear and self-deception in regard to the natives (who greatly outnumbered and surrounded them) had been wrapped away from the light of reason. For the moment these ugly things had been dragged out into the sun, and I was much struck when the saying 'He has taken me off to a T' was reported to me as having been said by a man who chose to see himself in an unlovable and unimportant character in the book.[1] Quite recently I was amused to hear that *Turbott Wolfe* was still kept under lock and key in the public library at Durban, sharing that honour with Rabelais, Boccaccio, the *Origin of Species* and some illustrated books on classical sculpture: but, as Herman Melville remarked, 'Those whom books will hurt will not be proof against events . . . Ill or good men cannot know. Often ill comes from good, as good from ill.' That I had known what I was doing and had known also that the execution was not particularly elegant is shown by one of the two epigraphs to the book a quotation from Hermann Hesse which was intended as an apology, not as a boast:

'When the unconscious of a whole continent and age has made of itself poetry in the nightmare of a single, prophetic dreamer, when it has issued in his awful, blood-curdling scream, one can of course consider this scream from the standpoint of a singing-teacher.'

[1] 'They go on abusing your book,' wrote George Sand to Flaubert apropos of *L'Education Sentimentale*. 'It has shown too well the disorder that reigns in people's minds. It has rubbed the open wound; people recognize themselves too well in it.'

Three newspapers took no part in the chorus of vilification. I had no objection whatever to being told by one of them that the book was the most vital novel about the country since *The Story of an African Farm*, and by another that it was vigorous, and marked both by 'sombre prophetic vision' and by 'a half sensual, half dreamy glow' that signified 'a poet in the making.' There were several persons unknown to me who wrote to various newspapers in order to explain that I deserved some consideration, for, said one of them, 'he has defied public opinion and fusty usage and has made us see the larger issues with a poet's vision.' And in Natal, where I was being most decried, an Englishman, later of repute as an authority on African problems, published a long and perceptive account of what I had been driving at.

While the hullaballoo was going on, I received a sparkling letter from my favourite uncle Franklyn, who had now settled for good in Spain. 'You have managed to catch an effect,' he wrote, 'where tedious people only catch malaria.' Then the reviews began to come in from London and New York, and very gratifying they were. In England the book was first noticed by Desmond MacCarthy, who said it had prevented him from looking out of the window of a train for three hours. What more could a writer ask? The *Nation* explained that it was 'volcanic' and 'although not what is usually called a great book' was an important one; and a reputable writer said he was tempted to call it a work of genius, though he did not quite yield to the temptation. If the nineteen-twenties were as feverish as they are sometimes represented as having been, I think it is something that a reviewer, right in the middle of that period, should have singled out my novel as 'a book with a temperature.' Not that I had expected it to be called soothing, fragrant or dewy. 'Look elsewhere for your bedtime story,' was the wise warning of the *New York World*. But the American reviewers were really too generous to be convincing, and I was already too well aware of my limitations to have my head turned by finding great names in the same sentence as my own.

Even my father was beginning to be impressed. 'If you want to go to the Devil,' he said quite affably, 'you must go to the Devil in your own way.' Although, reasonably enough, he had little belief in writing as a means of making a living, and although he was somewhat concerned at my having, as he put it, 'stirred up a hornet's nest,' I think he was not without a sort of pride in what I had done. Conventional in many ways, he had nevertheless always regarded himself as something of a rebel against convention, and could sympathize with his rebellious child. Also there were particular passages in *Turbott Wolfe* which gave him pleasure because we had shared some mood or experience from which they were derived. My mother was more frankly pleased with the whole proceeding, for she had done much to encourage my bent and I think hoped that by following it I might lead a useful and happy life. Besides, parents who are aware that their own lives, however satisfactory, have not given them full scope for their potentialities, take a particular pleasure in the possibility of natural and fruitful developments in their children. But it now became evident that although I might remain some time longer at Entumeni I should not remain there indefinitely.

There had been few breaks in the routine for any of us, but in the course of my visits to Durban to buy what economists call consumers' goods, for the supposed benefit of the Zulus and the modest profit of the Plomers, I had explored various aspects of the life of that port, from the villas of the ruling caste on the Berea to the obscurer nocturnal animation of back streets, from the Indian bazaars to the purlieus of the docks. During one of these visits I made the acquaintance of the poet Roy Campbell.[1] Some years older than me, he was a Scotch South African who had been to Oxford and had married an Englishwoman, and whose talent had already made him some reputation in London and also in Paris, where a responsible critic had said, '*Il procède de Marlowe et de Rimbaud.*' He and his wife were living on the south coast of Natal in a somewhat isolated place where they invited me to go and stay with them. I paid them one or two short visits from Entumeni, and

---

[1] A quarter of a century earlier, my mother, when ill soon after arriving in Durban, had been attended by his father, the leading local doctor, who won her gratitude by lending her his carriage when she was convalescent.

learnt of a project to produce a literary magazine, which had found a backer and in which Campbell was to play a leading part. He now invited me to go and live with them and help with this enterprise.

The south coast is said to have suffered from 'development' in recent years, but in those days much of it was unspoilt. At one point there was an estate, Umdoni Park, belonging to a sugar magnate, who had built upon it two somewhat imposing houses. He lived in one, and in the other, which he destined to become a kind of South African Chequers, lived the widow of Louis Botha. His son, a young man who had been at Oxford and later in attendance on General Smuts at the Versailles Conference, was the backer of the proposed magazine, and it was in another house on the estate that the Campbells were living. This house had been occupied previously by a landscape painter, and in his studio, at a short distance from it, I now took up my abode. It stood on a slope overlooking the Indian Ocean, which was only a few yards away. I was of course no stranger to this coast, or to its climate, which in winter is surpassed by few, and I was glad to be there and to be the guest of a generous, gifted and very entertaining friend with whom I had interests in common.

At Umdoni Park I wrote, among other things, a long story, *Ula Masondo*. Much more coherent and objective than *Turbott Wolfe*, this was an account of the effect upon a primitive native of going to work in the gold mines of the Rand. Both these productions have influenced or have been imitated by other writers, so it would be gratifying to think that, apart from any æsthetic merits they may possess, there may have been something seminal about them. However, Croce says in his autobiography [1] (a book of which the austerity is almost shocking to an image-making or mythopoetic rather than purely philosophical mind) that a thought never produces an effect but always a collaboration:

'Just as the thought of a single writer is born of the collaboration of earlier with contemporary history, so that same thought when (as we inaccurately say) it issues from him and communicates itself to

[1] Translated by R. G. Collingwood. Clarendon Press, 1927.

others, passes through an historical development that is no longer his, but that of all who welcome it and improve upon it, or even reject it and misunderstand it and controvert it and ignore it: in a word, think for themselves.'

The first number of the magazine, *Voorslag*, appeared in June, 1926. The title had been chosen before my advent, and signifies a whiplash — not that it was intended to interest amateurs of *le vice Anglais* but to sting with satire the mental hindquarters, so to speak, of the bovine citizenry of the Union. Most of the first number was written by Campbell and myself, either under our own or fictitious names. It also contained an article by General Smuts on 'Beauty in Nature,' which advanced the proposition that 'beauty would be there even if we were not there to behold it,' and that scientists, by interpreting it too exclusively in terms of utility — sexual selection, and so on — had neglected 'values' for 'facts' and had accordingly left unexplored a large and fascinating problem.[1]

Literate South Africa was mostly somewhat puzzled by *Voorslag*. It had been prepared to welcome Campbell's reappearance as a poet, for it thought that poets lived in a kind of cloud-cuckoo-land and had nothing to do with everyday life, but it was disconcerted to find him praising *Turbott Wolfe* and collaborating with its author. The tone of the press was on the whole respectful, bewildered and slightly cautious. The second number, again mostly written by Campbell and myself, was more satirical than the first, differences arose with the promoters as to the future policy to be pursued, and not choosing to compromise we left them to pursue their own fancies. The magazine dragged on for a few months, but after our departure had not enough vitality to sustain it. We had derived a good deal of amusement from the enterprise and perhaps, like twentieth-century Bushmen, had left a few vivid paintings on the walls of that dark cave, the mind of the white South African.

[1] Speculation of this kind has been to General Smuts what his paint-box has been to Mr. Churchill. Some years later I gave some account of Smuts's career and qualities: it has been called just. See *Great Contemporaries*. Essays by Various Hands. (Cassell, 1935.)

Apart from *Voorslag*, Campbell had been writing some of his finest poems, including *The Serf*, *The Zulu Girl* and *Tristan d'Acunha*. When the last-named piece appeared in the *New Statesman*, that journal printed an appreciative letter from T. S. Eliot, which besides being a well-deserved compliment was a remarkable instance of Eliot's learning and acumen. He wondered, he said, whether Campbell had heard of a poem on the same subject by a German poet named Kuhlemann. Now it so happened that I had read to Campbell, one evening at Umdoni Park, some extracts from a letter written to me from Oxford in February, 1922, by my old Rugbeian schoolfellow, D. R. Gillie, including a translation of a few lines from Kuhlemann's poem, and a mere phrase or two in these had kindled Campbell's imagination. A good example of 'collaboration' in the Crocean sense.

Among the contributions to the second number of *Voorslag* was an essay in Afrikaans by a Dutch friend I had made in Durban, Laurens van der Post, one of the sons of an impoverished nobleman who had emigrated from the Netherlands and had become a landowner and State official in the old Orange Free State. Van der Post, a young man of much charm and intelligence, was at that time a journalist.[1] When I arrived at Durban after leaving Umdoni Park at the end of August, 1926, the Campbells were proposing to return soon to Europe, and I was thinking of accompanying them, when something occurred which put me on quite a different track. In the pursuit of his profession, van der Post had made the acquaintance of Katsué Mori, a Japanese merchant captain whose ship was visiting the port of Durban and who had expressed a wish to meet me. On the 30th August van der Post and I paid a visit to Captain Mori in his ship and had a long and interesting conversation with him, the upshot of which was an invitation to both of us to go with him to Japan, where he would remain a fortnight before his next voyage, a period long enough for us to take a tourist's quick glance at the country. Van der Post had no difficulty in securing the consent of his

---

[1] The author of a distinguished novel, *In a Province*, (1934), he served in Abyssinia in 1940–41, and, as a captain in the Intelligence Corps, was reported missing at Singapore in April, 1942.

newspaper. As for me, I had to make up my mind quickly, since Mori was sailing in three days' time. I knew that if I accepted I should not be content with a fortnight in Japan and that if I refused such a chance might never recur. To commit myself to such an adventure at such short notice and almost without resources would have seemed harder if I had been older or of a less enquiring turn of mind or less impressed by Mori. On Thursday, 2nd September, 1926, the *Canada Maru*, a small cargo ship, left Durban for Kobé with van der Post and myself as the only passengers.

Before I describe the voyage and its consequences, I will return briefly to the subject of my family, because the rest of this book will lead in another direction. When I left Africa my brother was just fifteen, and his ambitions, though unlike mine, were not fixed in Zululand. He soon decided to go to the United States, my parents paid his passage, and without any extraneous help he was soon, by sheer force of character, earning his own living in New York. After some years he became a Canadian citizen and at present holds a commission in the Royal Canadian Naval Reserve: in May, 1943, he was in command of His Majesty's corvette *Sunflower*, when she rammed and sank a U-boat. Both the young birds having left the nest, my parents felt neither inclined nor able to carry on the establishment at Entumeni, nor, since it had served its purpose, did they wish to delegate the running of it to anybody else, so they sold it and returned to Europe for good. Still in middle life, they were able, in the dozen years that remained before 1939, to travel on the continent of Europe, where I sometimes visited them. It became their custom to winter abroad and to make the most of England in the summer, though it seemed to them an England inferior to that they had known in earlier years. They were not free from vicissitudes, which I do not propose to describe here: I will say no more than that I am indebted to them both for infinitely more than my mere existence.

Part III

NOT BY EASTERN WINDOWS ONLY

1. THE VOYAGE

I WAS twenty-two and van der Post was even younger. He was then unmarried, and I had no compelling ties. Unlike me, he could make the voyage an exercise in his profession, but I, though all but penniless, had inherited a fair share of my father's impulsiveness and wanderlust; I had a longing to see more of the world and no wish or necessity to remain longer in Africa, much as I loved it in spite of all its wrongs. It would be correct to assume that Captain Mori had been pleasant and persuasive. What requires some explanation is Mori's motive, or combination of motives, in pressing us to go with him to his own country.

Mori was at this time in his late thirties. He came of the Samurai class in the southern island of Kyushu, had been educated at Etajima, the Japanese naval college, and had entered the Imperial Navy, with which he had served in the Mediterranean and elsewhere during the war of 1914–18. His upbringing, education and experience had been determined by duty, tradition and convention, by 'custom and ceremony,' and had produced a balanced and capable man with formal manners and of dignified appearance. His mind was active, his behaviour generally prudent and deliberate, not to say calculating, and his body vigorous. He was sturdily built, not particularly short, very erect, with an ivory-coloured skin (very occasionally flushed with alcohol or excitement) and a broad, stylized face, the eyes rather far apart, the features regular, the bony structure broad without being coarse or heavy, and the maxillary muscles noticeably developed. To support his dignity he wore a sparse moustache and a beard consisting of perhaps twenty or thirty fine black hairs which appeared like the lines of an etching on the point of his chin: the fact that he sometimes joked about this appendage, caressing it as he did so with a shapely and well-kept hand (the fingers rather more spatulate than is usual with his race), was one of several indications that he did not take himself entirely seriously all the time — in fact there was a streak of winning *naïveté* and boyish playfulness in him. If he had set out to fascinate us he could not have been more successful than he was by simply being himself. He gave the impression of being master of himself and of his surroundings, his ship was as spotless as his person and appeared to be run as efficiently as a battleship, and he was evidently as good a husband and father as he was an affable companion. We were the more drawn to him by our wish to try and make amends for insults to which he had been subjected at Durban because of his non-European aspect, and which he had suffered, though deeply offended, with dignity.

The *Canada Maru* belonged to the Osaka Shosen Kaisha, one of the two leading Japanese shipping lines, and Mori had been selected to open up a new and regular cargo service between Japan and South and East Africa. It was plain from the first that his mission was not narrowly limited to the transaction of commerce: since he had been charged to open the way for closer trade relations with those countries, his task was to some extent diplomatic. He was confronted in both countries with a strong racial prejudice and with commercial distrust as well: it had not, for instance, been forgotten that short-sighted Japanese exporters, some ten years earlier, had sold to merchants in Africa a large quantity of very cheap pencils, which, when sharpened, had been found to contain only half an inch of lead.

On his very first voyage to Africa (this was the second), Mori had had some success as a diplomat. The evidence hung on the wall of his cabin in the shape of a framed and signed photograph of an obviously English couple — a tall man, dressed in an expensive-looking suit, standing on a lawn, with his wife beside him in tweeds, both of them hatless and, I rather think, with some kind of terrier at their feet. It was not a particularly interesting photograph and if in a dentist's waiting-room one had noticed it in the

Tatler one would not, except from some personal interest in the couple, have looked at it twice: but this was not a dentist's waiting-room, it was Mori's cabin, and the photograph was a trophy, almost a scalp. It represented, he explained, the Governor of Kenya, who had (by Mori's account) been gracious and cordial, and had gone so far to promote 'good relations' as consenting to accompany Mori as his guest and passenger on a short coastwise voyage. This triumph at Mombasa had no doubt won Mori the commendation of his employers and his Government, and he had no doubt been anxious to achieve at Durban some comparable feat. I suppose van der Post and I were the best he could do, and he seemed to be bearing us off to his far country very much as in the days of Captain Cook exploring navigators used sometimes to carry home for exhibition in Europe indigenous inhabitants of the Pacific islands. We were very young, it was true, and had no official status, but we had one quality very rare among white people in South Africa, a complete absence of racial prejudice — and that emotion was one of the obstacles, perhaps the greatest, in Mori's way. Rarer still, we exhibited a sympathetic curiosity about Japan and its people. Also, he judged us to be not without influence. Van der Post was on the staff of the principal newspaper at Durban, and I had written a book and helped to produce a magazine, both of which had become widely known there and had obtained notice much further afield. As a civilized man, Mori knew the power of the written word; as a man of the world, he knew its potentialities as propaganda.

Since Mori thought that we might be useful to his country by helping to remove the difficulties in his way, he naturally made himself very agreeable to us, but it was not possible to judge how far his winning ways were to be attributed to his wish to make use of us, and how far to true human feeling, for he was affectionate as well as attentive. The comedy in the situation was that while he thought he was making use of us for his own ends, we thought that we were making use of him for ours. There was no deception on either side, since there were no commitments: it might be called a case of mutual aid. What interested us was the unexpected adventure and the chance of seeing Japan, though we should not have taken it unless we had liked Mori for his own sake. A further element of comedy was that by treating him as an equal — that is to say, as being an equally human being — just as we had treated the natives in Africa, we were, in a sense, putting him, as a 'coloured' man, on their level, though the Japanese look down with contempt on negroes and other dark races as barbarians.

In the light of later events, Mori's mission may appear ominous and even slightly sinister, but in those days Japan had until quite lately been for many years in alliance with England, and if van der Post and I were friendly towards him as a man, we were the more polite to him as a sort of ally. My ignorance of Japan and the Japanese was profound, and until I met Mori I had given them little thought. In the far-off Spondon days, during a visit to South-sea, I had seen a large battleship, a complicated structure, gliding through a golden morning mist, and had regarded it with some detachment merely as a strange and impressive spectacle. 'Look at the pretty flag, Billy,' they said. 'The rising sun! That great big ship belongs to the plucky little Japs who fought so well against the naughty Russians. Yes, they are our friends, and perhaps some day you will go and see their pretty country, where the houses are made of paper and the ladies wear chrysanthemums in their hair.' If I had later occasionally seen Japanese in London, I had never spoken to one, and had simply been brought up to this romantic, period conception of their race as 'quaint,' 'plucky,' clever little people living in excessively picturesque surroundings, their womenfolk dainty and petite, with names like Nanki Poo, holding silk fans in the daytime and paper lanterns at night. Later on, from Loti, one had gathered that daintiness was happily united with easy virtue. I had read a few books by or about Lafcadio Hearn, two or three travel books, one or two dubious novels, and a couple of metallic sonnets by Hérédia, and had lacked sufficient curiosity or opportunity to enquire further into the nature, habits and surroundings of the Japanese. My ignorance and the remoteness of their country and outlook made it all the more interesting to be going there in company with some of them.

There is no doubt that the Japanese, long ago perceiving Western sentimentality about them, did their best, right up to 1941, to exploit it for the purposes of propaganda, and behind a barrage of cherry blossoms they gradually built up their heavy industries for their great design of conquering the world in the name of their 'divine' Imperial dynasty. But the Japanese, like everybody else, live a double life, and it was not necessary to know Mori long to perceive that in him — as perhaps in every Japanese militarist, business man or political shark — there was a sensuous æsthete, to whom for instance the blossom of the cherry was far more than a symbol of patriotic mysticism, and for whom it had associations with amorous dalliance in exquisite landscapes, with childish memories, with nostalgia for the lost romantic past, with the sight and sounds of home.

Our first port of call was Kilindini. Mori went ashore in a topee and a well-cut suit of cream-coloured silk and carried in his hand an ebony stick with a silver top. These accoutrements were becoming to him and did not make him look a dandy but very much the *soigné* samurai. While he was attending to his business and cultivating 'good relations' to prepare the way for a Japanese economic penetration of the country, van der Post and I explored Mombasa. We asked a nice young Englishman, retrenched a year or two before from the Indian army, whether there were any good books to be had about Kenya. Glancing furtively over his shoulder, he admitted the existence of the work of Dr. Leys and offered to lend it to us if we would promise to tell nobody that he had done so. This made us laugh, because we knew the book well, it had formed our ideas about Kenya, and I had reviewed it in *Voorslag*. Between other diversions, van der Post and I played tennis on a concrete court, through fissures in which tropical weeds protruded; the balls, long past their prime, had lost their bounce and taken on a protective colouring to match the Dark Continent; the game was therefore in slow motion and full of hazards and had an unreal, dreamlike quality. Even more unreal, in a sense, was the dinner to which we were entertained, evidently at Mori's behest, by a Japanese merchant and his wife. I have never eaten a larger or better meal, and course succeeded course on a Russian scale and of a French perfection: what made it unreal was that we were all acting parts not precisely defined.

Mori meant to cultivate his 'good relations' with the Governor, announced that he was going to Nairobi to see him, and invited us to go too. From the windows of the train we watched the abundant fauna—bounding antelopes, cantering zebras, and giraffes which regarded the train with a mild superciliousness verging on indifference, their heads protruding through the tops of trees against a background of the sun-dazzled equatorial snows of Kilimanjaro. In Nairobi, which seemed a sort of tropical version of a Middle Western pioneer township, the imposing hotel in which we stayed was thronged with equally remarkable beings—an American professional big-game hunter; boyish fortune-hunters from the lesser English public schools; an adventuress in a cloche hat and jodhpores, who, out of bravado, rode into the dining-room on a spanking chestnut mare, dismounted airily, and tossed the reins to the nearest waiter; tanned but anxious-looking young couples of the stranded gentry who rattled round to the banks in Ford cars to try and increase their overdrafts; a dressy but superannuated lady novelist looking round with haggard eyes for copy and a new husband; well-bred young women out from England to visit landowning relations; a Balkan speculator; a touring bishop. The partitions between the bedrooms were thin and endowed with marked acoustic properties, and at night the drowsiest ear could not help receiving some startlingly intimate lessons in biology.

In the morning Mori invited us to go shopping, and we went with him to an establishment kept by an Indian taxidermist, evidently the local Rowland Ward, to whom trophies of many a *safari* were brought to be mounted. Picking his way among horns, tusks, antlers, bottled serpents, trays of glass eyes, and huge hairy carcasses stuffed with rigid realism, Mori gravely approached the proprietor and we heard him say (for the Japanese cannot always manage the letter 'l'), 'I desire some rion's whiskers.' Van der Post and I looked at each other with a mild surprise, but the taxidermist, a stately person in flowing robes, did not bat an eyelid; he treated the request as naturally as if Mori had asked for a zebra-skin kaross or a stuffed crocodile, and presently handed over an envelope in which he had placed some long, off-white bristles. When I asked Mori what he wanted them for, he said he had a friend in Japan who possessed a lion's skin, but the whiskers had unfortunately moulted and been swept away by a too assiduous maid, and it had been much hoped to replace them — but only by the real thing.

Mori had made known his wish to pay a courtesy call on the Governor, and he was planning to take us with him, intending no doubt to introduce us as Japanophils and to show that he was on easy terms with other whites. Hanging about the hotel, gnawed at by desperate and only half hopeful expectation like a middle-aged man waiting for a young and unfaithful typist under a station clock, Mori waited for the invitation: then the shattering news came that the Governor was ill and could not see him. I have no idea whether the illness was diplomatic or not, but Mori had no doubts on the subject, and we gathered that the telephone message he had received from an A.D.C. was not soothingly worded. He took it as a rebuff, almost as an insult, that the man whom he had entertained in his ship and who had been so cordial should now refuse to see him either officially or unofficially after the long journey up from the coast.

It is a mistake to believe that the Japanese are adept at hiding their feelings, for though a disciplined, they are a temperamental race. On the journey up to Nairobi, Mori had been calm, confident and playful; on the journey back to Mombasa he was silent, broody and bitter, and for him at least the zebras now trotted and the antelopes pranced in vain. When we got back to Mombasa we learnt that the ship's carpenter, a mild, flat-faced country lad, had died suddenly. Here Mori saw an opportunity for a kind of revenge. The dead boy, he resolved, should not be cremated or buried at sea or equally obscurely in some cemetery for 'coloured' people: no, he should lie among the decomposed remains of some of his ex-allies as an equal.

> 'Sceptre and crown
> Shall tumble down
> And in the grave be equal made
> With the poor crooked scythe and spade.'

Difficulties were raised, but Mori the diplomat got to work, and so it happened one sultry evening that the Anglican burial service was read over the corpse of a Japanese peasant by a hot and irate-looking Anglican clergyman in a surplice, probably a cricketer, while Mori and van der Post and I stood by with the crew of the *Canada Maru* — well-behaved and in spotless white ducks, and looking slightly spellbound, like good children at a classy wedding — to witness this unexpected end of some poor mother's son, this triumphant vindication of Japan as a Great Power. As for Mori, he had such a mingled expression of solemnity and satisfaction on his face that he might have been burying a rich and childless uncle. He looked like a cat that has just finished a large piece of its favourite fish.

When we put to sea again we had some more passengers, a party of Japanese with gold teeth and cameras, who had been ostensibly shooting a film of big game and were full of conventional anecdotes about hair's-breadth escapes and big charging brutes with wicked little red eyes. They had also filmed us getting out of the train at Nairobi, much to the interest of our fellow-passengers, who had not been able to make us out at all. One of the party was the caricaturist's Jap — a squat, citron-coloured person with huge teeth set horizontally and fan-wise in his head and with horn-rimmed spectacles hugging a bridgeless nose. He surprised us by always wearing in the tropics long woolly pants of the kind which at school we used to call fug-pipes, and over them a short blackish silk kimono. The big-game boys joined us at meals, but otherwise we did not see much of them.

Meals, it may be said, were Japanese, and by this time we had become quite used to chopsticks. As well as quantities of rice, dried seaweed and pickled plums, we had also picked up a little of the language. In the afternoons Mori used to shut himself up in his cabin (no longer adorned with the Governor's photograph) and indulge for an hour or so in solemn ritualistic chanting from the Japanese classics: this was evidently not merely a cultural exercise, since his voice, a virile bass, was strenuously produced — to the benefit, he assured us, of his internal organs and nervous system. The purser was reading Bergson and the wireless operator Einstein, but the cleanliness and efficiency of the ship did not suffer and to a landsman's eye were superlative. In the evenings one of the officers used to play that haunting instrument the *shakuhachi*, a kind of bamboo flute with great purity of tone, and as the mast-head of the ship stirred rhythmically about among the stars on those calm, warm southern nights, the long-drawn notes seemed a classical lamentation, exquisite and resigned, for some irrecoverable age of primordial peace, an evocation of what the Japanese call *awaré* — which has been translated 'the ah-ness of things.'

In an empty hold displays of *judo* and *kendo* ('sword-way') were staged for our benefit, and Mori, dressed in a masked helmet and a jerkin with breastplates, wielding a two-handed sword and uttering blood-curdling yells, not only became barbaric and mediæval but revealed himself as a formidable athlete. One night by full moon a feast in Japanese style was held on the deck, and much *saké* was drunk. One of the big-game boys sang some lachrymose love-songs in the style of a cat in rut, and van der Post and I obliged to the best of our ability (which in my case was small) with music-hall ditties and Afrikaans folk-songs — *Vat jou goed en trek, Ferreira!* and so on. I also essayed a solo in Zulu, which sent my thoughts back to Entumeni. Presently Mori, flushed with drink and in some *déshabillé*, performed with great vigour and technical skill what was obviously a war-dance; and looking at his clean and muscular feet one felt that he would like to plant them on the neck of a defeated enemy. For a few minutes the atmosphere was uncomfortable; equivocal looks and remarks were exchanged by the Japanese, and we knew without a doubt that he was dancing in honour of *der Tag*. A momentary but ineffaceable impression.

At Singapore we saw the sights, shook off innumerable pimps, and had a banquet in the Chinese quarter; off the precipitous eastern coast of Formosa we were tossed about like a cork in a high-powered typhoon; and in due course we glided, on a clear autumn day, to our anchorage off the port of Moji. The ship was instantly infested with reporters, who were much more interested in us than in the fug-piped cameraman and his chums, and each was equipped with a visiting-card, a smile, and, as we afterwards learnt, with great powers of invention. Almost the first thing we saw when we went ashore was a shrine at which a Russian shell taken in the Russo-Japanese war had been mounted on a pedestal, very much as in England captured German guns were mounted, after 1918, in open though not in sacred places. This object was a good introduction to the study of the nefarious Japanese cult, or religion, of emperor-worship and militarist nationalism.

Our first evening, however, was to be devoted to night life, and it was the beginning of the most strenuous fortnight I have ever spent. The scene of the revels was an elegant and luxurious pleasure-house. Formerly a rich man's villa, it stood in its own grounds, which were formally laid out in the best conventional taste, and everything, indoors and out, was exquisitely ordered, for the Japanese know how to make cleanliness the setting for glamour and how to divorce vice from squalor. Mori was our host, but was later reimbursed, I trust, by his employers or his Government, because even by the standards of a sailor long absent from home the night must have been an expensive one. Deprived of our clothes and supplied with clean kimonos, van der Post and I went off to take a hot bath and then joined Mori in the best room, where we sat on silk cushions on the floor round a low table of red lacquer. There were three other guests, local friends of Mori's. One of them had just returned from a mushrooming picnic in the country. He was unlike any Japanese we had yet seen, a *gros gaillard* in a white shirt and shorts, six feet high and strongly built, with a smooth tawny skin and a neck like a young bull's. Like so many toughs, he had a poor head for liquor, and long before midnight he was rolling about the floor, and rather too playfully worrying, like a young but overgrown dog, one of the little prentice geishas, who was perhaps rather frightened but did not lose her head. These little creatures had their faces thickly made up with wet white, their little tongues now and then peeped out of their painted mouths, their eyes and the pretty ornaments in their coiffures twinkled and sparkled, and their movements were as mannered as their clothes were sumptuous. Mori was something of a matchmaker and had evidently primed the most attractive and intelligent of the geishas to make up to me. She was in fact pretty, gentle and quick-witted, and had none of that affected ingenuousness which often makes geishas rather boring. I think the idea was that I should fall heavily at the outset for Japanese womanhood and accordingly for Japan, but matchmaking is such a gamble, and just as people often give as presents what they themselves like rather than what the recipients want, Mori had chosen the bait he himself would have taken. All the same she was a very nice and obliging girl and may be said to have literally laid herself out to please — nor was she unsuccessful. We had been eating an excellent and prolonged Japanese meal and drinking enough *saké* to float a sampan, and in between times there were songs, dances and various forms of fun and games which I need not specify. At some unearthly hour a dapper little local photographer appeared with a camera, a tripod and magnesium flares to record the occasion, and after a considerable struggle (particularly with the mushrooming hearty, who was at last propped up in a semi-recumbent position of which he was probably unconscious) we managed to form a more or less presentable and photogenic group. The result is before me as I write and is a credit to the photographer and to all but two of his subjects: Mori, I may say, looks perfectly self-possessed while I have a deceptive air of innocence. In the morning, not entirely free from a hangover, we were offered some sinister-looking pieces of a fish called *fugu*, which is supposed to be a delicacy — unless you eat the wrong bits, when it is lethal. In fact, a well-known athlete had died of eating *fugu* there at Moji only the week before. It was really not the sort of thing to tempt a 'morning after' appetite; it was too suggestive of a breakfast with the Borgias; and although we ate some of it, this act of politeness cost us an effort, since it did not please our palates. However, we falsely expressed ourselves grateful for being offered a dish so uncommon and so appetizing.

Later in the day we sailed through the Inland Sea for Kobé, admiring islets covered with pine trees, speculating on distant factory chimneys smoking purposefully, and in due course looking through binoculars at Mori's own house on the beach at Tarumi and at his wife and child waving as we passed. From the moment we set foot ashore we were caught up in a whirl of entertainment and sightseeing. At Osaka we were taken by Mori to be introduced to the heads of the shipping company, who gave us another slap-up dinner with sophisticated urban geishas in attendance. Excursions to castles, temples and 'beauty-spots' were designed to attune us to the picturesque; other excursions were arranged to impress us with what was modern. We were taken, for example, to see a model hostel for workers in a textile factory, but all that we saw and heard of their lives filled us not with admiration but horror and pity; we were taken over the premises of the *Osaka Mainichi* very much as foreign delegations visiting London are sometimes taken to Printing House Square; we were shown all over a mammoth department store; accommodated in a brand-new American-style hotel with waffles and maple-syrup for breakfast and iced water on tap in every room; repeatedly photographed — on the roofs of high buildings, in groups, and even in bed; and interviewed not only by the leading newspapers but by those less well-known, such as the *Yorodzu Choho* and the *Jiji Shimpo*. The reporters continued to show rare imaginative power, representing us in a light that never was on sea or land and attributing to us opinions and intentions of which we were amazed to read, but which we hoped might prove diverting to millions of tired commuters in the industrial cities.

It was a relief to spend some quieter hours pottering among the faded splendours of Nara and Kyoto and tasting in ancient surroundings the absolute tranquillity and cool melancholy of the Japanese autumn; it was a relief to rest our eyes on moss and the reflections in still water of scarlet maple leaves, to refresh our ears with the sound of running water in wooded valleys, and to contemplate, in the intervals of feeding deer in the cryptomeria groves of Nara, superb ancient sculptures, shapes by no means Praxitelean whose gilded smiles nevertheless did 'fill the hushed air with everlasting love.'

But then Tokyo was waiting, with more reporters and photographers, more sightseeing, luncheon with a millionaire, an interview with a Cabinet Minister, cocktails at the Imperial Hotel, and, even stranger, a gathering of the Rotary Club, not made up of bluff, back-slapping tradesmen but of formidable and silent magnates, to whom I was constrained to make a speech, which though civil was, I must confess, not free from irony. By the time the fortnight was up we had visited Nikko, the most conspicuous of Japanese 'beauty spots'; Isé, the most sacred shrine and headquarters of the national mumbo-jumbo; as well as Arashiyama, Momoyama, Hiyei-san, Hakoné, Miyanoshita and several other places. Most of all, perhaps, we enjoyed an early morning in a boat on Lake Chuzenji: it was a late autumn morning, and a few red and yellow leaves fell like dead butterflies through the mist and floated on the clear water, through which we could see the lake-bed of coloured pebbles.

It is interesting for a private person, just once in a lifetime, to go through the sort of experience that falls to public and political persons when they visit foreign parts officially. Looking back, I am struck with the amount of physical and nervous energy that had to be brought into play, and even more not merely with the number and variety of the things we did, places we visited and people we met, but with the strong, various and useful impression we received. The upshot was that van der Post was able to take away with him a picture of the country and people much less superficial than that to be obtained by an ordinary tourist in the same time, while I, who elected to stay in Japan, found that I had an excellent rough idea to begin with. Mori had been a good impresario, and it cannot often happen that two young foreigners, after a fortnight in a completely strange country, can claim to have seen glimpses of so many aspects of its existence. Had those two weeks been my sole experience of Japan, however, I should have formed a far less favourable opinion of the country and the people than I did in fact form after two years.

2. KAMI NERIMA

HAVING seen off Mori and van der Post on the departing *Canada Maru*, I found myself, so to speak, alone in Japan, with enough money to live on for two or three weeks, no friends or influence and only the merest smattering of the language. I therefore returned from Osaka to Tokyo with the intention of earning a living. It did not occur to me to make my presence known to our embassy or consulate, or to apply for help to the Cabinet Minister or other bigwigs to whom I had been introduced. I did, however, present myself to that fine poet and good-hearted man Edmund Blunden, to whom I had a letter of introduction and who was then occupying the chair of English literature in the Imperial University. He received me with much kindness and I established myself temporarily and not, I hope, too obtrusively under the same roof, that of an unpretentious hotel not far from the University. Here I took at once, as much from necessity as choice, to the Japanese style of living, sitting and sleeping on the floor, eating Japanese food and suffering a little from the cold. The view from my window was lacking in grace — the tall iron chimney of a public bath-house and a cold and distant sky — but the life of the hotel was not undiverting. Without much effort I obtained part-time work, as a stop-gap, on the staff of an institution with a name like the croaking of a bronchitic frog, the Gwaikoku Go Gakko, or School of Foreign Languages, my only qualifications being a love of the English language and perhaps some natural aptitude for teaching. The students were alert and friendly, easy to teach and pleasant to know. I also gave private lessons to a Japanese scientist, and a Marquis Hirohata proposed that I should tutor his children; he offered me a house in his grounds, but I did not wish to lock myself up in the bosom of one family.

I found myself with plenty of leisure to explore Tokyo and get the hang of things, but being needy was anxious to obtain a better and full-time job. The excellent Blunden made this known at the University and before long an opportunity presented itself. I went to see Professor Sanki Ichikawa, a philologist of international repute who was head of the English faculty and who, sitting with his back to the light, looked at me as searchingly as if he were an oculist and treated me to one of his characteristic silences, long, inscrutable and slightly disconcerting.[1] Whatever he saw in my right and left eyes, it fortunately did not prevent him from offering me a post at the Tokyo Koto Gakko, or Higher School, which, it was explained to me, might be called the Eton of Japan. Then again, it might not. Of recent foundation, it was perhaps the nearest thing in Japan to an English public school, but the similarity would not have occurred to me unless it had been pointed out.

At this juncture, a genial student at the University, Sumida by name, attached himself to me and constituted himself my factotum in return for the chance of bettering his English. It was a useful arrangement for us both, and encouraged by Sumida and my new job, I took a house near the village of Kami Nerima, on the Musashi plain outside Tokyo, out in the fields but within reach of a speedy electric train. The winter was delicious. Dry snow like sugar lay thickly on the landscape and outlined the bare branches of paulownias and the evergreen foliage of red-berried nandina bushes in the garden; not far off stood a grove of cryptomerias, cocoa-brown at this season, and thickets of tall bamboos, less mysterious but not less beautiful with the snow to lighten their depths.

In the nearest house lived a family named Shimoju. By a remarkable coincidence they were connections of Mori's, the head of the family, an ex-officer of the Imperial Guards, being Mori's wife's uncle. There were two sons and two daughters, the eldest son being in the army and in his spare time painting very much after Cézanne. They were a most cheerful and unpretentious family, and while Sumida (whose standards were somewhat exacting, for a speck of cigarette ash on the floor would send him scurrying for a brush and dustpan) was trying to get us a suitable servant, Mrs. Shimoju and her daughters insisted on coming to do all the housework for us, even the cleaning of shoes and the scouring of pots. It was difficult

---

[1] Ten years later, when I had the pleasure of editing his wife's travel-diary, published in England under the title *Japanese Lady in Europe*, her flow of narrative reminded me, by contrast, of this mysterious interview.

to know how to show proper appreciation of this great kindness.

Unfortunately my acceptance of a post at the Koto Gakko had led, really through no fault of my own, to unpleasantness. There was apparently in the educational world a feud about which I knew nothing, and the Gwaikoku Go Gakko accused the Imperial University of seducing me from their service. There was a great coming and going, a plotting and counter-plotting, but I stuck to my plan and incurred the displeasure of the authorities at the Gwaikoku Go Gakko by giving them notice of my departure. Some time later I learnt that this had led to my being slandered to my former students, who eventually came to me in a body of their own accord to tell me that they would believe nothing against me and to apologize for the behaviour of the authorities in their school — an instance of Japanese loyalty by which I was greatly touched, for, whether I had behaved rightly or wrongly, I was a foreigner, and xenophobia was already slightly on the increase. By the time I had settled down, and the day after these boys had first been to see me (for they often came again) one of them wrote to me:

'I am now very grateful for your yesterday's warm reception . . . To tell the truth, I expected that we should meet with more starchy, formal treatment which is usual between the people who belong to other nationalities, so I was rather afraid of seeing you. It was interesting for me to find you accustomed to the Japanese manner of living, and seeing you live in a simple way like a man who was thoroughly acquainted with the world I couldn't help smiling. But I believe the life you are leading now will not be unpleasant for you, because I perceived that you have something of the genuine Japanese character in your spirit — that is, the indifference about the world's affairs, the despise for social talents and a calm and self-possessed attitude.'

Complimentary: but this letter has the same slight note of condescension that may be heard in an Englishman's praise of a foreigner for not behaving like a foreigner; it hints at a conscious superiority. Much has been said about the 'inferiority complex' of the Japanese, and much of what has been said has been justified. Keen observers, on the other hand, have sometimes stressed that the Japanese do really feel, even if they have taught themselves to feel, on a loftier plane than other races, and that this feeling has been a strong motive power in their great imperialistic gamble. Both these feelings exist and are no doubt susceptible of analysis. Modesty and arrogance, diffidence and assurance, can exist or alternate in one breast, so why not in a whole race? The conscious superiority of the English as a race comes partly from insularity and partly from a long history of security and wealth: it is comparable to that particular kind of quiet assurance which can be found in individuals with a family history of the same kind. The Japanese sentiment of superiority is also that of an insular people, but more homogeneous and for many centuries far more isolated than ourselves. Suddenly finding themselves exposed to a large and dangerous world, it was natural that they should not only cling together, but regard themselves, so long exclusive, as different, believing themselves in some ways stronger and in some ways weaker than others. They have often argued that the Western races have been their superiors in mechanical achievements but that they themselves have been spiritually on a higher level. They have also argued that it was their mission to combine the best of both civilizations. Having proved, in much less than a century and by an unprecedented effort, that they could master and adapt to their own purposes the mechanical arts of the West, they still tended to believe in their spiritual superiority, so it naturally became a temptation to them to believe that they were better in every way. They not only yielded to the temptation but instilled that belief into their young.

In February, 1927, Mori came to stay at Kami Nerima, was most solicitous for my welfare, and strongly vexed at my having been disturbed by the pedagogues' vendetta. Though by no means rich, he most generously offered to maintain me at his own expense if I cared to abandon teaching, and Sumida instantly expressed a readiness to devote himself to my service without any recompense: but I preferred to go on earning my living. I was indeed overwhelmed with kind attentions. A friend of Mori's lent me a seaside villa at Kamakura, and before Mori himself went to sea again I went to stay with him and his family at Tarumi, near Kobé: he said I could stay there as long as I liked, or for good. The house was on the beach, among clean-smelling pine trees by nature contorted into formal growths like ideographs, and with a view of the island of Awaji, set between a calm sky and the calm waters of the Inland Sea. Waking in the morning and lying in bed listening to the wavelets lapping at the shore and watching the sun scattering early spangles on the indolent water, one felt that Tarumi would be a good place to live and die in.

Before returning to Tokyo, I made the acquaintance of Sumida's father, a simple provincial gentleman, modest and affable, and I also went to spend a night with an acquaintance at Mikagé, between Kobé and Osaka. In the evening we were sitting quietly with several other people in the main room of the house, which was open to the garden, when I was spellbound by a vase which solemnly began to dance: it tottered, paused, righted itself, pirouetted, and then rolled over. This seemed funny and inexplicable, but the floor was rocking slightly, and suddenly the whole house creaked, swayed and shuddered; there was a sound of glass breaking, then a universal dull rumbling, followed by distant shrieks; then a deep silence. I found myself alone in the room: everybody else had rushed prudently into the garden. This was my first experience of a considerable earthquake. Luckily the epicentre was a good many miles away: two thousand people, the papers said, had been killed, and more than twice that number injured.

It was springtime at Kami Nerima. The fields round the house were green with young corn, larks performed overhead, and violets came out by the wayside. A mile away a whole field of sumptuous peonies were soon in splendour, beyond the terminus of the electric railway was a hill covered with pine trees beneath which the ground was thick with flesh-coloured wild azaleas, and at the foot of the hill ran a broad stream over which dangled pendent bunches of white wistaria the size of a man. In the opposite direction lay the vast wilderness of Tokyo, infinitely spread out, one of the largest cities in the world, with innumerable little shops extending for miles and miles, each over-staffed with eager assistants apparently thriving on the smell of an oil-rag. It was a city electrical with life and, at least to me, of inexhaustible variety. Before I began work at the Koto Gakko, I was taken to two licensed fortune-tellers. The first was the widow of a somewhat scandalous novelist. She was a very old woman with very thick spectacles and hands like a turkey's claws. 'Even though you were born of a good family,' she said, 'your life will always be very complicated.' She told me among other things that the middle of my life would be the happiest part (how am I to know which is the middle?) and that I should not stay more than two or three years in Japan. The other fortune-teller was male. He told me I was temperamental and likely to contract a disease of the liver; he also foretold the exact date of my departure from Japan, an event which was then not even in contemplation. When I asked him which would be my best route back to England he replied with candour, 'I regret that I am not acquainted with the geography of the world.'

The Koto Gakko looked like one of those up-to-date factories on the Great West Road, and outside it, on a pedestal, was a bronze bust, not, as at first appeared, of the Neanderthal man (for it was from a distance a trifle prognathic) but of, perhaps, the founder of the school. In the masters' common room I had the pleasure of fraternizing with as agreeable a set of men as could be wished. With one exception, or possibly two, they had that streak of innocence or *naïveté* which makes the Japanese so endearing when you get to know them. This trait was naturally more marked among the students, particularly the younger ones. The curriculum was stiff, and as they grew up the boys tended to get tired and a little desperate, their adolescent burgeoning cramped by sheer overwork and an overwhelming imposition of duty. That they should have had to learn English as well as so much else greatly increased the strain on their minds, which were naturally agile: how greatly may be illustrated by two answers given by Japanese students to questions in an examination. The first was 'What do you know of Robert Louis Stevenson?' 'Robert Louis Stevenson,' the answer ran, 'was a famous Scotch poet who invented the steam engine, and because he

suffered from a disease of the lungs he was always known as Puffing
Billy.' The other student, asked what he knew of *Moby Dick*,
answered that it was a nickname given to Charles Dickens, because
he was always moving his lodgings. It will be agreed that these
answers, though laughable as howlers, are not lacking in ingenuity.
Many pretty examples of the misuse of foreign languages by the
Japanese, especially in the sphere of commerce, have been collected
from time to time. My friend Sherard Vines discovered some
alleged whisky labelled 'Rabbit Brand, as supplied to the Nobleman' — the Nobleman's opinion was unfortunately not recorded —
and I long treasured a label from a bottle of a proprietary brand of
soy, got up to look like Worcester Sauce. The inscription on the
label was partly in French, but copied from a bottle of hair oil, so
one learnt with surprise that the consumption of this delicious sauce,
containing the choicest oriental spices, would not only remove un-
desirable *pellicules* from one's *chevelure*, but would impart to it
suppleness, brilliance and an agreeable perfume.

More interesting really than the difficulties which faced the
student in learning English was the ability with which, as a rule, he
surmounted them: if there was much, in his distant and fragmentary
view of English civilization, that remained absurd or inexplicable or
merely barbarous, he often acquired a remarkable facility in reading
and writing our difficult language. The contrast between the two
civilizations could be illustrated by comparing the trends of education. An English boy begins — or used to begin — his life with end-
less discipline, with 'Little boys should be seen and not heard' and
'Now, Master Geoffrey, don't pick your nose, don't fidget, don't
speak with your mouth full, and don't be so cruel to poor pussy.' At
his preparatory school he is — or was — ruled and regulated in all
things. At his public school he gradually begins to feel a little freer,
has more time to himself, and can to some extent follow his own
inclinations. At the university, or wherever he goes after leaving
school, he enjoys as a rule something very like freedom in his spare
time — not absolute freedom, for there is no such thing, but freedom,
within limits, to do what he likes. With the Japanese boy the process is reversed. When a mere child he seems extraordinarily free,

prattling and roaming about at his own sweet will, seldom lectured, nagged or corrected, and yet behaving not in the least disgustingly. He then goes to a primary school, is popped into a little uniform, and indeed is quite likely to wear it for the rest of his life. By the time he gets to a secondary school he is overwhelmed with work and obligations and discipline of one kind and another, and by the time he gets to the university or out into the world he has to be a cog in the national machine or perish. The English boy tends to develop late, for racial, social and climatic reasons; the Japanese boy tends to develop early, his body ripening earlier, and experience — for instance, of women and of the difficulties of life — coming to him sooner, so that he is often a man before he has left school.

Though a trifle older in years and more variously experienced, I was certainly in some ways younger than some of my students. Between them and me was the strong bond that ties people of the same generation, and since their characters, manners and generally their ideas were sympathetic to me, I was able to associate with them as equals and friends in school and out; there was no question of keeping order, because it never occurred to them to behave in a rowdy or slovenly way; nor of keeping my distance, because I had no motive for doing so. They came from various strata of society, and among those dear to me were Honda, who had lived in England, his father being a diplomat; Shidehara, whose uncle brought honour upon his name by advocating, when Foreign Minister, a liberal policy towards China; Shiomi, whose father was a peasant; and Fukuzawa, whose father was a yeoman. I first got to know them well in the summer holidays, part of which I spent at a hostel belonging to the school at a place called Ikénodaira, away up in the mountains of the interior. In the winter the house was used as a headquarters for ski-ing and other winter sports, and in the summer for walking, climbing and so on. During the boom at the end of the war of 1914–1918, a number of *narikin*, or new rich, had built themselves villas at Ikénodaira, but most of these were now empty or derelict. The most imposing, however, was inhabited in the season by one of the numberless offshoots of the heaven-sent Imperial family, and the armed sentries in khaki at the gates struck a discordant note in an otherwise placid scene.

The chief feature of the hostel was a room on the ground floor which had been converted into a shallow bath through which a hot spring flowed all the year round. Providence had made it just the right temperature and much time was spent quietly wallowing and gossiping in this benign water. Nothing stimulates well-being and benevolence like a sociable hot bath, and since hot springs exist all over Japan and I spent all my holidays in travelling about the country, I passed much time in them. They are best perhaps in winter when the sun is shining on the snow, or when the plum trees are coming into blossom a few yards from one's nose, the rest of the body being under the water, and the body of a congenial companion by one's side. At Ikénodaira there was a mountain to climb, with a rest-house to sleep in half-way up, and at the top, far above the birch-woods and alpine flowers, a rocky platform from which at dawn there was a prodigious view. The countryside, fresh and temperate while Tokyo was sweltering in the *nyubai*, abounded in the flora and fauna which have to be known in order to appreciate Japanese poetry. Flowers like the *hagi*, or lespedeza, and birds like the *uguisu*, the so-called Japanese nightingale, have to be seen or heard before their delicate and varied associations for the Japanese mind can be even guessed at.

Later in the summer I went to stay with Sumida's family at Hiroshima on the Inland Sea, and so learnt something of the life and appearance of a large provincial town, and of the warmth of provincial hospitality. Among the ornaments of the house was a large wooden plaque engraved with a single gilded ideograph. This object hung over a sliding door leading to the lavatory. When I asked what it meant I was told that it meant Perseverance: I gathered, however, that its situation was fortuitous and it was intended as a general moral precept rather than as an encouragement to the constipated. Perseverance was certainly needed to find a pair of wooden clogs in the town to fit me, and in the end they had to be specially made. Back in Tokyo in the autumn I ran into an English business-man of my acquaintance, who asked where I had spent the summer. When

I told him I had been staying with some Japanese friends at Hiroshima his astonishment was great, and he was slightly incredulous. 'Well,' he said, 'I have been fifteen years in this country, and no Japanese family have ever asked *me* to stay with them.' He was an amiable and unprejudiced kind of man, but all his social or business contacts with the Japanese had been at places of business or public entertainment.

From Hiroshima we went across to Miyajima and gave ourselves up to the delights of swimming, using the same beach as the cadets who had come over, as they did every year, for a swimming season from Etajima, the naval college. Burnt to an apricot colour by the sun, they were extremely hardy and athletic, which was no wonder in view of their almost unbelievably strenuous physical régime. At the same time they had serious, anxious faces as the result of too much brainwork and too great a sense of duty and responsibility. When we were not bathing or idling we used to go out in a boat or stroll about in the village or in the woods. I remember the astonishment of two Indian visitors at seeing a young white man dressed in a Japanese fisherman's hat, a cotton kimono and high clogs; I suppose they were used to seeing Anglo-Indians, stiff-necked in stiff collars, and Poona-minded. Later in the same summer I made a wonderful journey with my friend Honda to Hokkaido, the northern island, and to Lake Towada, in the north of the main island, a journey of which I have given some account in my book *Paper Houses* under the title *Yoka Nikki*.

This was a good life — periods of not uncongenial work, for which I was well paid but which yet allowed plenty of time for other activities or for none, alternating with long holidays in which to explore and savour the country and cultivate private life. If I was mainly concerned with the Japanese and their culture, I devoted much time to reading European literature, both ancient and modern, for Marsh Moor and Entumeni had kept me back in this respect. And I did not want for European society. I do not care as a rule for those who, in foreign countries, huddle together, play golf or bridge, swap gossip and cultivate to the point of exaggeration their own national customs and habits of mind. I had not been long in Japan before I heard with some amusement that I was reputed in such circles to have 'gone native.' In fact I had neither the desire nor the need to cut myself off from the society of Europeans. I was on friendly terms with several English married couples and with an Englishwoman married to a Japanese, and among my chief blessings in those days I count the society of two Europeans in particular. First, the witty and learned Sherard Vines, a poet of distinction (neglected, in my opinion, by a reading public too easily hypnotized by the parrot-like repetition of names and too incurious to find things out for itself), and author of *Yofuku*, a markedly original book on Japan, of *The Course of English Classicism*, and of a satirical novel, *Green to Amber*, which gives a scintillating picture of English provincial life just before Munich. Secondly, the painter Anna von Schubert, a woman of the rarest intelligence and sensibility. I had long felt the want of the society of civilized European women, and here was one who was a civilization in herself. Years later I had the good fortune to bring her and Virginia Woolf together in London, where an exhibition of her paintings was, alas, postponed by the outbreak of war in 1939.

3. HIGASHI NAKANO

SUMIDA's parents having, according to the custom of the country, arranged a wedding for him, and my Sabine farm (as Blunden jocularly called it) at Kami Nerima being a little far out, I took a house much nearer the middle of Tokyo, in the region called Higashi Nakano — more of a built-up area, but peaceful, with quiet by-ways among gardens full of evergreens. The house, of one story, had one room in 'foreign style,' which I turned into a study, but was otherwise Japanese. When you came in, you took off your shoes and left them in the hall. The rooms all led into one another, being separated by sliding partitions covered with thick white cardboard lightly sown with motifs of gilt pine-needles, silver sprigs of flowering grasses, and so on. If one wished to give a party or to air the house one could remove all these partitions and turn the whole building, with the exception of the hall, kitchen, bathroom and lavatory, into a single room. Japanese rooms are not cluttered with furniture, so any room can be adapted for any purpose at any time. When bed-time comes, the maid opens a built-in cupboard with sliding doors, takes out your bedding, and spreads it on the springy grass mats, or *tatami*, with which the floors are covered; and after once getting used to this way of sleeping it seems grotesque to climb at night on to the back of a wooden quadruped. On the garden side, a narrow verandah of polished wood ran round the house. Between this verandah and the rooms were sliding paper screens, or *shoji*, with glass panels let into them; between it and the gardens sliding glass doors; and outside them again sliding wooden shutters. So, according to the weather or your mood, you could shut the whole house up like a box and be entirely snug and private within, or you could throw it open to the sun so that to sit indoors was virtually to sit out of doors. This was all as reasonable as it was usual, and it is time we too learnt to make our houses more adaptable to our much more changeable climate. The chief weakness in the Japanese style of living is the inadequate heating in winter. I relied at first on the usual charcoal braziers, but they are rather cold comfort and are apt to asphyxiate the unwary, so I found it better to make use of oil stoves or electric fires. I should still prefer to wash outside the bath and then to simmer peacefully in clean water in a deep wooden tub, for the touch of wood is pleasanter against the body than the surface of a European bath.

At Higashi Nakano I had set up house with Morito Fukuzawa, whom I have already mentioned. A year or two younger than me, he was handsome and of a slightly melancholy disposition, but with an agreeably ironical turn of humour, and of a hedonistic and scepti-cal frame of mind which I found congenial. Furthermore, his inclinations were literary, and he spent much time initiating me into the literature of his country, both ancient and modern. We read much poetry and much modern fiction, in which there were strong influences of Russian and French naturalism; we also read Saikaku, the seventeenth-century novelist, who was so candid that modern editions of his work sometimes consist largely of asterisks. We also went to the theatre — the marionettes, which have to be seen to be believed; the classical, difficult and highly formal *No* plays; and especially the popular *Kabuki* theatre. I have heard it said that Japan is the only country where the theatre is living in all the forms of its evolution — it is as though in England one could see at any given moment everything from a glorified Punch-and-Judy show, a masque, or a mediæval religious mystery, by way of stylized Shakespeare and Restoration comedy, to Chekhov, acrobatic ballet, or the latest art-theatre freak or whimsy. Japan almost took away my appetite for the English theatre: there the art of acting, which is hereditary, has attained perfection, and I have always thought it strange that Lafcadio Hearn (who so far 'went native' as to become naturalized and who is said to have had his professional salary heavily reduced in consequence) never went to the theatre; perhaps the explanation is that the poor man was blind in one eye and could not see much with the other. Before leaving this subject, I may say that the most singular spectacle I ever saw in the Japanese theatre was an imitation of the Oberammergau passion play. This was given in Tokyo in 1928. Much was made of the two roles of Saromé and Magudara-no-Maria (i.e. Salome and Mary Magdalene), who figured as what were in those days known as vamps, rather than as *femmes fatales*, and I shall not soon forget the painless crucifixion of a dapper Japanese Christ in a red wig.

I have alluded to the censoring of the novels of Saikaku. Prudishness seems to have been imported by the Japanese with Western civilization, but in my day had not made very much headway except in bureaucratic circles. It sometimes took extraordinary forms. At an exhibition of sculpture in modern Western style by native artists the middle of the main hall was occupied by a nameless something covered with a dust sheet, to which was affixed the following notice: 'This figure is improper. In order to view it visitors must lift the covering.' Needless to say there was a long queue waiting to inspect what turned out to be a banal and lumpy nude, about which the only impropriety was its creator's lack of talent. Then again, one summer in the country, a friend of mine was reproached by the local policeman for exposing his back at a window. He was in fact wearing a loin-cloth and was merely sitting on the window-sill in order to enjoy what freshness there was in the air. This incident is all the stranger since the Japanese as a rule see no shame in exposing their bodies, and bathe together as a matter of course. As a Japanese once said to me, 'You Europeans think it disgraceful to expose your bodies, but you shamelessly expose your minds. Everybody knows how men and women are made, so we see no shame in uncovering our bodies. We think it improper to uncover our thoughts.' This was said only half seriously, in a tone more whimsical than priggish, but there is something in it. From such a belief, so far as it is consciously held, it follows that the Japanese can be engagingly candid in matters over which we should be somewhat reticent. One day I invited home to dinner a colleague at the University, where I had been giving a lecture. 'Excuse me,' he replied, 'but I found this morning that my bowels were rather loose. This hot, rainy weather always makes my bowels loose. May I, therefore, defer acceptance of your kind invitation until my bowels are no longer loose?'

Another exhibition in Tokyo in my time was of so-called 'proletarian' painting. Those were palmy days in Japan, those nineteen-twenties, for 'dangerous thoughts' could then, up to a point, still express themselves with impunity. The paintings were not good; they were large, crude, realistic and enthusiastic. The subjects were heroic portraits or allegories or scenes of riot, historical or imaginary, designed to glorify the struggles of the working class for political power. One canvas, crowded with embattled figures, attracted particular attention because a number of small flaps of white paper were stuck on to it here and there, but only by their upper edges. On lifting up these flaps, one saw that in each case they were covering representations of wounds or blood. They merely drew attention to what they were meant to conceal; they were certainly not intended to placate the squeamish, but to veil 'dangerous thoughts,' to which they naturally only lent the attractiveness of what is forbidden. It is a curious fact that at this time so mild a book as *The Private Papers of Henry Ryecroft* was banned for its supposed power of promulgating such thoughts, but so far as I recollect, it advances nothing more than a rather weary hedonism, and that mostly by implication.

While I was in Japan the Government set aside three million yen in a single year to 'improve national thought.' One-third of this sum was assigned to the Ministry of Education to develop a system of spying in the schools and universities. The spies were entrusted with the smelling out of socialistic and communistic tendencies, particularly where these had led to the formation of secret societies. There was indeed at that time a fashion for Communism among the young, and the *mārukusu-boi* (='Marx-boy') was no rarity, though it is a question whether his profession of Communism was not generally marked more by long hair, a Bohemian way of life, and a proper restiveness under a growing authoritarianism than by a mastery of the stodgy chapters of *Das Kapital* and other canonical works.

It was not until after I had left Japan that official repression of 'dangerous thoughts' reached its greatest intensity. Six years after I had left Japan, one of my former students wrote to me about the fate of two others. The writer had a singularly sweet nature.

'My dearest friend M —,' he wrote, 'had been working secretly for labourers and farm-workers against the present policy of the Government. He was somewhat successful, but he worked too much. A physical crisis fell upon him. He lay in bed unconscious for about two months. Afterward in this February he was captured in a police station and is yet at present. Also O —, a dearest friend, came out this September from the confinement of a year and a half in a prison.'

The writer himself had become tubercular and had been sent to a mountain resort to recuperate. 'There,' he said, with an exquisite choice of words, 'I realized for the first time the sweetness and delicacy of breathing air in.'

If adherence to a so-called communism became frequent among those young Japanese who were rightly rebellious against the narrowing régime, it was by no means their only heresy. Some sought escape or relief by adopting an æsthetic or contemplative formula, modern European or ancient Chinese, by which to guide their lives. As one of my friends wrote to me:

'Men have shut themselves in material mechanism, not organism. They have forgotten and lost their own souls. In this condition, how can men examine their own selves and respect each other? A revolt against mechanism or universalization is the creed of some young Japanese.'

Clear-sighted, the poor devils, the young idealists, they were to have their counterparts, their unknown brothers and sisters in the innumerable pacifists and anti-Fascists of Europe and America, the volunteers in the Spanish Civil War, the Bible Christians of Germany, the neo-Yogis of California, the millions of protestants against the earlier manifestations of Axis smash-and-grab — Manchukuo, Abyssinia, Austria — who hoped rather than believed that the world could be saved by some other method than war, the world that was to be so nearly lost.

Since this is a kind of autobiography, I will allow myself to put and to answer the questions, What did I believe? How did I influence my Japanese friends? And how did they influence me? Young as I was, I was at least old enough to have formed some views about life in general and about such matters as religion and politics. In Tokyo I was able for the first time to enjoy and profit by those long discussions and arguments on all kinds of topics which I might have enjoyed if I had gone to Oxford, those talks which so greatly help a young man to find his level and develop the muscles of his mind. If I now put forward some of the opinions which had germinated in me before I arrived in Japan and which, under its influence, put out roots and shoots in me before I left, it is not because I wish to convert the reader but because they are an essential part of my existence.

I have made it clear that I was bred an Anglican Christian. Largely thanks to my mother, to the fathers of the Community of the Resurrection, and to a love of English literature and architecture, I have never lost an affection for the cult, but somehow I feel I was not born to be a Christian. Beechmont, and those strong tendencies in English civilization which had made Beechmont possible, had made puritanism permanently loathsome to me, and its progeny of cant insufferable. I disliked particularly the Christian attempt to reconcile suffering with virtue: as Darwin remarked, 'the number of men in the world is as nothing compared with that of all other sentient beings, and they often suffer greatly without any moral improvement.' No, it was not a Christian with whom my Japanese friends had to do. To become an atheist would at any time have seemed to me presumptuous, and I do not see how a man can be without humility before the immense mystery of the universe. It seemed to me that the world was ruled by natural laws, some of the less important of which were known, and though even these, in their purpose, were incomprehensible, one had to accept them without enquiring vainly into their significance. The world appeared too beautiful to be an accident and too hideous to be a design, yet it obviously was a design, unaccountable and inalterable.

If I must give myself a label, I will call myself a determinist. When, in Japan, one is woken up in the night, as often happens, to feel the house rattled or rocked by an earthquake, one does not shout or even murmur that one is the master of one's fate or the captain of one's soul. An interest in heredity and some perception of its power would in any case have prevented me from believing much in the independence or self-command of the individual. Heredity makes a a man what he is, and what is environment but a phase of heredity?

Hearing that a woman of my acquaintance had once in Dorset got a wild bird entangled in her hair and that it had proved to be that rare migrant, a blue-tailed bee-eater, somebody said that it must have been after the bees in her bonnet, but other people said, as one does, 'Of course that *would* happen to her: nobody else would either get a bird caught in her hair, or, if she did, such an excessively rare bird.' In fact the things that happen to us, including our deaths, are not merely the appropriate but the inevitable things.

A friend of mine in recent years used to dream very often, generally about unusual themes. In the morning he would relate what he had dreamt about — briefly, for he was intelligent enough to know that, except to specialists, the lengthy relation of dreams may bore one's hearers. If he dreamed of, let us say, the Empress Josephine, inevitably in the course of the day we should be confronted with some portrait of her or come across an allusion to her. Some otherwise unforeseeable event of almost every day, important or unimportant, invariably cast its reflection into his consciousness the night before. This might be raw material for an experiment with time, but to the determinist, who is bound to be aware of the unity of existence and the inter-relation of phenomena, time, one might almost say, is no object. If he sees the extraordinary as the habitual, he also finds the habitual fascinating. It is not habit that makes the world go round, but habit is an expression of the forces that do, and in the balance or conflict of opposing or varying forces he seeks to discover evidence of the design of life. 'The happiest man in the world,' wrote the Japanese author Natsumé Soseki in his copy of *Also Sprach Zarathustra*, 'is he for whom necessity becomes freedom itself . . . All is fate and all is freedom at the same time.'

The idea of progress was one in which I had been brought up to believe, but which I had already discarded. Progress implies perfectibility, which appears incompatible with life as we know it, and therefore ludicrous. The conception of utopias is only useful as a form of criticism of the way the world is being managed and as a possible influence leading to a temporary improvement. 'Liberty begets anarchy,' said Balzac, 'anarchy leads to despotism, and despotism back to liberty. Millions have died without securing a triumph for any one system. Is not that the vicious circle in which the whole moral world revolves?' If that is what he believed, it did not prevent him from continuing to examine the whole moral world or from finding the vicious circle as diverting as a merry-go-round.

Since Balzac's time it has become necessary to distinguish between anarchy and anarchism, which is perhaps the most beautiful political theory. The chief argument against it is that it is impracticable, but that has perhaps yet to be proved; its chief weakness appears to be its assumption that human nature is essentially good — a doctrine perhaps as extreme and unbalanced as that of original sin. Only a good man can be a real anarchist, but it is a theory more easy to admire than to believe in. To a liberal mind, no doubt, the best system of government is any which makes for the greatest good of the greatest number — but who is to decide what is the greatest good? The art of government is in practice merely the art of choosing lesser evils. The anarchist would say that there is no such thing as a good government, and it would not be easy to contradict him. As for communism, it never attracted me, and if I had lived in their day I would sooner have dissented with Bakunin than conformed with Marx.

These opinions I have more plainly set out than I could have done in my early twenties, but even then I had taken up, because it was my nature to do so, a somewhat detached and sceptical attitude to both religion and politics. I had no facile optimism or rosy hopes but, on the other hand, no want of energy or *joie de vivre*. An absence of hopefulness, in itself perhaps derived from physical causes, may tend to inhibit effort, particularly in public or political matters, but the lessening of effort is not necessarily a bad thing, if we may judge by the two greatest public efforts of our time, the two world wars. We live in a period when work has become a mania and idleness almost a crime, but it is just as well to remember that the best things the human race has done hitherto would have been impossible without leisure and what would now be called idleness. Gathering that I was what she chose to call a fatalist, a woman once said to me, 'Don't you brush your teeth, then?' — by which no doubt she meant that if what is to be is to be, why bother to do anything at all? I explained that to be negative and inert was to me inconceivable. As for myself, I regarded my function in life as that of an artist. This was not to make any large claims. The artist is what he is, he may be good or bad, important or insignificant, but it is his function to try and make something, to add new forms to life, to show life in a new light, to perceive and illuminate some small part of the universal design.

The nature of happiness was a subject which my Japanese friends liked to discuss. I remember once suggesting that clearheadedness, a highly developed consciousness, might make for one form of happiness, enabling one to free oneself from as many illusions as possible either about the world or oneself. But those unfortunate young men, crammed with lessons, already feeling the burdens of duty and responsibility and the increasing pressure of nationalism, and contrasting their lot with that of the simple peasants among whom some of them had grown up, were inclined to believe that it would be happiest to live like a frog at the bottom of a well, knowing nothing of the outside world and keeping cool in pleasant isolation. But, talking on into the night, we would agree that happiness might consist in belonging to a community confident of its existence; in feeling respect for that community and being respected by it; in doing the work, both of hands and head, for which one was best fitted, and yet having enough leisure; in being neither rich nor poor to the point of misery; in being free from envy and spite; in having good health, being happily married, and feeling confidence in the future of one's children; in the consciousness of loving and being loved; in being able to enjoy some change, variety and unexpectedness; and in maintaining a certain awe of the unknowable. We agreed that nobody could expect so much, and that such happiness as we enjoy is partial and intermittent — so we passed round the *saké* bottle and sent for more, growing mellow and bland, and gathering rosebuds while we might.

If I influenced my Japanese friends, it was probably in much the same ways that they influenced me — in the direction of a cheerful hedonism and scepticism, but even more in the direction of heightened perceptiveness, of creativeness through works of art, or towards the social act on behalf of an individual or community against official or social repression. There was one act against which I certainly and consciously sought to influence them — the act of suicide. I have heard it said that the rate of suicide was no higher in Japan than in other countries. I do not believe it, for, be official statistics what they may, the fact remains that suicide — sometimes single, sometimes double, sometimes even multiple — is commonly resorted to by the Japanese for reasons that seem to a European trivial or insufficient. In those strata of Japanese society with which I was least unfamiliar suicides were annoyingly common; again and again they seemed a waste of promising or potentially happy and useful lives, and I lost no chance of saying so. To-day I am less sanguine in the matter. I might hesitate to dissuade an intending suicide, and there are circumstances in which, whatever the Christian religion or English law may prescribe, I should regard it as only human to help a person to bring about his or her end. To try and judge whether, by dying, an individual in adversity might or might not be throwing away chances of happiness or usefulness is not, it seems to me now, a responsibility to be lightly assumed, but I still cannot sympathize with a patriotic or face-saving suicide. I once found out by chance that a young man who was staying in my house in Higashi Nakano took about among his toilet things a cut-throat razor and a bottle of arsenic in case a mood should decide him to save himself the trouble of ever having to take anything about with him again. I persuaded him to hand these lethal objects over to me and did away with them; fourteen years later he was a prosperous business man, inclined to plumpness, and with a thriving family of children. I really don't know whether that was a good development or not, particularly in the light of the following letter, which I received at Brighton in the late nineteen-thirties from a Japanese acquaintance in London. He was coming to the end of an official sojourn in this country.

'How do you do?' he wrote. 'I hope you are quite well. I am quite well now, but my death is coming nearer and nearer, because I must leave Europe about at the end of this year and then work as a slave for my family, which is quite the same as to die.'

Perhaps he was over-conscientious, for the Japanese custom of arranging marriages on behalf of the contracting parties instead of letting them choose each other, has much to be said for it, and once having complied with the formality, a Japanese of spirit can kick up his heels in other directions if he feels so inclined. As for the bride, it is her duty to do what she is told, wait on him, run his house and raise his children.

Whether the instance I have given of a potential suicide becoming a 'successful' citizen is a good or bad turn of events I do not, as I say, pretend to know, but I tell myself that I had a hand in it. That the assurance may not be empty is shown by a letter I received from another of my Japanese contemporaries, some years after I had left the country. He wrote that he had had a sudden and violent bleeding from the lungs, and had recovered after five months in bed.

'While in the sickness bed,' he wrote, 'very often I thought of you, remembering that at Higashi Nakano we talked with you on suicide and you showed the different opinion from ours . . . Your opinion had much to do with my heart. As you well know, the Japanese people think very slight of life . . . I also might have done the same at the expectoration of blood if I had not heard your opinion.'

The house at Higashi Nakano was a home to me in the best sense. I added to my income by university lecturing and by writing, so I could live as I liked, modestly but not meanly. I took pleasure in entertaining young men or women whose society I enjoyed or who needed a temporary refuge from family or other troubles. Space was limited, or they might have been many instead of few. Two characteristic inmates of the house on a more than temporary footing were a cat called Bimbo (= Poverty) who had sprung from nowhere, and a girl with a baby face and childlike disposition who had had a stormy adolescence and was glad of a haven. She was subject to hallucinations — her father's face would appear suspended in the hedge and supernatural cats were discovered in the cupboards, she saw fireworks at midday and heard bells at midnight — but she was a cheerful little person and quite a good cook.

I did a great deal of reading and writing in that house and a great deal of merrymaking. A married woman who came to live in the next house with her husband (she was singularly plain, had attended a university in America, and now lectured either to Buddhists on sociology or to sociologists on Buddhism) once politely asked me, when I met her in a train, why such *dramatic* noises came from my house. When I asked her to define them and expressed a hope that they did not unduly disturb her, she only tittered and bowed several times from the waist; but I suppose she had heard us larking about, or perhaps one of our *saké* parties had been a little too wild. Let me pause to honour that clear and noble drink, which is made from rice and sipped when warm, tastes a little like some very dry sherry such as Tio Pepe, induces the most agreeable intoxication, and never, in my experience, leaves anything the next morning but a feeling of well-being, even after being consumed to excess.

Among our neighbours was a poet and art-historian called Yoné Noguchi, a lean and sardonic-looking person, rather like a Spaniard, who had an air of having burnt his candle at both ends. As a youth he had emigrated to California, where, soon after his arrival, he had been gazing into a shop window when a heavy hand descended on his shoulder, and spun him round: he found himself face to face with a burly Californian, who, presumably to show his racial antipathies, spat in Noguchi's face — an attack as unexpected as that on Pearl Harbour in 1941. However, after a career of dish-washing and so on, the young man was taken up by a local poet, 'grey' if not 'good,' Joaquin Miller, who seems to have encouraged if he did not teach him to write English. The result was a book purporting to describe autobiographically the adventures of a Japanese girl in the United States. This ambidextrous production had some success, and in due course its author appeared in London and issued a quantity of verses in a bizarre English of his own. They were invertebrate but sensuous and novel, and serious pronouncements were made upon them by the writers and critics of the day, from Hardy downwards. To-day they are no doubt almost forgotten, but monographs by Noguchi on Utamaro and other artists are possibly of more lasting value. At one point in his career he married, I believe, an American woman, but I last heard of him as a confirmed xenophobe.

A rare but to me much more important visitor was Mori. At Durban, during one of his periodical calls at that port, both my mother and my brother, before leaving for Europe and America respectively, had made his acquaintance. He had in fact become a friend of the family. My mother was greatly impressed with his courtesy, charm and intelligence, and he found the same qualities in her. For each of them the encounter was with a kind of being never met before, yet they were immediately at ease with one another. Good manners are, of course, an international language; they had both had formal upbringings; my mother appreciated him for being a polished man of the world, so like, yet so unlike, a European of that sort; and Mori told me that she reminded him of a Japanese lady and was superior to any other European woman he had met. He was pleased with my brother for being so tall, humorous and sensible; my brother rightly thought him 'deep.'

At Durban the local attitude to the Japanese had improved, partly by Mori's own efforts and partly by those of van der Post who, in the press and on the wireless, had been describing his impressions of Japan and gently hinting that the Japanese were highly civilized before white South Africans had ever been dreamt of. In East Africa, too, things were better, and in April, 1927, Mori had been able to write and tell me that the hotels at Mombasa, partly as the result of a *démarche* by himself, now accepted Japanese guests. The *Mombasa Times* had also helped by referring to him editorially as 'an old friend of ours.'

All was not well, however. On 13th January, 1928, the *Natal Advertiser* reported an 'unfortunate incident' in a Durban tea-shop. It appeared that 'a well-known and popular Japanese gentleman, widely respected as a cultured and courteous man,' who had the entrée to 'the leading restaurants and hotels,' had nevertheless been 'placed in a very delicate position,' or, more bluntly, publicly ordered out of a tea-shop by an offensive woman. A few days later the paper printed a letter from Mori, describing the incident with considerable restraint. Being a seaman by profession, he said, he had been all over the world but had never 'met such a manner' before. He ended by asking, 'Is not the world changing day by day, and everything exposing its intrinsic value, disregarding its race value?' Alas, an undue regard for 'race value' was soon to become megalomania in his own country and drive her into an imperialistic war.

It was nearly always possible for me to see Mori during his brief sojourns in his native land, and at other times we kept in touch. His letters, arriving from distant places, always contained pleasant touches. Returning a book I had lent him, he wrote, 'Please excuse damage done to the cover by my pet rabbit (*sic*). He was given to me by an Indian friend in Mombasa, and seeing me with the book so much he must have known it was something good.' His letters mingled affection and anxiety. He called me 'the genious, the world-wide treasure', and wondered always if I was still getting on all right in Japan, for he felt he had rather abandoned me and that I might be feeling lonely or neglected. 'I have done very little to you during your stay in Japan,' he wrote, after I had been in Tokyo a year. In fact he must have been much lonelier than me, and during his long voyages he used to turn over many things in his mind which I am quite sure he did not discuss with his subordinates.

He was impressed by the renewed hullaballoo in South Africa over the second book by 'the genious,' *I Speak of Africa*, and he began to compare his career with mine. He was very nearly old enough to have been my father, yet it sometimes appeared to him that I had so far made better use of my time than he had. This was odd of him, for his career had been honourable and useful; full of courage and enterprise, he was accomplished in ways beyond my attainment. Addressing me as his 'dear friend,' he wrote to me somewhat wistfully on his thirty-ninth birthday, remarking sadly that the Japanese expectation of life is short, and that he had perhaps only a dozen more years to live. He compared himself to an ephemera, 'which fulfilled the meaning of his life, there is nothing to be grieved for.' Then he quoted a Japanese poem, and followed it with a translation:

> 'Don't call it an ephemeral life!
> I have done my duty. An empty body
> Dies away, without grief.
> Look at that blossoming cherry —
> A flower must fall.'

'Therefore,' he continued, 'only concern of mine is to have a flight even for a day, but not a mere longelity (*sic*). Indeed, how innumerable ghosts scrambling on in this world!'

Once at Higashi Nakano as I lay awake in bed, *more japonico*, between Mori, who had come to visit me, and Fukuzawa, who lived with me, they both being asleep, I pondered on the difference between them. Awake, they were a trifle formal in their manner to one another; I think they felt mutually a kind of respectful disapproval, tinged perhaps with a slight jealousy, for each knew that the other had a special claim on my affection. As I lay listening to their tranquil breathing, and warmed by the proximity of their bodies, I thought of them as the two poles or antitheses of the Japanese character. Mori was the man of action and duty, perfectly disciplined, all self-control and efficiency; a nationalist and, I suppose, a militarist; a quiet but fanatical believer, I had never doubted, in the 'divine' mission of his race; Mori stood for power, war, violence and injustice in the interests of a visionary and doubtful good. Fukuzawa was the intellectual, a temperament, melancholy and gaily sardonic; an æsthete, perhaps an artist, his life made up not of public duties but personal relationships; he stood for peace and quietness, for living and letting live, for internationalism, for the immediate and tangible good, for everything (as William Allingham put it)

'we prize
For mirthful, gentle, delicate and warm.'

The dualism of the Japanese nature which, for me, was typified by these two friends, became ever clearer. They were the two aspects of the Japanese double life. It would have been convenient to be able to divide the Japanese into Thugs and Gentles, but too simple, and erroneous besides, for the thugs were often largely gentle, and the gentles often tainted by the traits or tenets of the thugs. I have even heard it said that every Japanese is a split personality.

In the story, *A Brutal Sentimentalist*, which appeared in my first book about Japan, *Paper Houses*, I tried to realize a not impossible conflict between the two strains in one breast. The volume in question reached Japan when I was still there and was soon after translated into Japanese. It provides some detailed and accurate reporting on a few phases of Japanese life and character; the canvas is small but the painting is careful. When it appeared I received congratulations from some Japanese acquaintances on my insight into the character of the female of their species, towards whom their attitude was of course disdainful. Of the Japanese male they thought me less understanding, no doubt because, regarding themselves as superior entities, they did not like being analysed or criticized. (I had already heard exactly the same criticism of a novel about Japan then being widely read, *L'Honorable Partie de Campagne*, by a Frenchman named Raucat.)

It is outside my scope and experience to write of Japanese military matters, but from such knowledge as I had of Japanese soldiers I was convinced (and I should have thought it would have been obvious to any moderately observant foreigner) that they were not to be underestimated and that Japan would be in the future, as she had proved herself in the past, formidable as an enemy. An army held together by racial mysticism, an army of fanatics, must necessarily be dangerous, and there were signs of other kinds of cement, not unknown in the history of other military nations. It was common to see two buck privates in uniform strolling about hand in hand with a far-away look in their eyes, and I was credibly informed that this was not an expression of ordinary matiness but of an emotion to some extent encouraged in the armed forces, no doubt in the belief that greater love hath no man than this, that he lay down his life for his Emperor, but that there will be an extra incentive if by so doing he is also laying down his life for his friend. Such intense relationships have of course a place in the samurai tradition, sometimes as a substitute for conjugal love, sometimes as an adjunct to it.

4. THE TORCH TO TIES

WITH habit and increasing knowledge, with the pleasures of society and solitude, of travel, of the theatre and the bath, the café and the geisha-house, of the climate and the changing seasons, each with its own flora and formalities, with enjoyment of the fine and applied arts, the life of the streets and of the remote countryside, of popular festivals and the company of children, I was becoming more and more adapted to Japanese life and ideas. The gesture of a masked actor, the gnomic poem of a Zen sage, the lonely place in an autumn forest carried the mind away into mysterious spheres where the arsenal and the stock-jobber were as if they had never been. Yet the most commonplace happenings seemed on an uncommon plane. If, for instance, one went to have one's hair cut, the work was done with the utmost deftness, and skilful massage so quickened the circulation and soothed the nerves that one emerged with a new head and finer senses. The hands of most English barbers seem by contrast as heavy as those of a hedger-and-ditcher.

. So absorbed had I become in my surroundings that several times, when writing to my parents, I remarked that it was two or three months since I had spoken to a European. When I caught sight of stray Europeans, they looked odd or even grotesque. I had grown used to the stylized Japanese face, and the mongrel features of Europeans, by contrast, looked irregular. Their complexions were not clear, their gait was ungainly, their manners were casual and uncouth, their voices too loud, their opinions too outspoken. Once or twice, too, at close quarters, one noticed their peculiar smell. But I was one of them myself, therefore I must seem odd or even grotesque and perhaps odoriferous to those who shared my daily life. Goodness knows one was prodigiously stared at in public, and one's naked body excited frank interest in public baths. Yet in photographs where I appeared among groups of Japanese I was not particularly outstanding: true, my hair had not grown straight and black, but my cheekbones and facial expression were not unlike theirs and my eyes looked slightly Mongoloid. I had a happy sense of community with the Japanese; I lived with them and in their fashion and was a part of their society; I worked for them and played with them; love and habit had made them part of me. Nevertheless, I had not 'gone native' and could not. When at one time I contemplated marriage with a Japanese girl, I saw clearly the complications that might arise. I was aware of the anomalous existence of exiles everywhere and of their seemingly inevitable unbalance and distorted perspectives; and I felt, like a familiar pain, intermittent but recurrent, a keen sense of isolation from my own kind and their culture. I valued my three or four European friends and my less few European acquaintances. It seemed a little strange that some were dark and some fair, that some were tall and some short, that some had snub-noses and some hook-noses, but they were my brothers and sisters, I could discuss the Japanese quite freely with them, I could chatter and did not have to talk simply and with a deliberately clear enunciation, like a teacher of elocution, avoiding obscure allusions and slang; in short, I felt at home with them.

Such, then, was the latest form of my double life. I saw that it might be possible for me to make in Japan a happy and useful career, to make a good livelihood without undue effort, to learn much and perhaps to write much and originally about the country and the people, but I felt that this could hardly be my destiny, this remote and insular seclusion from the world, and that I must return to Europe and whatever trials of poverty, patience and obscurity might await me, simply because I belonged there. It was a case of

> 'Put the torch to ties though dear,
> If ties but tempters be,'

but the stronger temptation was from stronger ties. It would no more have been possible for me to remain in Japan, though in many ways it was to me, for all its faults, an earthly paradise, than it had been possible for, let us say, Herman Melville to remain in the Marquesas. But the decision was not taken early or irrevocably; I wavered and wondered, and turned over all sorts of projects in my mind. I refused the offer of a chair of English literature in a provincial university, because I did not wish either to commit myself to an academic career or to bury myself in the provinces, but after eighteen months in Japan I made a new contract extending my stay by a further year, and I still did not know whether, when the year was up, I should return to Europe only for a visit or for good.

My hunger for the fruits of European culture grew with the

books it fed on, and was sharpened by occasional sights of European paintings acquired by Japanese collectors, and by a particularly good exhibition of modern French pictures, which included examples of the work of several nineteenth-century masters and the first painting I ever saw by Rouault. When, however, in 1928 an exhibition was held at Uéno Park of ancient Chinese paintings no clear-eyed spectator could have hankered for Europe. The exhibits included the rarest and most splendid masterpieces that could be obtained from collectors both in Japan and China (the two countries were then not at war, and Chiang Kai-shek had been on a visit to Tokyo.) Most had never been publicly shown before; some had been illustrated in the best monographs on Chinese painting; all had been selected with the highest discrimination. This show alone would have been worth a voyage to Japan.[1] The noble profundity, the symbolism, the directness, the plant-like grace and freshness of these paintings gave me the strongest inkling of the grandeur of Asiatic civilization that I had yet had, and I wished I could spend some years in China to learn even a little of what it had to teach. But how many lifetimes would one need, how much luck, health, money and knowledge even to smell the richness of old civilizations and to embrace living bodies to which they had given birth (for it is only through love that one can taste)? It seemed for a moment shattering that one might die without so much as a glimpse of, let us say, China and Persia and Russia, the Mediterranean countries, Portugal, Ireland, Morocco, the West Indies and Latin America. Then one understood the futility of globe-trotting; one must build up images out of the little one could know and the more one could guess; there could be fruitfulness within narrow bounds. It would be better, perhaps, to be like the Japanese poet Basho, or like White at Selborne, and to hear with a thrill of pleasure a frog jump into an evening pond than to diffuse energy in vain and spread one's faculties thinly over more than they could cover. The important thing was never to lose the appetite for life and art, never to lose heart or curiosity.

[1] Among the exhibits was Yen-Hui's *The Wizard T'ieh-Kuaï*, a painting of so high an order that it could only have amazed the greatest European masters

In the summer of 1928 I went with a Japanese companion to Lake Kawaguchi, and while there visited the house of a decayed samurai family in an old, weird and secluded village. The slightly degenerate heir was reported to be disposed to sell some antique bibelots and works of art which he had inherited, and I paid a call on him with a view to buying something to give to somebody as a present. A pale, tallish and haunted-looking young man of about my own age, wearing a kimono of faded dull blue silk, he received me with elegant manners and an appearance of pleasure, entertained me to a meal, which was served by an elderly maid with a face as impassive as a mask, and then took me to see a large and ancient temple rich with carvings and gildings but slowly rotting under a mantle of mosses and ferns. When he produced his treasures he said nothing about selling them but asked me to choose whatever I liked and he would give it to me. It seemed only polite to choose something not too rare or costly, so I picked out a pair of *saké* bottles which, though pretty, seemed to fulfil this condition. My choice seemed to please him and we fell to drinking together. He behaved rather strangely in his cups, and the uncanny atmosphere of his house and garden and of the old temple beyond it was not in the least dispelled by the warming effect of the liquor on the cockles of the heart. The sibilant sound of a sliding partition somewhere in the house, followed by a low-voiced argument and a sound of weeping suggested the presence of a neurotic invalid or *séquestrée*, some victim of nerves or male tyranny. My host listened a moment, smiled wryly, said 'It's always the same in this house — I'm glad, very glad, to meet a foreigner,' and poured out some more *saké*. He was in the end reluctant to let me go and wished me to come and stay with him. So I might have done had I remained in Japan, though my uneasiness remained undispelled.

From Kawaguchi unfamiliar views were to be had of Fuji-san, that strangely ubiquitous peak. Professor Chamberlain, the Japanologue, recorded that an infuriated tourist once referred to it in print as 'that disgusting mass of humbug and ashes.' Cant is indeed a besetting Japanese fault (as indeed of certain other insular peoples) and the intrusiveness of the mountain and its hackneyed associations used at times to cause me the same irritation, so that when I had occasion to write of it I would peevishly spell it Foodgy, as if to debunk it; but it is a peak with so many moods and aspects — now menacing, now ethereal — that it melts away prejudice and the eye learns to require it as part of the landscape and to miss it when it is not visible.

After a brief sojourn in that dreadful mountain-resort Karuizawa, which was full of foreign dregs but where I had undertaken to lecture to a Japanese summer school on a literary topic, I went on to Chuzenji, in company with Fukuzawa, to see Anna von Schubert, whose beauty and talent, wit and wisdom, which would be radiant anywhere, shone to especial advantage against a background of diplomatic and big business Europeans taking refuge from the summer sultriness of Tokyo and Shanghai. One met them walking in the rain with an air of constraint, and if one ventured to swim in the lake there was a danger of being brained by one of the beastly little sailing boats in which they spent most of their time, never tiring of competitive races, and disturbing the superb landscape with a restless geometry of triangular white sails. It was not without pleasure that we saw a pompous English colonel who had been vainly fishing in the lake, using dragon-flies for bait, succeed in catching after much delay and exhaustion of patience, a bat.

After returning to Tokyo I had the unforgettable experience of seeing a film called 'The Last Days of Tolstoi,' taken at Yasnaya Polyana not long before his death. I do not know if there are other copies of this film in existence. It was incomparably the most exciting 'documentary' I have ever seen, and the most important relic. In those few crude shots of the nobleman pretending to be a peasant, the whole legend came to life: those simple gestures were the gestures of genius. Tolstoi walked down the garden path looking stolidly before him, beside him his bulky wife, heavily skirted, smiling and looking into his face as she vainly tried to get a smile in return. She picked a flower and tried to fasten it in his blouse, but he brushed her hand aside like a nuisance, and in that gesture the whole horror of the final flight was impending. The terrible prestige of greatness! Imagine even a few feet of film showing Goethe, in his habit as he lived, or Voltaire, or Shakespeare, or Beethoven, or Rembrandt.

Before I left Japan, early in 1929, I received from Mori a *kakeji*, or scroll, inscribed in the admired calligraphy of one Rai Kyohei: it was a treasured family possession. Here is a translation:

'To make oneself pure in heart,
To reach the essential reality of things,
To let others think of themselves,
Not to envy the merit of others,
Not to boast of oneself,
Not to think oneself wise,
To try and find good people and at once reject bad ones,
To help merciful government, and to uplift the degrading customs
    of the world.'

A difficult programme, but a specimen of conventional Japanese idealism, derived from ancient Chinese tradition and hard to reconcile with the bloody dogmas of armed force.

From Singapore, Mori wrote to say good-bye:

'The three years sojourn of you in Japan, I expect, will be remembered by the world for ever as the epoch-making of the genious. It was a blessing for me to have met you at Durban and contributed something to this matter, but I must be ashamed for having undone my duty for the genious.'

It is hard to see how he could have done more for me than open his heart, his house and his purse: I can only hope that he was not ill repaid. He brought me to his country and I learned to love half its life; if I hated the other half, that was not Mori's fault. The love has been an infinite enrichment, the hatred has been justified by events. Suppose we 'reach the essential reality of things' and find it twofold, what are we to do then? What can we do then except be glad that at times it seems single?

Japan is not the only foreign country from which I have had to tear myself away, but it was the first and the pangs were great. Any traveller who is happy in some pleasant place is likely to play with the thought of staying there for good, even when he knows he cannot. So it was with George Wheler, who travelled in Greece in the seventeenth century — and nobody who has known and loved Greece can fail to sympathize, reading how Wheler, visiting a hermit on the slopes of Helicon, was by him brought

'delicate white Honey-combs, with Bread and Olives, and a very good wine: to which he set us down in his Hutt, and made us a Dinner, with far greater satisfaction, than the most Princely Banquet in Europe could afford us. For the Quiet and Innocency of their Life, the natural Beauty of the Place, the Rocks, Mountains, Streams, Woods and curious Plants, joyn'd with the Harmonious Notes of Nightingales, and other Birds, in whole Quires, celebrating, and as it were, welcoming that forward Spring, to speak the truth, so charmed my melancholick Fancy for a time, that I had almost made a Resolution never to part with so great a Happiness, for whatever the rest of the World could present me with. But, in conclusion, it prov'd too hard a task for me, so soon to wean my self from the World.'

Having felt impelled to return to Europe, I do not feel remorse at having come away from Japan. If I had decided to stay and make my life there, it would have been the double life of the exile; I should no doubt have 'gone native' more and more; I should have seen the disgusting rise of militarism to supreme power and the total eclipse of liberal ideas; I should have seen my friends persecuted and might myself have been victimized or deported; and if I had contrived to remain contentedly there, little more than twelve years would have passed before the country, in the hands of its warlords, was committed to its desperate expansionist war; I should then either have been tortured or bumped off, or both, on some trumped-up charge of espionage or the propagation of 'dangerous thoughts,' or else shipped back to a Europe which I should not yet have learnt to know and from which I should have become greatly estranged.

In Japan I often grumbled and complained at what seemed to me the shortcomings of Japanese life, which indeed could in many ways and with justice have been compared unfavourably with life in Western Europe; but it is as common for a traveller to do that in a foreign country as it is for him to praise that country when he returns to his own. It seems to me that I have been very fortunate to have known and enjoyed, in youth and in time of peace, spells of existence in Africa and Asia, and later to have seen something of immeasurable Russia, of independent Poland, of Germany before Hitler, of Italy before she was brought to ruin by the ridiculous Mussolini, of France before the collapse, and above all Greece. Civilization has many dialects but speaks one language, and its Japanese voice will always be present to my ear, like the pure and liquid notes of the bamboo flute in those tropical evenings on the Indian Ocean when I heard it for the first time, speaking of things far more important than war, trade and empires — of unworldliness, lucidity and love.